The Expressway World

The Expressway World

Richard J. Williams

polity

Copyright © Richard J. Williams 2025

The right of Richard J. Williams to be identified as Author of this Work has been asserted in accordance with the UK Copyright, Designs and Patents Act 1988.

First published in 2025 by Polity Press

Polity Press
65 Bridge Street
Cambridge CB2 1UR, UK

Polity Press
111 River Street
Hoboken, NJ 07030, USA

All rights reserved. Except for the quotation of short passages for the purpose of criticism and review, no part of this publication may be reproduced, stored in a retrieval system or transmitted, in any form or by any means, electronic, mechanical, photocopying, recording or otherwise, without the prior permission of the publisher.

ISBN-13: 978-1-5095-6010-3

A catalogue record for this book is available from the British Library.

Library of Congress Control Number: 2024947561

Typeset in in 11.5 on 14 Adobe Garamond
by Fakenham Prepress Solutions, Fakenham, Norfolk NR21 8NL
Printed and bound in Great Britain by CPI Group (UK) Ltd, Croydon

The publisher has used its best endeavours to ensure that the URLs for external websites referred to in this book are correct and active at the time of going to press. However, the publisher has no responsibility for the websites and can make no guarantee that a site will remain live or that the content is or will remain appropriate.

Every effort has been made to trace all copyright holders, but if any have been overlooked the publisher will be pleased to include any necessary credits in any subsequent reprint or edition.

For further information on Polity, visit our website:
politybooks.com

Contents

Illustrations vi
Acknowledgements vii
Preface ix

Chapter 1 The Expressway World Revisited 1

Chapter 2 New York: The Expressway in Ruins 23

Chapter 3 Los Angeles: The Expressway as Art 49

Chapter 4 London: The Activist Expressway 73

Chapter 5 São Paulo: The Expressway Occupied 97

Chapter 6 Madrid: The Expressway as Public Space 121

Chapter 7 Seoul: The Return of Nature 145

Chapter 8 Glasgow: Living with the Expressway 169

Notes 190
Select Bibliography 221
Index 223

Illustrations

Cross-Bronx Expressway, New York City	xiv
The Rose Fitzgerald Kennedy Greenway, Boston	16
'Truck and Car Fall as West Side Highway Collapses', *The New York Times* (16 December 1973)	23
Miller Highway Remnant at West 72nd St., New York City	25
Paul Rudolph, Lower Manhattan Expressway, New York City. Bird's-eye perspective section. Rendering. (ca. 1970)	38
Thomas Heatherwick, Little Island, New York City (2013)	45
Marylin Jorgenson Reece and Carol Schumaker with the I-405/I-10 interchange under construction. *Los Angeles Times* (6 April 1964)	49
California Department of Transport Division of Highways, I-405/I-10 interchange, photograph 16662-6 (14 January 1966)	58
I-405/I-10 interchange, Los Angeles	63
Scaffolding Play St. Marks, 1968	73
Costume Under Motorway, 1968	75
Hawkwind, *X In Search Of Space* interior gatefold, 1971	87
Acklam Road skatepark, Westway, London	90
Prefeitura Municipal de São Paulo, perspective drawing of Elevado Presidente Costa e Silva, São Paulo, 1969	98
Minhocão, São Paulo	108
Ciro Miguel, proposal for Parque Minhocão, São Paulo, 2013	112
Madrid Rio from the Puente de Toledo, Madrid	121
Las Colmenas housing and the M-30, Madrid	124
Dominique Perrault, Puente de Arganzuela, Madrid Rio (2011)	133
Cheonggyecheon restoration, Seoul (2003–5)	145
Kim Swoo-Geun, Sewoon Sangaa, Seoul (1967)	151
Cheonggyecheon restoration, Seoul (2003–5)	157
MVRDV, Seoullo 7017, Seoul (2017)	162
M8 at Charing Cross, Glasgow	169
M74 at Tradeston, Glasgow	182

Acknowledgements

Richard Anderson, Pedro Fiori Arantes, Stuart Baird, Joe Banks, Rosa Barba, Anne Bartolotti, Hugh Campbell, Ana Claudia Castro, Dongho Chun, Athos Comolatti, Neil Cox, Christina M. Crawford, Mark Crinson, Juan Cruz, Vena Dhupa, Alistair Fair, Jamie Forde, Richard Freeman, Ginés Garrido, Miles Glendinning, Ben Highmore, Dominic Hinde, Alex Hochuli, Claudia Hopkins, Andrew Houlachan, Paul Jenkins, Eunju Kang, Sepideh Karami, José Lira, Ana Maluenda, Daryl Martin, Peter Merriman, Nate Millington, Michael Moorcock, Felipe Morozini, Rory Olcayto, Jen Orpin, Ada Penna, Paul Routledge, Iain Sinclair, Paul Sweeney, Richard Thomson, Igea Troiani, Jon Trux, Christopher Turner, Jan Urquhart, Tom Vague, Abby Williams, Alex Williams, Tim Wilson, Ruth Verde Zein, and Sharon Zukin.

I would also like to thank the staff of the following institutions for their hospitality, help in locating research materials and for many excellent suggestions: the Burns Library at Boston College, Kendra Stoll at the CalTrans library in Sacramento, Anthony Ng and Mohammed Rashidfarokhi at CalTrans District 7, the Centre for Alternative Technology in Machynlleth, the Colegio Oficial de Arquitectos de Madrid, Ewha Woman's University in Seoul, the Faculdade de Arquitetura e Urbanismo Universidade de São Paulo, the University of Liverpool library, the Glasgow City Archives at the Mitchell Library, the Getty Research Institute library in Los Angeles, the New York Public Library, Ouvidor 63 in São Paulo and the Universidad Politécnica de Madrid.

Thank you, finally, to the journals *City*, *Sophia*, and the *London Review of Books* for letting me publish some of my preliminary thoughts on the topic of the expressway world.

The project was generously supported by the Leverhulme Trust, who provided an International Research Fellowship based at the University of São Paulo in 2022, and the British Academy, who equally generously

ACKNOWLEDGEMENTS

provided a Senior Research Fellowship for 2024, as well as a Small Research Grant in the same year. As ever, the University of Edinburgh provided consistent support throughout.

Finally, I have to thank Eileen Kinsman most of all. The book is for her, with love.

Preface

Imagine an expressway. You are standing on a concrete pedestrian bridge and you're looking down on it, onto six lanes of slow-moving traffic, some of it stationary. In the distance off to your right is a modern city centre, dense and compact with office towers; you can pick out a few of the names of the occupants from this distance – the accountants KPMG, a Hilton hotel, the big names of capital. You're some distance away from that world, both physically and psychologically, and you're also well distanced from what you know to exist to your left, a mile or so away, an area of solid Victorian housing with leafy streets and cafes. You're somewhere else here, the only pedestrian in the vicinity, and the only other humans you can see in the immediate locality are drivers and the occasional passenger, glimpsed behind glass. The traffic is a constant roar; you can smell it too, especially when a truck downshifts to drag itself out of a crawl. Nothing much grows here, apart from weeds poking through cracks in the paving. It's a scene you can find all over the world – for many, an everyday form of devastation.

It might seem perverse to make a case for places like these, but more often than not that is exactly what I do in this book. The expressway I describe above happens to be in Glasgow, Scotland's largest city and one that embraced the automobile with unrestrained enthusiasm in the 1960s and 1970s (it came close to erasing all of its Victorian centre at one point in favour of a car-oriented plan). Glasgow is a good case, but it could equally be Lagos or London, São Paulo or San Francisco. The expressway world is ubiquitous and global, and almost any city of any size that you can think of has an urban quarter like this. The expressway world, as I call it here, borrowing a label from an American critic Marshall Berman, is that place where the devastation is most acute.[1] It's where a highway slices through the city, dividing it from itself ('severance' is the term highway engineers use to describe this effect). The expressway can take various forms in this zone – it can be built at grade level, or buried, or even sometimes tunnelled at great expense. Most commonly, however, it is a bridge, an elevated structure of a kilometre or more, built in precast sections in concrete or steel, and raised up on piers. As engineering structures, they can be hugely impressive. Writing in all seriousness in 1971, the English architectural critic and historian Reyner Banham called the 405/10 junction in Los Angeles a 'work of art'.

In terms of history, the expressway world is still in many places being built. African cities, pumped with Chinese capital, are enthusiastically building such structures, Indian and Chinese cities too. But this book is mostly about structures from a moment when the private car represented the future of transportation and cities everywhere were being reconstructed in its image. This is a few years from the middle of the 1960s to the early 1970s, a period before the oil crisis of 1973 when that car-oriented vision fell out of fashion. We mostly don't care for that expressway world now, that world of the 1960s. On its construction, we might have been able to see its structures as works of art, and before they got clogged up with other people's cars to experience them as seamless flow. But the expressway world mostly has negative associations now – pollution, waste, noise, visual and physical separation. The M8 is for many an urban disaster that must be simply abolished.

I am not so sure. The expressway world can be richer and more complex than it might first appear. In the following chapters, there are examples of expressways that have become – through activism, or imaginative political action, or benign neglect – urban places in their own right. You can find numerous adaptations of the expressway world too, ameliorations of its worst effects, and imaginative appropriations, as well as cases where nothing has happened at all. But above all you will find that the expressway world is something *lived*, involving the interaction of individuals and institutions in ways its designers may never have intended. In that it is very like the nineteenth-century railway environment with its arches and viaducts, now much prized by developers. There is no reason the expressway world can't also become that if we want it. Roads are a resilient technology. Almost anything with wheels can move along them: bikes and buses as well as cars and trucks. You can sit and walk, or run on them, if permitted, which admittedly is not often. In a few places you can occasionally sunbathe. There has even been more than one idea to turn one into a swimming pool, miles long.

Arguments for abolishing the expressway world abound. However, abolition, I think, is mostly fantasy. It can be done, at vast expense, but it may end up being as totalising a solution as what it replaces. There can be losses as well as gains. As Megan Kimble, an American journalist, writes in a recent book, we need to be cautious, even when we think abolishing the expressway is the right thing to do. 'We should tear down urban highways', she writes. 'But *how* we tear them down also matters.'[2] Or, implicitly we end up with more of the same, more highway power being inflicted on those without that power, more division and inequality, just of a different form.

This book therefore tells stories of accommodation with the expressway world, of ways of living with it, and of directing it slyly to new uses. Some of the most arresting cases here, such as São Paulo's Minhocão, manage to keep apparently mutually hostile interests in play, sometimes over decades. That is evidence of the possibility of a different kind of expressway politics, neither advocacy nor abolition, but something else.

There's also some mourning here in this book too, for some readers no doubt misplaced, but nevertheless there because the expressway world one way or another is in decline. The cities that embraced it most enthusiastically in the 1960s have turned equally enthusiastically against it. I think what Megan Kimble describes in *City Limits* is the coming orthodoxy, however long it takes to come about. Paris, under the mayoralty of Anne Hidalgo has turned its riverside highways into beaches. England's second largest city, Birmingham, is making a pedestrian-friendly boulevard out of its orbital ring. Every weekend Brasília, the most autophile of all the twentieth century's new towns, turns its central expressway into a park. It is often said that 'peak car' has been reached in the rich world – the young, some say, can no longer afford cars, nor aspire to have them, nor even see the point in learning to drive.

It is nevertheless still occasionally possible to experience the expressway world as it was intended to be. Around car-mad Glasgow one can, if the timing is right, sense the miracle that its expressway designers imagined. On a summer's evening, starting from the heart of the Victorian commercial city, you head westwards towards Charing Cross where in a minute or two you can pick up the M8, which sweeps you up almost immediately and south over the broad expanse of the river Clyde. It's an exhilarating move on the rare occasions that the traffic is on your side. In

PREFACE

twenty minutes the expressway drops down to the estuary and the view suddenly expands, dotted with islands and ferries, with the mountains of the West Highlands forming a vertiginous backdrop. This is a different world all of a sudden, both connected and metropolitan through the expressway, and also wild. The expressway world, for all its difficulties on foot, is also this.

I am a driver at least some of the time, and just occasionally I also experience this miracle – sometimes the journey westwards as described, sometimes in the other direction, where the Kingston Bridge swoops across the river before plunging deep into the engine room of the Victorian city. With luck, it is a quintessentially modern, Futurist experience. But it's also rare for the driver, and costly for everyone else. It nevertheless *is* the expressway world, and the task of the book is to hold on to the reality of that experience, along with all the other contradictory and difficult experiences that contribute to it. You can be both a driver and a pedestrian, and activist and a consumer, an enthusiast and a critic. The expressway world isn't a single world, but multiple and overlapping ones, and the stories the book revolves around are stories of complexity, both/and not either/or.

One last, but important thought: the original designers of the expressway world were, in their own ways, totalitarians, some more openly than others. Their solutions were total, all-encompassing, intolerant of dissent. The critical response to the expressway could also be as totalitarian, not to mention costly. We're not now going to demolish concrete structures everywhere given the amount of carbon embodied in them, as well as the now well-known costs of demolition. So, most likely we are going to have to learn to live with them, just as we did with nineteenth-century railway viaducts – and that experience from the 1960s onwards shows the variety and imagination of the possible responses.

I wrote this book in a city, Edinburgh, which most unusually has remained almost entirely untouched by the expressway. Edinburgh for better or worse chose not to remake itself in the image of the car in the years following the Second World War. It flirted with putting an expressway through its medieval Old Town, paralleling development in Glasgow, its rival to the west. In the end, it elected to do none of it, and the city's streets remain largely those of the distant past. On this question, the city remains inordinately pleased with itself, as it is with its resistance to most other aspects of the modern world. But this conscious refusal of the expressway has had consequences. It has been harder to do the large-scale pedestrianisation schemes that can be found in Glasgow for example, and from the point of view of a driver, or bus passenger, the city's traffic is agonisingly slow. And, perhaps more controversially, the refusal of the expressway world has also meant the refusal of the kinds of urban spaces this book describes, which, highly imperfect as they are, have qualities that bear consideration. The expressway world is a place as much as any other urban place, and it has value, admittedly often eccentric or difficult, but value nonetheless. To make sense of the expressway world now, we need to be open to that possibility – and the following chapters are therefore an exercise in open-mindedness. Between retention and abolition there are ways of living with the expressway world that may have lessons for how we learn to live with the rest of the built environment.

Cross-Bronx Expressway, New York City. *Photograph by Richard J. Williams.*

CHAPTER 1

The Expressway World Revisited

Back in 1982, the American philosopher Marshall Berman published an electrifying and much-cited account of the Cross-Bronx Expressway, the notorious section of Interstate 95 that slices across the northern part of New York City. The traffic was violent, he wrote, 'fast, deadly fast', everyone on the highway 'seized with a desperate, uncontrollable urge to get out of the Bronx as fast as wheels can take him'. But it was not just the drivers' behaviour that disturbed him, but the violence the highway did to its surroundings. It was a blasted, inhumane place: 'hundreds of boarded-up, abandoned buildings and charred and burnt-out hulks of buildings; dozens of blocks covered with nothing at all but shattered blocks and waste'. An ordeal for anyone, he went on, it was 'especially dreadful for people who remember the Bronx as it used to be: who remember these neighbourhoods as they once lived and thrived; until this road cut through their heart and made the Bronx, above all, a place to get out of'.[1]

Built between 1948 and 1968 the Cross-Bronx Expressway was an extraordinary act of will of one man, New York's political colossus, Robert Moses. The violence Berman saw was Moses's, nowhere clearer than in a notorious speech given in May 1964 at the World's Fair. Moses – chair of the Triborough Bridge and Tunnel Authority and at least eleven other key committees, perhaps the most powerful single figure in New York City's history – was recovering from a prostatectomy at the city's Roosevelt Hospital, so he had the speech delivered by an aide. Radical surgery was on his mind: it was easy enough to build roads in a Canberra or a Brasília, he said, where nothing previously existed, but 'when you operate in an overbuilt metropolis you have to hack your way with a meat ax'.[2]

Berman understood that sentiment all too well because the severed neighbourhood was precisely the one in which he himself had grown up. Moses's actions felt like a personal attack. 'The Expressway World', the title of Berman's chapter on Moses, was part of a larger argument about modernity, depicting it as destruction and chaos, rather than progress: as the book's title put it, borrowing a phrase from Marx and Engels, 'all that is solid melts into air'.[3] The expressway was a key image in this argument, the heart of two of the book's chapters. For Moses and strong men like him, the expressway was the purest embodiment of progress. For critics such as Berman, it was the destroyer of worlds.

There are plenty of reasons to go along with Berman. Expressways once built are more often than not somewhat toxic objects. Many of them are associated with dictators, or populist strong men, or just men like Moses used to getting their way (a warning: this is a book populated with big, not always entirely good, men). Many of the expressways in the book are associated with now unfashionable ways of doing things, like driving everywhere. In many cases, the urban expressway represents a peculiarly modern dystopia, the image we reach for when we want to represent scepticism about progress. Often enough the urban expressway in image is captured at a moment of embarrassing failure: the popular protest at the moment of inauguration, or the persistence of the traffic jam that the expressway was supposed to solve. There have been catastrophic structural failures, such as the collapse of Los Angeles's I-5 during the 1994 Northridge earthquake, or the deadly disintegration of Genoa's Morandi bridge in 2018, or the inundation of Houston's I-45 and I-69 by Storm Beta in 2020, or in 2024, the destruction of the Francis Scott Key Bridge carrying the I-695 in Baltimore after a ship collided with one of its piers.[4] Or there have been recent, and well-publicized cases where an expressway destroys the part of the city that it is meant to serve. In Giza, Cairo, the new Teraet Al-Zomor Bridge is said to pass less than 50 cm from the flats on either side, an act of urban warfare by any standards (Egypt's Ministry of Housing argued after the fact that the flats had been illegally built, so the residents had no rights).[5]

The images of the Giza bridge are somehow uniquely horrifying – the expressway is literally in the bedroom! – but the dystopian expressway was already a long-established cultural trope. As early as 1958, the great American urbanist Lewis Mumford depicted the expressway as a uniquely destructive force. 'Perhaps our age will be known to the future historian as the age of the bulldozer and the exterminator', he wrote; 'the building of a highway has about the same result upon vegetation and human structures as the passage of a tornado or the blast of an atom bomb.'[6]

The failed expressway has become an important political trope too. There are now innumerable acts of political resistance, from the American freeway revolts of the late 1950s onwards, successful in stalling portions of San Francisco's freeway system. The activist Jane Jacobs's work in resisting the Lower Manhattan Expressway in the 1960s is legendary. In London, the popular understanding of expressways is almost entirely in terms of failure. Its Motorway Box of 1965, an eight-lane, eighty-kilometre expressway on stilts, famously never happened.[7] It was one of the academic and planner Peter Hall's Great Planning Disasters, as his 1980 book had it.[8] Elsewhere in Britain, popular resistance to the M11 and M77 motorways killed any substantial road-building programme from the late 1990s onwards.

Disaster, failure, dystopia: it has become difficult to see the urban expressway in any other terms. Whether we are concerned with them in academic, political or cultural representations, the treatment of the urban expressway has become almost universally negative. As Michael Dnes has put it in a book on London's expressways, their treatment has focused 'overwhelmingly on their rejection'. 'Seen from a distance', he continues, 'the rise and fall of urban road projects appears to be a story of threat and redemption, or a revolution that cast out one flawed view of the world and established a new, better approach to managing transport in the city.'[9] In other words, we know better now.

If anything, the mainstream approach to the urban expressway is more negative now than at any time in the past. In *Carmageddon*, Daniel Knowles describes the urban expressway as a 'tourniquet on a healthy limb', a way of killing a healthy city. Cars are getting too big, cars unequivocally 'make life worse', carmakers are 'evil', traffic can't be beaten and all roads lead to the ground zero of racial capitalism, Detroit.[10] Megan Kimble's recent study of anti-expressway activism in Texas is unambiguous about them as agents of racist governance. Built, at least in part, to separate impoverished African Americans from the rich city, for the sake of racial justice alone, she writes, they must be torn down.[11]

The Promise of the Expressway

But before we get into the critique, what precisely do we mean by an expressway? It is a road, of a peculiarly modern kind. Designed exclusively for motor traffic, sometimes only restricted to the private car. It has limited access points, which is to say that it can only be reached on wheels via carefully engineered on- and off-ramps. Its carriageways are strictly separated, by a space where cars cannot drive, or by crash barriers; you can't cross from one side to the other in the usual way. Pedestrians are forbidden. It's designed for speed. There are huge signs designed to be read at a glance. As Peter Hall put it, these elements are remarkably consistent, even at the level of signage with 'distinctive lower-case lettering, that became part of a new global visual symbolism'.[12] Their very ubiquity would subsequently be an attraction for pop artists such as the American Ed Ruscha, keen on anything popular and mass produced.

The first expressway with these recognizable global characteristics was, Hall thought, most likely the Automobil-Verkehrs- und Übungsstraße (AVUS), a ten-kilometre route through Berlin's Grunewald, completed in 1921. Germany's Autobahnen, proposed during the Weimar period, and built enthusiastically by the Nazis from 1933 as a job creation scheme, were early evidence of the same, although (Hall points out) the engineering of these early highways could be primitive: 'they run like a roller-coaster over every undulation in the landscape … on- and off-ramps are too tightly engineered.'[13]

The US built a handful of expressways at the same time (the Arroyo Seco Parkway, Los Angeles, in 1939; the Pennsylvania Turnpike in 1940) but it did not build with much enthusiasm at least until the passing of the Federal-Aid Highway Act of 1956 and the initiation of the Interstate highway system.[14] Most of the cases in this book date from the later 1960s by which point the expressway had become an orthodoxy, invisible in its normality, even as it brutalized the existing city.

The expressway can take various forms in the city zone: it can be built at grade level, or sunk below ground, or tunnelled, the latter invariably the most expensive option. Most commonly, however, it is a bridge, an elevated structure of a kilometre or more, built in precast sections in concrete or steel, and raised up on piers. As engineering structures, they can be impressive or highly intrusive or both. The terminology varies a good deal. There are quite a number of labels in English, with equivalents in other languages – 'motorway' in British English has a precise legal definition and set of engineering standards, 'interstate' and 'freeway' likewise in the United States. *Autobahn* in Germany, *autopista* in Spanish, *autostrada* in Italian, *autoestrada* in Portuguese have similar meanings. There are some cultural differences depending on the time and place the terminology is used, along with variations in design standards.[15] I use 'expressway' here, partly to refer to Berman, partly because it has generally urban connotations, partly because it can be found in use in various locations at various times – it is intentionally transcultural and transhistorical.

The expressway was once all wonder and promise. The promise is there in vestigial form in early modernist urban visions, in, for example, the Italian Antonio Sant'Elia's *Città Nuova* ('New City'), a highly mechanized urban vision sublimating high-speed circulation (Sant'Elia was a Futurist whose founding manifesto of 1909 opens with the perverse celebration of a car crash).[16] It is there more clearly in Swiss-French architect Le Corbusier's *Ville Contemporaine* of 1922, an imaginary, but highly influential city of three million planned as a grid of identical skyscrapers set in open parkland.[17] Through the middle of the *Ville Contemporaine* the architect planted a great expressway, dead straight, six lanes wide, featuring grade-separated crossings. There was an anachronistic triumphal arch at one end, but this city was otherwise uncompromisingly automotive.[18] Le Corbusier liked cars: his 1923 manifesto *Vers Une Architecture* compared car design approvingly with the evolution of Greek temples and he actually designed a car in 1936, the *Voiture Minimum*, although none was ever built.[19]

The expressway world is there, in a distinctly early Soviet form in Mikhail Okhitovich and Moisei Ginzburg's 'disurbanist' proposals of 1929 and later, which imagined cities in their traditional sense replaced by lightweight pods strung out along highways; the car would predominate.[20] The expressway world found a well-known American form in Frank Lloyd Wright's 1932 Broadacre City, described in the provocatively titled book, *The Disappearing City*, in which the expressway would be the means of effecting a radical decentralization of American cities, partially realized by a combination of accident and design after the Second World War.[21]

Of early visions of the expressway world, probably the most popular was the *Futurama* exhibit at the 1939 New York World's Fair, sponsored by General Motors, and projecting a world twenty years in the future in which its products would be ubiquitous. An accompanying book, *Magic Motorways*, appeared in 1940. The author of both was a visionary theatre set designer, Noman Bel Geddes, a man (as the book's disarming cover blurb read) 'of almost unbelievable energy, irascible and unpredictable'.[22] Approximately five million stood in line for the sixteen-minute *Futurama* show, making it by far the most popular attraction in World Fair history. It took the visitor on an immersive ride into a future America, criss-crossed with high-speed motorways filled with quick semi-autonomous cars, equipped with secondary safety devices to make accidents inconceivable. New York might be connected with San Francisco in twenty-four hours, indicating an average speed of more than 160 kilometres per hour, and a sleepless night, although Bel Geddes implied that the journey might be at least partly automated. It was a seductive vision, no more so than in the sections depicting urban life. Here, repeatedly, Bel Geddes was anxious to keep drivers and pedestrians apart with two separate circulation systems, distinct not only in method but in mood: 'people saunter above – cars speed below' reads the caption to a perspective drawing of a future city block.[23] He replanned the metropolitan city around colossal expressways, punctuated every ten blocks with a skyscraper, each enormous block 'a complete unit in itself'. That would not only be desirable but necessary: crossing the street would otherwise be suicide.[24]

Bel Geddes depicted the city as a machine, and its circulation sublime. In the United States that vision led directly to the 1944 Act of Congress establishing the national highway system. At the level of urban governance, it certainly helped embed the automobile-focused vision of the American city that Robert Moses was already building in New York.[25] The city, in these breathless fantasies, is all automobility. As Robert Caro's biography of Moses shows in relentless detail, Moses was a visionary as much as Bel Geddes. He could support his arguments for highway building with any amount of data on traffic flow and revenue streams to the Triborough Bridge and Tunnel Authority – but he achieved much of what he did by force of rhetoric.[26]

Fantasies like *Futurama* are tremendously important, communicating unfamiliar and complex ideas to a mass public. Bel Geddes's core ideas were legible and memorable: the supremacy of the car, the separation of pedestrian traffic, the sublimation of traffic flow. Echoes of these modernist fantasies can be routinely found throughout the postwar period, some more plausible than others. The new capital of Brazil, Brasília, is a city of half a million structured around a fourteen-kilometre expressway, the Eixo Rodoviáro, a symbolic and functional urban spine along which a large part of the city's housing was strung out, along with some of its principal monuments. It is inescapable and spectacular in both the plan and real life. Lucio Costa, the plan's architect, was clear about the imagery. Brasília, he wrote, was to be the capital of 'the autostrada and the park', a motorized vision that assumed, without being very specific, much greater car ownership.[27] Costa did also build a colossal, multilevel bus station above a buried expressway, a Futurist spectacle. From the terrace of the bus station, probably the city's most complex and animated public space, an extraordinary mechanized ballet plays constantly, as hundreds of buses make their way in and out, while cars flash by on the expressway below.

Automotive fantasies could be retrofitted onto an existing city, as they might have been in Berlin via the English architects Peter and Alison Smithson. In their competition entry for Berlin Hauptstadt in 1958, they proposed a thrilling experience for drivers as an expressway plunged them at speed beneath an urban megastructure, and they hoped an equally thrilling experience for pedestrians who would be able to look at the traffic. 'Cars as spectacle', they wrote 'look down to the roads. People as spectacle: look up to escalators and terraces.'[28]

The perspective drawings they supplied for the competition had something of Brasília in them in their celebration of the expressway, as both structure and fantasy. They might have lost the competition, but a not dissimilar fantasy would show up, for example, in Cumbernauld, a new town to the north-east of Glasgow, similarly oriented around an expressway over which was erected a megastructure housing a modern town's essential functions. In an undeniably exciting perspective drawing of it published in 1963, the town centre was approached at speed in a Ford Thunderbird convertible.[29] It was an optimistic image for a part of the country that was both poverty-stricken and damp – but it was a widely disseminated and compelling fantasy.

Traffic in Towns

These visions, unbuilt and built, were essentially Futurist, speed-obsessed and uncompromising. There were quieter visions too. The expressway world might also be a means of giving the pedestrian a better deal, at least in theory. In Britain, this came first in the form of the Buchanan report on the predicted growth in road traffic. Commissioned in 1960 by Ernest Marples, the Transport Minister in the Conservative government of Harold Macmillan, it reported at the end of 1962, and an abridged version of the report appeared in paperback the following year as *Traffic in Towns*, becoming an unlikely bestseller. Its tone could be somewhat apocalyptic. Sir Geoffrey Crowther wrote in the introduction of a 'national emergency'.[30] Colin Buchanan, the report's author, had already claimed that nothing less than 'civilised life (was) at stake'.[31] The precise threat was the growth in traffic volume, with traffic already unmanageable at the time of publication – the traffic jams around Christmas 1958 seem to have been a turning point. Volumes were predicted to grow by 300 per cent by 1980, based on the then reasonable assumption that every household would very likely soon acquire a car. There was a political dimension too, which Crowther described bluntly: 'a majority of voters in the country will soon be car owners'.[32]

Traffic in Towns had some startling solutions. London's Fitzrovia – the area bounded by the Euston Road and Oxford Street – would be largely demolished, to be replaced by an elaborate double-decked megastructure, with expressway-style roads at ground level and pedestrians at an upper level. Where that could not be done, Buchanan proposed retrofitting areas with a raised platform, separating pedestrian from car traffic in the same way. Life at car level need not be excessively gloomy, he wrote, proposing holes punched into the pedestrian platform to admit light, and shop frontages that could animate the below-grade scene.[33]

If *Futurama* imagined a city of flows, principally from the driver's perspective, *Traffic in Towns* concerned itself more with the pedestrian. A photograph of Paris depicts the Place Vendôme as a rubbish heap of cars. We need, Buchanan wrote somewhat despairingly, to respect 'the simple act of walking'.[34] To facilitate this enhanced pedestrian realm, traffic needed to be directed somewhere else. Having done its job, pedestrian life could be liberated. The expressway world could also be this.

Expressways as Power

Any book about roads is also a book about power. Roads enable power but they are also pictures of it. Before anything or anybody moves along a road, it exists as a representation of political power, perhaps in its most primitive form. A line joins two places on a map and power flows. Robert Moses, perhaps the single most important political figure in the history of New York City, understood this – his bridges and tunnels, turnpikes, parkways and expressways were *the* material forms of his political authority. Brian Larkin, an anthropologist, has written precisely of infrastructure as a means of making power visible, beyond the theatre of the debating chamber. 'A road's technical function is to transport vehicles from one place to another, promoting movement and realizing the enlightenment goal of society and economy as a space of unimpeded circulation', he writes. But it can also be a fantastic object that exceeds any practical function. Roads 'operate on the level of fantasy and desire', key currencies of political power.[35]

The expressway world is therefore full of stories about the projection of political power, by men such as Robert Moses, but also by organizations, such as Glasgow City Council at the height of its municipal pomp, or the California Division of Highways, all visionary in their different ways. That power might be used to build the expressway world, as it is in many of the cases described in this book, but it may also be used to create spectacular alternatives to it; in terms of the expression of power, there is not always much difference between the creation of the expressway world in the first place and its replacement. That is the story of Alberto Ruiz-Gallardón in Madrid, or Lee Myung-bak in Seoul, both the subject of later chapters. The forms may be new, and on the face of it progressive, but they are nonetheless the expression of political power, for precise desired effects.

Thinking about power also means thinking about resistance to power. The expressway world might have been the expression of authority, but it also produced new forms of resistance to authority. This means, for example, the work of Jane Jacobs, a New York-based journalist and community activist, whose ground-breaking book *The Death and Life of Great American Cities*, published in 1961, described the residual power of citizens in the daily occupation of their neighbourhoods; they knew things, and could see things, and had (to the outsider) invisible networks of trust that could operate to maintain order.[36] Effective power, she showed, could be distributed in new ways. Social networks could also be repurposed to deter political authority, as Jacobs showed in relation to the resistance to the Lower Manhattan Expressway, and after she moved to Canada in 1968, in relation to the Spadina Expressway in Toronto, both of which were cancelled in the early 1970s, in some part as a result of her work. It makes sense to think of the power of the expressway world residing in these places too; similarly, later anti-roads activism in the UK, for example in relation to the M3, M11, M74, and M77 expansions, ought to be considered integral to the expressway world, rather than simply in opposition to it. Such actions have produced a different kind of expressway world, even if they have not prevented it coming into being.[37]

Power in the expressway world might also simply mean use or occupation. Through use, places change over time, as the geographer J.B. Jackson repeatedly argued in his role as editor of the journal *Landscape*. By the middle of the 1960s he was regularly writing about roads as culture; a 1966 lecture described the messy automobile-oriented sprawl at the edge of American cities as producing unlikely but vital forms of modern social life.[38] For Jackson, the parking lot might even be a new form of civic space (he was an optimist). Ideas like that have had enduring appeal for academics in cultural studies and adjacent disciplines – expressways, and roads in general, have increasingly come to be read as cultural objects, their richness deriving in part from their very ubiquity.[39] The geographer Peter Merriman's book on the construction and politics of the M1 motorway through England's spine is a documentary of an anthropological place, produced by its users as much as its designers;[40] Joe Moran's book on roads is similarly an account of lived places. For Eric Avila, a specialist in Californian racial politics, the spaces of the expressway have scope for appropriation by the apparently powerless.[41] In these cases, occupation is a form of power, and the expressway world a production of its everyday use as much as its design and construction.[42] That occupation could involve care or even love, as a recent anthology has it.[43] The expressway world therefore represents various forms of power – traditional political authority invested in individuals and institutions, resistance to that authority from below, and everyday forms of occupation, all of which matter, above all in how they relate to one another.

Expressways as Culture

The expressway world is also culture. Culture matters here because it is representations – in art, design, advertising, television and, above all perhaps, film – that condition reality; we learn to see things in image before we can see them in real life. Katherine Shonfield, an architectural theorist, wrote extensively about this question. In her book *Walls Have Feelings* (2000), she wrote how 'fictions' (for her, especially film), could be used 'to reveal unseen workings of architecture'.[44] A film might represent a building in ways the architects could not have envisaged, particularly when it comes to attributing meaning: in films, she writes, 'architecture is inevitably self-consciously loaded with meaning', perhaps because film-makers typically spend so long looking at the results of what others have built. 'I am struck', Shonfield continued, 'by the way a film maker will commonly spend much longer determining how the artefacts of architects and other urban designers are to be filmed than was originally spent designing the artefacts in the first place.'[45]

One of those 'artefacts' is precisely the expressway, long an obsessive image for film-makers. (We can argue about the reasons, which may be that the Western film world's capital, Los Angeles, has so many of them, or that their experience through the windscreen is already quasi-cinematic – that is another book.)[46] A great many of those cinematic representations of the expressway have been dystopian. Typically, it is jammed and choking (Federico Fellini's *8½*, Jean-Luc Godard's *Weekend*, Joel Schumacher's *Falling Down*, Damien Chazelle's *La La Land*), ruined and littered with abandoned cars (Mimi Leder's *Deep Impact*, Fernando Meirelles's *Blindness*, George Miller's *Mad Max: Fury Road*), the site of repeated family trauma (Wim Wenders' *Paris, Texas*), or a stand-in for an authoritarian state (Héctor Babenco's *Kiss of the Spider Woman*). It's a stock disaster movie trope, a straightforward means of representing civilization turned on its head. Those negative, sometimes catastrophic, representations arguably connect to the way we think about the expressway now.

The expressway on film can also be highly ambiguous, open to contradiction. One of Shonfield's key cinematic examples is Jean-Luc Godard's 1967 film, *Two or Three Things I Know About Her*, filmed in Saint Denis, a suburban commune on the northern edge of Paris. The Périphérique orbital expressway, then under construction, repeatedly appears without explanation in the film. It's a strange, somewhat surreal object, and the relationship with its surroundings in the film, Shonfield writes, is 'one of absolute difference'.[47] 'Godard's Périphérique', she continues, 'sweeps through the city at high level, ignoring the vertical spatial hierarchy of the buildings it cuts through, isolating them and rendering them forlorn objects subordinated to the road's curvaceous power.'[48] Buildings are reduced to 'commodities', dissolving traditional urban hierarchies, much as the film does generally. But the film doesn't judge, and instead largely accepts the Périphérique, its strangeness telling us something about the contradictions of the modern urban condition. It makes its oddness visible, and it shows a public learning, somehow, to live with it. For the anthropologist Marc Augé, the Périphérique was the embodiment of the 'non-place'; Godard shows it becoming its opposite.[49]

In Andrei Tarkovsky's *Solaris*, a 1971 treatment of a Stanislaw Lem novel about the human encounter with a sentient planet, a hypnotic, wordless sequence depicts a drive on Tokyo's fantastically illuminated expressways. It bears no relation at all to the rest of the narrative, let alone the book on which it is based, but it speaks eloquently of Tarkovsky's fascination with the expressway as a magnificently strange, sublime object. It represents – one supposes – something of the director's surprise as a Soviet citizen abruptly exposed to hyper-capitalist Japan, but it also simply recognizes a new kind of nature.

For other film-makers the expressway has often enough been a *terrain vague*, a zone where things are possible or can be said that are otherwise forbidden. Or it might become, by accident, something unintended. In the documentary film *Lagos/Koolhaas* made in 2002 by the architect Rem Koolhaas and the artist Bregtje van der Haak, the harbour expressway in the centre of the Nigerian metropolis is the focus of a film about the everyday lives of its inhabitants.[50] The expressway appeals to the film-makers here because its intense traffic has turned it into a place of commerce and socialization, a neo-public space rather than a means of circulation. Similarly, the São Paulo expressway of the 2006 documentary film *Elevado 3.5* by João Sodré, Paulo Pastorelo and Maíra Bühler, appears as a lived place, an unlikely but authentic home for a diverse population. Film is particularly good at doing this, but the expressway world has been a routine subject in art too, particularly for artists based in LA. In the UK, a Manchester-based artist Jen Orpin has lately made a career out of painting tiny, intensely detailed panels depicting British motorway bridges, each one laboriously describing overlooked infrastructure.[51] They picture the often intense lived experience of the expressway world, and its human associations and meanings. In Orpin's paintings, the expressway world has become anthropological place.[52]

Autogeddon

To engage with an infrastructural object like the expressway is to engage with one of the key symbols of the hydrocarbon economy, at a moment when that economy finds itself in a place of unprecedented uncertainty. The crisis pervades all thinking; we don't know where to 'land', as the philosopher Bruno Latour put it in a late essay on environmental thinking.[53] It has produced some striking gestures: California, long the epitome of the car-oriented society, passed a Senate Bill in 2013, which put an effective end to new expressways, with the explicit aim of reducing driving.[54]

The sociologist John Urry anticipated many of the present uncertainties about the expressway world in a 2007 book *Mobilities*. Urry used the term 'automobility' to describe a system of some complexity, much bigger than individuals and their vehicles, the latter being, he thought, relatively unimportant. The system, he thought all-encompassing, extending to anything from licensing to oil refining to motels and repair shops, anything from government to the tinkering of 'car enthusiasts'.[55] Automobility's costs were huge, he wrote, involving 'massive environmental resource use' as well as 'an extraordinary scale of death and injuries'. Noting 3,000 daily deaths globally through car use, he wonders if 'the freedom to drive' is not also 'the freedom to die'.[56]

A similar sense of crisis also pervades contemporary architectural discourse, to which this book is certainly adjacent. In September 2019, the British professional publication *Architects' Journal* started what it called a 'Retro First' campaign, arguing for retention and reuse over demolition, given the amount of embodied carbon in existing structures – it repeated the manifesto-like phrase from 2007 of Carl Elefante, a former president of the American Institute of Architects, 'the greenest building is the one that already exists'.[57] A quarter of the sessions at the 2024 iteration of the Society of Architectural Historians' annual conference in Albuquerque had some relation to the climate crisis.[58] Barnabas Calder, a contemporary architectural historian with a particular interest in climate change, has written of this disciplinary shift: until recently few architects in history would have 'interpreted their own buildings in terms of energy'. Since then, Calder notes in *Architecture from Prehistory to Climate Emergency* (2020), 'there is hardly any writing about contemporary architecture and cities that does not refer to sustainability as the central challenge of our time'.[59] 'Every tool', he writes in his activist conclusion, 'big and small, heroic and expedient, needs to be brought to bear on the urgent race to decarbonize.'[60]

Beyond architecture, the climate crisis prompts a reassessment of modernism. This is inescapably a book about modernism, and specifically how we deal with its legacy. The expressway world is a modernist world whose origins lie securely in the avant-gardes of the early twentieth century. Its principal forms – the high-speed road plunging dramatically through the heart of the city – are modernist.[61] In all of those projects as originally built, there are echoes of the modernist avant-garde's commitment to innovation, to 'defamiliarization and destabilization', to creative destruction, to use the economist Joseph Schumpeter's phrase. There is also an uncompromising quality about all the schemes as originally built. Blunt and tough, all damp-stained concrete and gloomy undercroft, they have a rarely discussed *mood* that is of itself modernist, a melancholia that is not explicitly cultivated but is always there and is inherent to the appreciation of modernism.

But, as art historian Hal Foster wondered in 2023, what happens when modernism ceases to be quite so central to the cultural imagination?[62] What happens when its ideals might start to seem 'to provide ideological cover for modernity and capitalism'? Or what happens, he writes, thinking in terms of contemporary environmental concerns, when 'the modernist insistence on acceleration' is so out of step with 'a world that needs, desperately, to commit to de-growth'?[63]

Foster imagined a cultural world in which modernism has faded substantially from view, along with what he calls its 'melancholic' attitude to the world and the moral power that goes along with it; we might, he concludes, be able to find a different future in which modernism can be more easily seen relative to other contemporaneous tendencies, and also more closely 'imbricated' (as he puts it) in capitalist modernity rather than as a challenge to it.[64] Foster writes about modernism in general, rather than architecture, let alone the specific example of the expressway. But what he says matters here, as do the other approaches: the culture that produced the expressway world is no longer central in the places that first built it up.

These academic concerns parallel a range of threats to the expressway world. The turmoil in the automotive industry does likewise. General Motors and Chrysler, for much of the twentieth century icons of American industry, both collapsed into bankruptcy in 2009, surviving only through US government support.[65] Both have since been eclipsed in terms of market capitalization by the electric-only startup Tesla, whose success has been in turn challenged by Chinese rivals such as BYD.[66] Electrification has turned the car economy on its head, along with the increasing automation of the driving experience. The production of cars collapsed worldwide during the Covid-19 pandemic, by as much as 50 per cent in some regions.[67] Cars have become very much more expensive than they were pre-pandemic, harder to insure, and harder to drive into cities. It has been said – although equally contested – that the richest world economies have reached 'peak car'.[68] A book by cultural historian Matthew Crawford, published in 2020, *Why We Drive*, pictures driving as an archaic skill, perhaps like equestrianism, soon to be a minority pursuit.[69] The political direction of travel is clear enough in the richest world economies, even those most dependent on the car. There will be no more unrestricted car use; road schemes increasingly have to justify themselves on environmental grounds; as products, cars are at the start of a genuine revolution, via new technologies of electrification and autonomy. What exactly is a car, and what constitutes driving, and whether either should be permitted in cities are increasingly open questions.

Expressway Teardowns

The negative view of the expressway world has produced the desire to erase it. And if that is the aim, one project in particular is an inescapable reference point, as well as perhaps an example of what to avoid. This is the so-called Big Dig, or the reconstruction of the central area expressways in Boston, Massachusetts, which took place between 1982 and 2007 at a cost, estimated and adjusted for inflation, of $21.5 billion.[70] The project involved the diversion of the two-kilometre elevated inner-city section of the I-93 interstate underground. A new linear park – the Rose Fitzgerald Kennedy Greenway, named after the Kennedy family matriarch and North End native – occupied the land previously taken up by the elevated structure. The original scheme was opened in 1959 and consisted of a largely elevated green steel structure known locally as 'the green monster' running north–south through the central city, carrying six lanes of traffic. Construction involved the displacement of 20,000 mostly poor residents from the inner city areas adjacent to Boston's North End, which Jane Jacobs had celebrated in *The Death and Life of Great American Cities*.[71] In operation, the Artery carried 200,000 cars per day, nearly three times its design capacity. Traffic crawled for ten hours out of every twenty-four. The accident rate was said to be four times the national average.[72]

Planning for the tunnel project began in 1982, and the whole project included a new river crossing and associated improvements to public

The Rose Fitzgerald Kennedy Greenway, Boston. *Photograph by Richard J. Williams.*

transportation. The tunnel construction process had to be invented on site and was immensely complex in order to maintain the flow of traffic throughout – temporary supports as wide as the tunnel had to be built under the elevated structure while the tunnel was dug, the original supports cut away, and the structure only demolished once the tunnel had been completed and the traffic rerouted.[73] The project was notorious for cost overruns, corruption and defects. The entire tunnel section was closed in 2006 after a poorly adhered section of concrete ceiling fell on a car, killing the driver.[74] It has also been a matter of popular debate whether the scheme improved traffic flows. A 2015 report in the *Boston Globe* indicated that journey times remained much as they had been at the start of the project, with the pinch points merely relocated outside of the inner city; some journeys might even take longer.[75]

The relocation of the expressway underground removed the sight and sound of traffic from the north–south corridor, creating in the process seventy square kilometres of new real estate, divided into at least thirty parcels of varying functions. The overall scheme involved at least ten landscape design firms, with the initial masterplan overseen by Utile, and opened in 2008. The park, in form of a reversed 'C', embraces Boston's city centre, and is divided into discrete, themed pockets, with a regular farmers' market; public art abounds. There were plans, later abandoned, for a museum on parcel 12 designed by the Israeli architect Moshe Safdie. A vast area of public space, it is overseen by a Conservancy, its day-to-day running supported by mostly private funds.[76] It is a remarkable project for its scale and its success in creating safe pedestrian space where there previously was none. It is also an exceptionally controlled space. Each of its parcels has a defined theme, and an imagined user; there is a bewildering list of prohibitions. In these matters, the Greenway is no different from the other highly controlled, neo-public spaces that have come to define rich-world cities. The control does, however, sit uneasily with the citizen-led approach underwriting expressway activism – the Greenway arguably replaces one form of authority with another. Whatever it does, the Greenway isn't any kind of return to the dense community life of Boston's North End that Jane Jacobs found so appealing, and that the Central Artery largely abolished.

On the Greenway Conservancy's webpage, there's a curious and revealing image depicting the site's reconstruction.[77] Heavily cropped, the top half shows the distinctive green-painted elevated structure, and dense traffic filling the roadway. It's the middle of the 1980s, judging by the style of the vehicles, the period when planning for the Greenway began. Below, there are acres of scrubby car parking, and to the left, one of the Artery's parallel feeder roads. The green of the metal is discoloured by rust, weeds poke through the concrete at the edge of the feeder road, the parking lot is forbidding. There are no people visible – this is a landscape of machines. But it's one of few images on the website that shows some history. It has 'authenticity', to appropriate a concept important in the work of Sharon Zukin, a sociologist. There's room for things to grow, like the weeds, in the gaps between the rules.[78]

I visited the Big Dig over several days in 2024, and I confess that I found myself inexorably, perhaps perversely, drawn to the unreconstructed fringes of the Greenway where the I-93 emerges from its tunnels and the overpass begins again – the spaces, in other words, where something of the old structure could be seen. Here in these admittedly bleak spaces, there was precisely the authenticity lacking on the reconstructed Greenway. It's hard to make any objective case for these spaces, but here at least I was free of the constant exhortations to behave in approved ways ('GATHER!' 'PLAY!' 'UNWIND!'), the surveillance and the pressure to spend money. Perhaps I should return – but the Greenway was of all the many expressway spaces that I visited for the book, reconstructed and otherwise, the one I most disliked.

The Boston experience, however protracted and costly, does represent some kind of model, as do the cases regularly promoted by the Congress for the New Urbanism (CNU) under the label of *Freeways Without Futures*. Here, since the early 2010s, the CNU has routinely advocated freeway teardowns as part of its programme of advocacy of traditional urbanism.[79] The 2023 iteration of the ten ongoing campaigns across the whole of the continental United States were at varying stages of development. In place of the elevated expressways came images of tidy mixed-used development, with generous planting, pedestrian and bike lanes, and a general air of middle-class contentment. Eighteen completed projects were listed, including Boston's Big Dig, and teardowns in Chattanooga, Milwaukee, Oakland, Providence and Rochester, along with, for good measure, the well-known projects in Madrid (M-30), Paris (Seine expressway) and Seoul (Cheonggyecheon).[80] CNU's somewhat imperial project might also have included Maastrict and Eindhoven in the Netherlands, both of which removed urban expressways and created parkland (and in Eindhoven's case, reinstated a canal) in the 2010s. These projects, now numerous and global, constitute an emerging, and highly photogenic orthodoxy. It appears to heal the urban body, and correct past injustices, and re-establish a lost order; its logic (as the CNU website makes clear) is also intrinsically connected with real estate development. Tearing down an expressway is a way of finding scarce inner-city land.

The Plan of the Book

This could easily be a book of gentrification studies, and it might have been had it concentrated on the United States. Instead, it explores a global range of possible responses to the expressway problem, only some of which can be described in gentrification's terms. Some are subtler responses, forms of accommodation or living with the expressway, or making culture out of it. The expressway is a global form. However, as Latour points out in *Down to Earth*, the global no longer represents an ideal, and the imagination of its future is acutely local.[81] The book therefore takes the local seriously, showing how the same basic forms can find themselves used in different ways.

The book's narrative begins in New York (chapter 2) on the West Side Highway, exploring the way this collapsed expressway produced different forms of accommodation and appropriation, before eventually being rehabilitated as a surface level boulevard. The chapter also covers the unbuilt LOMEX, or the Lower Manhattan Expressway: an extraordinary megastructure that would have divided lower Manhattan. Chapter 3 explores the intersection of the San Diego and Santa Monica freeways in Los Angeles, for Reyner Banham a work of engineering art, and the chapter explores its status in those terms. Chapter 4 considers London's iconic Westway, the elevated portion of the A40(M) as it crosses the West London suburb of Ladbroke Grove. The Westway has, I argue, been the site of the most intense imaginative forms of cultural appropriation – its substructure was extraordinarily well used from the start, and it remains an example of how to live with the expressway as well. Chapter 5 explores São Paulo's equally iconic Minhocão, which over a half century has turned itself from everyday expressway into urban beach. Chapter

6 considers the dramatic and costly transformation of Madrid's M-30, which created some ten kilometres of public space over a newly tunnelled section of expressway. Chapter 7 focuses on Seoul's Cheonggyecheon, perhaps the most extreme response to the expressway – the demolition of a highway and its expensive replacement with a reconstituted river, a highly rhetorical, although misleading restoration of nature. The final chapter explores the past and future of Glasgow's M8, at a moment when the poetics and politics of the expressway are unusually fluid. At the time of writing, the public conversation about its future was unfocused but highly imaginative, with all kinds of mutually contradictory desires in play.

Automotive fantasies no longer hold much appeal for younger consumers no longer willing or able to bear the cost of car ownership.[82] Of itself, the expressway no longer represents modernity, but a uniquely modern problem. This book explores the range of possible solutions, from doing nothing, to cultural interventions and appropriations, to the most elaborate forms of reconstruction. The expressway can be a crudely dystopian trope, but it can also be – as in Tarkovsky – something much more open and complex. Recovering that complexity is one of the principal tasks of this book, because in the popular discourse around the expressway, simple solutions predominate. Marshall Berman's outrage at the Cross-Bronx is entirely understandable, but it is also a simple view: he wants it gone. As do, increasingly, many others, looking to replace it with a park or garden, or a beach, as part of a larger, somewhat nostalgic project of recovering a lost urbanism. The concept of the fifteen-minute city, popularized by the architect Carlos Moreno and adopted in principle by cities as varied as Paris and Oxford is a good example; the Congress for the New Urbanism's *Freeways Without Futures* is another. There is no place for the expressway in that slowed-down, small-scale city vision.[83] We continue building urban expressways, especially in the Global South as Daniel Knowles has written.[84] But the direction of travel is clear enough, away from the expressway world and towards some other, yet to be determined future.

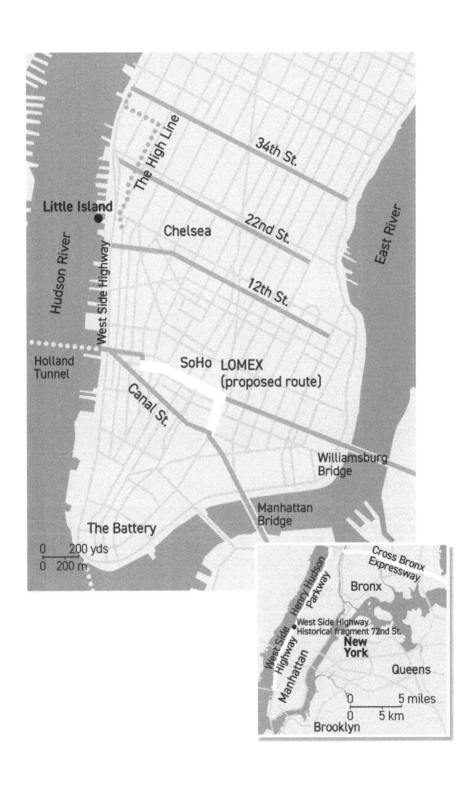

CHAPTER 2

New York: The Expressway in Ruins

'Truck and Car Fall as West Side Highway Collapses', *The New York Times* (16 December 1973). *Photograph by Ted Cowell. From* The New York Times. © *1973. The New York Times Company. All rights reserved. Used under license.*

It is an extraordinary image: on the right-hand side, in the foreground the tractor unit of an articulated truck lies on its roof, wheels helplessly aloft, the contractor's name, Edenwald, legible on the cab door. On the left a Ford LTD sedan car faces you, right side up, but battered and crumpled. Debris lies all around. Scan upwards, and there is a clue to the location – a winged Art Deco-style relief reads Pier 53 Market, indicating the industrial Hudson River frontage in lower Manhattan, the zone around 12th Street to be precise. But behind that is a chasm where clearly a road ought to be. In fact, you can make out the road, or what's left of it, with its white lines marking the lanes. But the whole section is in the wrong place, resting at forty-five degrees instead of horizontally and you puzzle to make sense of what has happened. A section of one carriageway has broken clear along one edge and collapsed, taking the vehicles with it. A firefighter looks on from the right, his distinctive helmet framing the scene. Back up on the surviving section of the roadway a crane picks forlornly at the debris. It's the expressway world, but definitively ruined.

The photograph, by a freelancer, Ted Cowell, appeared in *The New York Times* on 16 December 1973 and the event it depicted had occurred the previous day on the West Side Elevated Highway.[1] The precise location, at around Little West 12th Street in lower Manhattan, was once the heart of the city's deepwater port, but in 1973 an increasingly derelict area of wharves and warehouses. The highway, built in 1930, was in poor shape. As a 1974 State Department of Transportation put it, the 'use of salt and heavy volume of traffic have caused disintegration to large areas of concrete slab … in some cases portions of these slabs have fallen to the street below. The blacktop overlays are also in poor condition with potholes and surface cracking. That damaged concrete has been temporarily maintained by placing steel plates over the voids; there are over 70 steel plates on the deck.'[2]

Ironically, some patching up had just started. The truck in the image was involved in the $1 million repair job, carrying thirty tonnes of asphalt to another part of the highway. 'The connections between the transverse floor beams and the east main longitudinal girder failed', stated the 1974 report, 'causing a 70ft section of the northbound deck to fall onto West Street.'[3] The drivers escaped with minor injuries and, according to news reports, were discharged from medical supervision the same day.[4] No-one else was harmed, despite the spectacular collapse.[5]

It took forty-one years to sort out the West Side Highway, during which time almost everything imaginable happened to it: first of all nothing, then its informal adoption as a bike lane, its occupation by squatters, a megalomaniac replacement design followed by its cancellation, then demolition and reconstruction as a traditional boulevard, then destruction again thanks to the events of September 11, 2001, before its reconstitution again as a boulevard, this time with the addition of the

Miller Highway Remnant at West 72nd St., New York City. *Photograph by Richard J. Williams.*

Hudson River Park, a legal entity since 1998. In its current iteration, it has arguably been the focus of the city's most frenzied urban transformations of recent times. The park alone is by far the city's largest since the completion of Central Park in 1858. Destroyed and abandoned multiple times, the West Side Highway has since become choice real estate. In the middle of it all, a tiny fragment of the original highway still remains, at the park at 72nd Street – an abandoned spur, its steel frame, painted an institutional green, pokes out from under the modern elevated highway, a picturesque ruin.

Here the expressway world literally and metaphorically collapses. New York was not the only place this happened, but it was perhaps one of the most dramatic reversals of the expressway world, for the city was after all central to its formation. In 1940, the architectural theorist and historian Sigfried Giedion described New York's primacy in the development of automobile-oriented urbanism, particularly for its parkways that he particularly admired; New York's enthusiasm for expressways predated that of any other American city, contrary to later, Los Angeles-centric views.[6] (The historian of planning Peter Hall, writing much later, agreed.[7]) But if New York was an early adopter of the automotive model, and through the work of Robert Moses especially, its most enthusiastic builder, it was also the American city that most publicly abandoned the automotive model, partly through neglect, partly through lack of capital to continue it, and partly through anti-highway activism. The story of the West Side Highway and its aftermath is key.

There had been well-publicized, so-called 'freeway revolts' elsewhere in the United States, starting in San Francisco after the consequences of the passing of the 1956 Federal Aid Highway Act were properly understood (in 1959 San Francisco's Board of Governors voted to cancel seven of its ten urban freeways, under pressure from well-organized local opposition).[8] However New York's failures were arguably the most spectacular, and the most consequential, and they can be found as clearly as anywhere in the history of the West Side Highway. A highly imperfect urban space at every point, its imperfections themselves describe the history of the expressway world.

The Miller Highway

For Marshall Berman, New York's expressway world is, for good reason, coterminous with Robert Moses, the obsessive, all-powerful chair of the Triborough Bridge and Tunnel Authority from 1934 to 1968 and at least eleven other public positions in New York. It is Moses, who curiously never learned to drive, who remade the city in automobile terms, responsible for the Henry Hudson Parkway, the Cross-Bronx Expressway, and the Long Island Parkway system, 416 miles in all of intersection-free express roads, along with associated bridges, tunnels and parks. No other single historical figure comes close in making the expressway world.[9]

It is easy to attribute New York's experience of the expressway world to Moses, but the West Side Highway actually predates his period of influence. The city's first elevated expressway, it was first mooted in 1924 as a possible resolution of so-called 'Death Avenue' – the dense and dangerous traffic conditions on Tenth and Eleventh Avenues around the port, conditions compounded by the presence of the New York Central Railroad at grade level in the area. Al Smith, New York City's then Governor (and later Moses's great enabler) endorsed the plan in 1926, and construction of the first section, a mile and a half stretch from Canal Street to 22nd Street, started in May 1929, completed in November 1930.[10] For Julius Miller, Manhattan Borough President, the elevated highway was 'a personal crusade'.[11] (Miller liked elevated roads, and he had already built a significant one, the Park Avenue Viaduct outside Central Station.) Short, but innovative, the West Side Highway had three northbound lanes, and three southbound, the concrete and granite roadway supported by steel peers set eighty feet apart. The road surface sat thirty-five feet above ground, allowing for traffic to cross at grade level to and from the piers. To modern eyes, its exit ramps are terrifying – set in the centre of the structure to restrict the land take either side, they required slow moving traffic to pass into the fast lane before exiting. Notoriously tight turns and narrow lanes also proved to be killers.

Its imperfections notwithstanding, the Miller Highway caused much celebration. As *The New York Times* reported after its official opening on 13 November 1930, it was a model project that might be the first unit in a system of elevated highways encircling the city, perhaps even the nation.[12] The cost it reported as $6.5 million for the first section (the equivalent of $123 million in 2025).[13] It foreshadowed 'an era of speed in motor transportation' and more prosaically might help the immediate traffic situation in lower Manhattan. There was quite a parade. After speeches by Miller and others, the official cars set off for the on ramp at Canal Street, descending to ground level again via a temporary wooden structure at 22nd. The band of the 16th Infantry led the parade, followed by mounted police, and then 'a naval band, a detachment of marines and sailors, the provisional company of 165th Infantry, New York National Guard, field artillery, anti-aircraft units and detachments of men and equipment from four city departments. Police on foot, on motorcycles, in side cars and in emergency wagons with screaming sirens followed. Then came firemen.' There were 3,000 in all in the official parade, a big show for a short road, and a statement of intent.[14]

The Elevated was a practical project directed at decongesting lower Manhattan, but it was also an aesthetic one. On announcing the project in 1928, Miller said that the highway would provide 'charming views of the river and the opposite shores', and radically improve the experience for tourists from Westchester County travelling down to lower Manhattan and beyond.[15] The tourist gaze made concrete, it reconfigured the city as a sequence of motorized panoramas.[16] Miller was nowhere near as poetic as Moses later on, but he had similar aesthetic ambitions, and the project had a certain grandeur. It employed the architects Sloan and Robertson, whose recent work included the Graybar Building at 420 Lexington Avenue, a fantastical, pyramid-like office complex with Babylonian decoration. There was some fantasy with the first phase of the West Side Elevated Highway. The structure was steel, with concrete balustrades, a practical measure to keep the traffic on the highway, but also an opportunity for Art Deco stylings. The balustrade, Amy Finstein has written in an account of early American highways, 'was to be punctuated by small stepped posts along its length, emulating the forms of nearby setback skyscrapers. The lamp standards were to magnify this iconography, using gradually stepped steel plates to create tall, slim, pyramid-topped forms.'[17] This part of the programme was directed at motorists, 'syncopating' the driving experience.[18]

If the design programme unexpectedly considered the driver's aesthetic experience, it also had something for the pedestrian, with winged relief motifs regularly punctuating the concrete balustrade, and twenty-one cast iron cartouches announcing the cross streets.[19] There were 'two distinct constituencies' therefore: drivers moving at speed along the structure and pedestrians picking their way around at ground level, and the architects addressed them with different scales.[20]

There was cultural ambition, occasionally visible in images of it, such as the fine gelatin silver print of it at night in 1940, made by the artist Andreas Feininger, now in the Whitney's collection. A long exposure makes the car headlights into bright trails, an everyday photographic cliché now, but a novelty then.[21] In real life, the aesthetic part of the programme is clearly visible at Riverside Park at 72nd Street, where a substantial fragment survives, although curiously without much explanation. Emerging from a popular present-day dog run, it rises to fifteen or so metres, before being dwarfed by the present-day elevated structure of the Henry Hudson Parkway, the toll road that makes its way north. The present-day highway is straightforward and utilitarian (although busy with basketball courts and dog runs and cafes at ground level, it is no wasteland). The Miller fragment is a different kind of object; it curves westward away from under the parkway, a forest of broad steel arches, twelve in all, the verticals perhaps ten metres apart. The roadway part is still visible, but now just the horizontal supporting structure, describing a curve but in clunky straight sections. Steel drainage pipes thread their way through the whole thing but they don't detract from the overall effect, which is dark, complex and somewhat baroque, with echoes of New York's great civic architecture.

The West Side Elevated Highway may have been a Miller project, but Robert Moses did not waste time in subsuming it into his own, much grander, vision. As chair of the Metropolitan Conference on Parks, in February 1930 he presided over an annual dinner at the Commodore Hotel at which he outlined a $20 million programme of parkways, in which the West Side Elevated Highway had been absorbed.[22] From then on it was a fragment of the gigantic West Side Improvement Project, which restructured the west side of Manhattan as a series of parkways, linking Westchester County to the north with lower Manhattan and New Jersey.[23] Moses oversaw the whole West Side project from 1934 to 1937, opening it on 12 October that year with some pomp. Rarely prone to modesty, Moses said 'droves of cars zoom or crawl through Riverside Park and down the WSH and view the matchless, unspoiled Pallisades'. 'By comparison the castled Rhine with its Lorelei is a mere trickle.'[24]

It was a highway, but conceived of in terms of a leisure park, so news reports emphasized the amenities that accompanied it – the tennis courts, the playgrounds, the softball fields, the basketball and handball courts, the 13,000 mature trees, the 350,000 shrubs and the 140,000 feet of footpaths.[25] The drive itself was imagined as a pleasure ride, its sequence of unfolding visual delights framed by the car windscreen. It was also, Robert Caro noted, an argument in itself for progress, at least progress formulated on Moses's terms. To ride on the elevated portion of the West Side Highway was to be presented with a view of the congested industrial city with its pervasive filth and smoke, but at the same time to rise above it. A 'panorama of all that was wrong with the industrial era', wrote Caro, 'the reporters could still realize that they were not on those streets, that they were speeding downtown without even having to pause'.[26] You can see something of that in a widely reproduced postcard from the early 1940s in Columbia University's collections of the highway looking north from 46th Street.[27] The docks stretch out to the left, factories and warehouses to the right. There's a marked separation between the roadway and the rest of the scene; above it is the future, all light and space and motion, while below it is a dingy industrial chaos, the future and the past in one image.

The cost for the whole scheme, put at $24 million ($446 million in 2025 terms) in the news reports, was likely ten times that figure.[28] It was in any case a public relations triumph, and a remarkable piece of propaganda for the emergent expressway world – this was, in the reports, much less a prosaic solution to a safety problem, than a kinetic sculpture. In the language of the reporters, it is the quintessential modern experience, about flashing above the existing city, plunging into its depths, and rising up again to carve a path along its waterfront.

The limitations of the West Side Elevated Highway quite quickly became obvious, and *The Times* sent reporters in the 1940s to cover the problems it had been built in theory to resolve. A nasty curve at Gansevoort Street was responsible for six deaths alone in 1941, hence its new name, 'Dead Man's Bend'.[29] Perceptions of it changed – it became 'villainous' in Finstein's words, known for its 'inconvenient ramps, sharp turns, inadequate capacity, and decrepit condition', faults attributed to it well before the 1973 collapse.[30] There were reports and schemes to improve it, none very conclusive.[31] 'Monumental disrepair', as Moses described it in a grumpy pamphlet of 1974, clear in his view that nothing beyond neglect had been achieved since his involvement with it in the 1930s.[32]

The Miller Highway Occupied

Collapse was therefore predictable. Collapse also made the West Side Highway visible, in the clichéd sense that we only notice infrastructure when it stops working.[33] It had been in many ways invisible until then, a place one might go specifically to escape the formal city and its moral codes. And the collapse of the highway is also of a piece with New York's wider fiscal collapse in the 1970s (made into a media icon by the *New York Daily News* with its legendary 1975 headline, 'Ford to City: Drop Dead').[34] In the photographer Danny Lyon's images for *The Destruction of Lower Manhattan*, documenting the epic demolition works on the site of the World Trade Center in 1968 and 1969, the West Side Highway is a repeated presence. Sometimes it is directly imaged, sometimes glimpsed at the edge of an image or from a window; consistent with the desperate landscape Lyon describes in general, it is already, pre-1973 collapse, half-ruined.[35]

The 1973 collapse was followed by progressive closures of the roadway, first around 14th Street and then shortly after the entire section south of 23rd Street. Not long after that, an elevated section of the Henry Hudson Parkway was closed around 72nd Street, 'inflaming tempers', then all sections below 46th Street, and before long the whole structure was under threat.[36] Comprehensive demolition was discussed in 1976, and started the following year in October – and it would take until 1989 until the entire structure, except for the 72nd Street fragment, would disappear. In between the 1973 collapse and demolition, however, it took on another life. As the city pondered what to do and ran out of money, the West Side Elevated Highway inadvertently became something else – an informal playground, an impromptu garden, a place.[37]

The New York Times could report in 1974 that the southbound lane of the Miller Highway had, with no organization of any kind, already become the most heavily used cycle lane in the whole city, albeit an illegal one.[38] It could be dangerous. The same report described a boy's death one night by falling though the 14th Street gap. It could also be a more benign place, if an eerie one. Or it could, as another *The Times*' report described in 1977, be a place of impromptu artistic interventions.[39] It described an apocalyptic scene, 'all broken windows and dark interiors as vapid as an old movie lot', with artistic appeal; a visiting German painted the roadway with an image of the Twin Towers in aluminium paint, while ailanthus trees rose from the cracks, and down below in the meat-packing district prostitutes mingled with blood-spattered butchers. It might in short order, *The Times* continued, revert to a state of nature, 'a Rousseau landscape hanging right above the continuing traffic'.[40] The accompanying picture confirms the assessment. A young, affluent-looking male jogs towards the camera in running shoes, half-smiling, like a J.G. Ballard character perfectly at home in the dereliction. You can make out modern towers in the background behind him, and closest to the viewer, already luxuriant shrubbery taking over the roadway.

The West Side Highway's appearances in film continued the apocalyptic theme. It's there, repeatedly, in background shots in Martin Scorsese's *Taxi Driver*, the location of the filthy depot where the psychopathic protagonist Travis Bickle picks up his rented Checker cab. The steel structure and cement balustrade are clearly visible, as is the Art Deco relief work identifying Pier 57, along with glimpses of traffic creeping along the carriageways, but it's a means of framing the city's decay rather than an exemplar of progress; a grimy, man-made horizon, it limits the experience of the city rather than opening it up. Bickle's world is simply a larger version of the West Side Highway, a grimly claustrophobic city, collapsing under the weight of its own filth. In Sidney Lumet's *Serpico* (1973), the downbeat closing shot frames the main character, newly ex-cop, beaten and dejected under the West Side Highway while in the background, moored up at Pier 88, the colossal, dark bulk of the *SS France* looms.

The ruined highway also became a photographic subject at this point, in, for example, images by Jan Staller made around 1977 and subsequently acquired by the Museum of the City of New York.[41] In colour images made with a large format Hasselblad camera, the Elevated appears entirely depopulated, at dawn or dusk, a stark ruin, but a place in which (as the photographer described) there was a peace absent from the rest of the city, as well as big horizons; in other words in this work, and in the ad hoc improvisations of local joggers and artists, there was a value in abandonment. At the same time, next door in the abandoned dock buildings, other photographers such as Alvin Baltrop were documenting the impromptu queer utopia that had emerged in the ruins; the dereliction adjacent to the formal city had provided a space of unusual permissiveness, sexual or otherwise.[42]

LOMEX Detour

What we have so far is a story of ruins: a strangely designed, poorly executed, badly maintained highway that collapses out of neglect, only to find, if only temporarily, a universe of alternative uses – film set, homeless encampment, queer utopia, bike path. As the municipality retreated, others moved in. As much as the expressway world is a product of visionaries and authoritarians, it is also a product of improvisers and opportunists, bricolage as much as plan.

There was value, in other words, in not rebuilding the expressway world, in maintaining it as ruin, in forestalling progress. In New York, the most celebrated case of that prior to the West Side Highway was the Lower Manhattan Expressway (LOMEX), and we need to take a detour there to understand why – apart from a $2 million, 156-foot section – it remained entirely unbuilt.[43] Its rejection, as Marshall Berman described, was more than a local matter, but it signalled a broader rejection of the expressway world in the city, and the possibility of doing so beyond.[44] LOMEX's failure explains in large part why the West Side Highway was never rebuilt in its elevated form.

The first proposal for anything like LOMEX appeared in 1929 in the Regional Planning Association's *Regional Plan of New York and its Environs*.[45] Moses first seriously backed the project in 1941, and by 1960 had New York City's Board of Estimate approval, which means that it had become a real project. It had in any case become more financially appealing through the potential for Interstate funding from Washington.[46] There were incentives, in other words, for over-engineering; an interstate would attract federal money. The Lower Manhattan Expressway therefore became I-78, a Y-shaped scheme connecting the Holland Tunnel under the Hudson with two branches across the East River to Brooklyn, one to the Manhattan Bridge, the other to the Williamsburg Bridge. In Manhattan proper, it crossed the area later known as SoHo, characterized by late nineteenth-century cast-iron fronted warehouses, at that time zoned for industry, with correspondingly low rents. Many buildings lay partially vacant. It became popular with artists in the 1960s who valued the low cost, the big floorplates and the quality of the light. Architects, even modernists, increasingly praised it: Peter Blake, then editor-in-chief of *Architectural Forum*, called it 'one of the most spectacular museums of modern architecture to be found anywhere in the world'.[47] The colonization of loft buildings for cultural purposes was well covered in the mainstream media, and it made increasing appearances in film.[48]

The expressway plan got a boost in the early 1960s with the support of the Downtown-Lower Manhattan Association (DLMA), a pressure group representing the interests of business and financial services in particular. Chaired by David Rockefeller, conveniently the brother of then New York state governor Nelson, it aimed to protect Wall Street as the city's premier financial hub, where the Rockefeller bank headquarters continued – against prevailing fashion – to be located.[49] The DLMA saw SoHo as a threat. A 'grey zone' of economic social decay between the financial district and the wealthier parts of the city and the state; with a view to maintaining the health of the central city, it needed to be reformed.[50] It published its key prospectus in 1964: 'Lower Manhattan Expressway: An Essential Key to Business Growth and Job Opportunities in Lower Manhattan and New York City', the title alone a statement of the business agenda.[51]

Moses himself was bullish about it. In a revealing, pro-LOMEX pamphlet published by the Triborough Bridge and Tunnel Authority in 1965, Moses, his frustration barely suppressed, urged that there be 'no further delay in building the LOMEX'. 'The route of the proposed expressway', he went on, 'passes through a deteriorating area with low property values ... the buildings in this area are at least sixty years old, are in poor condition, and have numerous violations against them.'[52] There were two pages of admonitory photographs – dense SoHo streets clogged with traffic and overflowing trash, cast-iron warehouse façades rising imperiously. In a different context this might have been a visual argument for historic preservation. Here it was incontrovertible evidence for what had to be erased.[53]

By that stage, however, opposition was already well mobilized. It was a varied coalition, but not an unprivileged one, as Eric Avila has described, armed with 'college degrees, home equity, dual incomes, inherited wealth, flexible hours and contacts in media and government' – they had the time and the connections to make waves.[54] Their numbers included the architectural journalist and activist Jane Jacobs, author of the recently published *Death and Life of Great American Cities*, who formed the Joint Committee to Stop the Lower Manhattan Expressway, along with Gerald Mountain, the pastor of the church of the Most Holy Crucifix on Broome St. The scheme would have demolished Mountain's church, as he pointed out in numerous press articles.[55] (In a later meeting he complained: 'on the map my church has been replaced by fountains!'[56]) On 9 August in the evening during a downpour Jacobs led a successful march from SoHo to Gracie Mansion, the official residence of the Mayor of New York, at 88th Street overlooking the East River.[57] Eleanor Roosevelt, the wife of former president Franklin Delano, had already given vocal support.[58] Roosevelt had written to Mayor Wagner, complaining that, among other things, 'an alarming number of aged persons' might be displaced, while the area was 'known for its low crime rate'.[59]

A delay resulted – Jacobs appeared to have won a point.[60] The activist position gained popularity. John Lindsay, elected mayor of New York City in 1965, ran his campaign on a platform of opposition to the Lower Manhattan Expressway. The debate rumbled on, with innumerable skirmishes. In April 1968 at a New York State hearing on the project at Seward Park High School, Jane Jacobs was arrested and charged with disorder – frustrated at the conduct of the meeting, she invited fellow activists onto the stage as she spoke, and destroyed – or helped destroy – the stenographic record of the meeting. An ad in the *Village Voice* sought 'witnesses' for the strange events.[61]

The constituencies of opposition therefore included not only local residents and activist journalists, but also the (Democratic) political establishment and God. They also increasingly had art. As early as 1962, Stephanie Gervis wrote in the *Village Voice* of the potential of artists to kill the Broome St Expressway.[62] For 'Jackson', a Broome St-based artist Gervis quoted, New York had 'become the world's focal point for contemporary painting' and the expressway 'would destroy a series of the most fecund neighbourhoods'. For artists, the Broome St Expressway became a focal point of opposition certainly for it directly threatened their lofts, but opposition also substantially formed group identity. Prior to the expressway proposals, if art existed in the area, it was sketchy and marginal; after the Broome St Expressway proposals, SoHo was on its way to becoming the centre of the art world, not only in the city, but beyond.

An artist-led campaign against the Expressway, called simply Artists Against the Expressway, started up in 1969, co-ordinated by Julie Judd, married to the sculptor Donald – they owned a loft building at 110 Spring Street, now a museum.[63] The proposed expressway, only a block away from their building, was really too close for comfort.[64] The Judds understood that they and other artists might have some influence, and perhaps even power over their environment. Their campaign capitalized on the growing status of SoHo and the New York art scene in general, widely understood to have supplanted Paris as the de facto global art capital.[65]

During precisely the period the DLMA was promoting the expressway, New York's art world grew substantially in the downtown area, a new and increasingly dynamic pole of growth (there would be a more permanent shift of art world geography from uptown later in the 1970s). The urban historian Aaron Shkuda lists seventy-nine galleries that opened up in SoHo between 1964 and 1975, while artists were an increasingly visible population in the area.[66] (They were helped in part by changes to zoning regulations in 1970 that permitted 'certified artists' to install bathrooms in their lofts.[67]) In any case Mayor Lindsay had already declared the Lower Manhattan Expressway dead in 1969.[68] Nelson Rockefeller, still state governor, legally confirmed the decision in March 1971 when he signed a bill removing it from city plans. Referring to LOMEX, and an equally controversial plan for a Cross-Brooklyn Expressway, the governor's spokesman reportedly said, 'Now we're happy to see them buried.'[69]

The story of the Lower Manhattan Expressway is, on the one hand, a story about power and popular opposition to it, and it can be told as a courtroom drama. But it is also a story about urban moods and pathologies. At the beginning of the 1960s, in public discourse at any rate, the city was a thing to be simplified (think of Moses's 'meat ax'[70]). By the end of the 1960s, thanks in part to Jane Jacobs' activism and the publication of her book *The Death and Life of Great American Cities*, there was an understanding of the city as an ecosystem, in which the street, with its accumulated forms and rituals and mutually understood behaviours, was the central figure.[71] It was an anthropological rather than an economic understanding. Marshall Berman wrote much later on of Jacobs' presence as a 'shout in the street', in so doing identifying the city street, in all its lived complexity, as the locus of modernism.[72] It was not a straightforward battle between the privileged and the dispossessed, as Avila argues – there was the 'decisive role of class privilege' on the part of the anti-expressway activists: 'they fought powerful political and economic forces but they too maximized wealth and power to pursue their self-interest'.[73] It was in some ways one set of privileged actors battling another. But it decisively changed the prevailing politics around the expressway world, posing existential and lasting questions about its desirability and viability.

The Lower Manhattan Expressway threat created the perfect conditions for what in some ways finished it off, namely the influx of artists.[74] What we might now term planning blight – which is to say the threat to capital value posed by a future project – actively depressed rents in SoHo, precisely allowing the sudden and rapid migration of artists.[75] Once the threat of the Expressway was withdrawn, and processes to consolidate SoHo's status were initiated, capital values and rents subsequently rose – and ultimately, in the great artistic migration to Chelsea of the 1990s – the art world decamped again. The expressway world had created its nemesis: after LOMEX no further development occurred, nor, significantly was conceivable, such had been the changes in lower Manhattan, of principal actors, of demography, and of mood.

The Lower Manhattan Expressway has a strange coda. In 1967 the Ford Foundation funded the architect Paul Rudolph, until not long previously the chair of Yale's Department of Architecture and the designer of its building on campus, to study the possibilities generated by the Lower Manhattan Expressway. It was a parallel project to the politicking at City Hall – it had no official status and was focused on ameliorating the proposed expressway's effects. The result was a set of detailed pen drawings and models, all completed in 1972 at which point there was an exhibition, *New Forms of the Evolving City*. A comprehensive selection of drawings and photographs of the exhibition were published as a book with Ford Foundation help in 1974, but by this time the parent project was three years dead. 'People will no doubt be quick to point out that … this proposed highway corridor is no longer to be found on official maps of the city', wrote the book's author, Peter Wolf. He brushed aside such anxieties: 'These ironies, which will escape few careful observers' attention, hardly matter.'[76] The Italian design journal *Domus*, covering the Rudolph project in detail in 1976, similarly ignored the question.[77]

Rudolph's project was therefore an architectural orphan. It is telling that it should be the cover image of Reyner Banham's 1976 book *Megastructure: Urban Futures of the Recent Past*, a melancholy review of an architectural tendency that Banham – for all his initial enthusiasm

NEW YORK: THE EXPRESSWAY IN RUINS

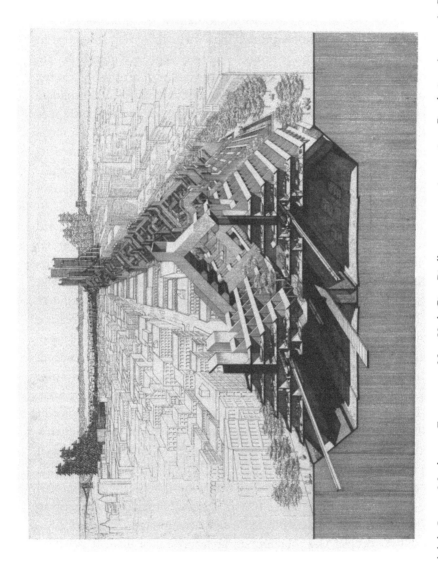

Paul Rudolph, Lower Manhattan Expressway, New York City. Bird's-eye perspective section. Rendering. (ca. 1970). *Retrieved from the Library of Congress.*

for it, especially the visionary work of the London-based practice Archigram – thought was dead.[78] He said little about Rudolph's image, except to use it as a way to problematize the meaning of megastructure. He quoted Rudolph in interview, the architect struggling to explain the megastructure work by historical allusion. It was, he wrote not altogether convincingly, like the Ponte Vecchio in Florence, a multifunctional chunk of city contained in a single form, both infrastructure and building at the same time.[79]

The image is by any standards astonishing. An enormous drawing, done by hand by Rudolph himself, it is of a type the architect made his own: a combination of single point perspective and section, showing at a glance the use and inhabitation of space, and the situation of that space in the landscape. The foreground takes a slice through the project, a vast triangular structure, with a linear atrium running all the way through from the Hudson to the East River, a distance of nearly three miles. In the far distance are the Manhattan (on the left) and Washington (on the right) bridges, their lattice-form towers both clearly identifiable. But in the foreground is something unlike anything else: two concrete structures filled with apartments and offices, set above the atrium, and below that, a monorail people mover system with cellular pods, and below that, six lanes of Interstate. Trees – somehow, in spite of the unpromising environment – rise from the atrium, while outside the structure either side of the reconstructed Broome Street, there is a linear park, a message that development can bring nature back into the devastation of lower Manhattan.

Rudolph did not lack ambition. In his script treatment for an unmade film on the project, his historical precedents for the project included no less than the Parthenon, Chartres Cathedral, St Peter's Basilica, Bath Royal Crescent, the Rue de Rivoli, the Spanish Steps, the Eiffel Tower and the Villa Savoye.[80] But more revealing perhaps was Rudolph's imagination of the driver/inhabitant of this extraordinary landscape. Obsessed with mitigating the driver's frustrations with traffic, or recapturing a sense of flow, Rudolph's city is only real when seen from a height. 'From the air the city seems serene and peaceful', he writes. 'The city is soundless, remote and abstract. We are uninvolved with the life below.'[81]

It is certainly exciting: Futurism meets the Death Star.[82] And although done independently of City Hall, it is easy enough to see how it might service the desires of the DLMA, and their value mining of lower Manhattan real estate. It is also diametrically opposed mood-wise to the emergent urban consensus around the best use of lower Manhattan, which was increasingly mindful of its existing surroundings. Rudolph didn't depict the inhabitants of this megastructure in any detail, but perhaps he didn't need to – this was a machine, its real inhabitants automata, circulating perpetually on their monorails. Even the structure itself appears to be in motion as it zooms towards the East River. It is as far from the complexly anthropological life of Broome Street as it is possible to get.

'So the 1960s passed', wrote Marshall Berman, 'the expressway world gearing itself up for ever more gigantic expansion and growth, but finding itself attacked by a multitude of passionate shouts from the street … bringing the gigantic engines to a stop, or at least radically slowing them down.'[83] In fact the conclusion to the LOMEX project seemed to be clear to local journalists as early as 1962. In a succinct assessment by Stephanie Jervis, first published in the *Village Voice*, the battle of LOMEX represented 'the endless Holy War against the spirit of Robert Moses'.[84] In that account, the war seemed genuinely winnable – not perhaps because Moses's power was on the wane, but because LOMEX had activated diverse and unbiddable forms of opposition – artists, activists, local residents – in other words, human beings rather than the highway schemes' motorized automata.[85]

Enter Westway

LOMEX was the first significant challenge to the dominance of the expressway world in New York, and it marked the effective end of Moses's authority. Almost immediately following its cancellation in 1971 came Westway, the official reconfiguration of the West Side Highway. No relation to west London expressway of the same name that is the subject of chapter 4, it was vast in ambition, encompassing not only a road, but mass transit, and a huge tranche of development land, reclaimed from the Hudson. Initially proposed in 1971, Westway involved the complete recreation of the west side of Manhattan, a project that if realized would have been – as the architecture critic Paul Goldberger wrote – as decisive for the form of the city as Central Park.[86] For one thing it meant the erasure of the rationale for Manhattan's existence in the first place, its old port. Westway would have removed all of its piers below 34th Street, and reclaimed the land to build a park extending as much as half a kilometre beyond the existing shoreline.[87] The West Side Highway in its various forms, including the Elevated and the Henry Hudson Parkway, would become a new Interstate, buried in a tunnel. There was financial logic, for an Interstate (as opposed to a city or state highway) would be eligible for Federal funds, amounting to 90 per cent of the overall cost. There was impeccable modernist logic too: the city as parkland, circulation, open space, the erasure of complexity. It marked the completion of the job started by Moses.

In 1974, with Parsons, Brinckerhoff, Quade and Douglas consultants, the New York State Department of Transportation published its monumental report on the project, setting out eight alternative schemes, with varying degrees of land reclamation.[88] It unequivocally recommended the biggest and most costly of them, estimated at $1.2 billion (about $8 billion at 2025 rates). There wasn't much architecture per se, except for some minimal boxes concealing the ventilation from the depressed roadway. Nor was there much human life: a perspective drawing outlining the design of one of the ventilation buildings, there is a small crowd, as if it were some kind of an attraction. But otherwise, judged by the Design Report, Westway is entirely depopulated, the city reduced to abstract motorized circulation – it speaks to the erasure of the city rather than its development.

Westway was the apotheosis of the expressway world. It had some serious architectural involvement, namely some proposed landscaping by Venturi and Scott Brown, that would have rendered the city skyline as a series of postmodern toys. It piqued the interest of developers including Donald Trump, who took advantage of the speculation around Westway to propose a multi-tower residential scheme that involved the somewhat bold relocation of the West Side Highway inland to allow tenants uninterrupted river views.[89] But it faced challenges from the start, including well-organized environmental opposition based on Westway's existential threat to the Hudson's population of striped bass.[90] Moses himself, out of office since 1968, was sharply critical, no doubt because he was no longer involved. The plan was a 'fiasco', he raged in a grumpy, self-published pamphlet from 1974. 'Has anyone bothered to consult any of those who have had intimate experience with the West Side since the time of the original improvement? ... Much of it is a hoax.'[91] He outlined, uncharacteristically, a cheaper alternative scheme.[92] Westway failed in 1985, the victim partly of well-organized legal opposition (much of it based on the environmental case), partly political inertia.[93] Sixty per cent of the funds allocated were redirected towards public transit.[94]

The Creation of West Street Promenade

With Westway stalled, the future of the West Side Highway started to look different. In 1986, the landscape architects Vollmer Associates were appointed to oversee a transformation of the highway, and a public commission on its future was established. The commission reported publicly in 1986, expressing the clear view that the highway should be replaced by a six-lane, surface level boulevard with associated parkland. It had taken into account particular concerns about the status of public space in any development, and the specific fear that the waterfront might be divided into parcels for luxury development, preventing public access to the Hudson (as had been the case with the 1976 Trump proposals). Compared with the Westway report, Vollmer's reads like an anthropological study crossed with a mea culpa, acknowledging in its opening pages the municipal neglect that led to the 1973 collapse, the subsequent failure of Westway ('lengthy, controversial, confusing'), and the degraded conditions in the present day.[95] Carbon monoxide levels routinely exceed federally approved levels; there are an appalling number of traffic accidents.[96] The report is something like an ethnography. A large part of it is demographic analysis, describing the composition and distribution of different populations along the route, including ethnically and economically marginalized groups.[97] There were twenty-three community consultation meetings, a measure of how – post LOMEX – planning needed to be done.

Progress was glacial. Vollmers produced a multi-volume Environmental Impact Report in 1994 on what was at that point known as The Route 9A Reconstruction Project. The appendices detailed 150 meetings held with community boards, and summaries of a further 275 meetings with other organizations, and commentaries on the proposals from politicians, leaders of commercial organizations and concerned citizens.[98] The report included the transcript of a public hearing in 1993, and written correspondence from a wide range of interested parties: bicycle-phobes ('they refuse to obey traffic regulations'), the pro-bicycle, Atlantic Chapter of the Sierra Club, the oldest environmental pressure group in the US, and representatives of the meat industry.[99] All human life, seemingly, was represented. After the battles of LOMEX, and then Westway, the expressway world was increasingly understood as place, rather than an empty development zone. That cultural transformation was increasingly represented in procedural terms; for projects requiring major land use decisions, the city of New York increasingly required consultation with community boards, transparency around decision making, and environmental reports and evaluations.[100]

The Vollmer report was followed by a somewhat saccharine piece of public relations for the separate but related project of the Hudson River Park, endorsed by then mayor of New York City, Rudy Giuliani, and Governor of New York State, George E. Pataki, and describing a masterplan by Quennell Rothschild Associates, with Signe Nielsen.[101] The park rationale was simple – the colonization of industrial land for leisure, turning abandoned piers into public space. It would, it was said, 'forever pay its way', its running costs covered by charging rent for public events.[102] The conversion of industrial land would 'heal an old wound' (for an old industrial city, it was striking to describe industry as injury).[103] Perspective drawings depicted the new park in a perpetual, Canaletto-like golden evening, accompanied by lushly suggestive text: 'Imagine a superb new public park ... grasses bend low in the breeze ... children scamper.'[104] It was a madly bucolic vision that made clear that, one way or another, the highway was now all about leisure.

The final outcome was in some senses perverse: a six-lane surface boulevard, almost exactly replicating what had been there before 1930. It was a remarkable reversal of the expressway world. Construction did not begin until 1996. In 1998, the Hudson River Park was created, the non-profit charged with overseeing the transformation of the former port area to public use, with individual piers intended for redevelopment as pocket parks, alongside a strip of parkland running between the highway and the waterfront more or less continuously from the Battery north to 72nd Street.[105] In 1999, Mayor Rudy Giuliani led the renaming of the highway as the Joe DiMaggio Highway, named after the baseball legend and sometime lover of Marilyn Monroe.[106] On 11 September 2001, as the works on the highway were coming to completion, three chunks of the collapsing World Trade Center fell onto the highway, causing widespread damage. Ambulances lined up on the section nearest the fallen towers. Much debate ensued about whether, and if so, how to complete the plan.[107] The work was eventually completed thirteen years later, in 2014. From the 1973 collapse, to the completion of works in 2014 it had therefore taken forty-one years to arrive at a solution, only two short of the forty-three years during which the original elevated Miller Highway was in operation. For half of its life in other words, the West Side Highway lay in ruins, broken and impassable, but also – in spite of itself – alive.

Fantasy Island

Visit the West Side Highway now and it is an area defined by leisure, a striking transformation from its earlier industrial life. This has happened partly since Westway's cancellation, and the creation of the Hudson River Park, but it has accelerated since the creation in 2005 of the Special West Chelsea District, one of eight special zoning regimes created in New York. Chelsea's case, like the others, was designed to support the development of the area 'as a dynamic mixed-use neighborhood', 'to encourage the development of residential uses', 'to encourage and support the growth of arts-related uses', and especially to support and develop the use of the High Line as a neighbourhood-defining piece of infrastructure. All its aims were directed at conserving the 'value of land and buildings' in the area, and therefore 'protect[ing] the City's tax revenues'. It was a straightforward real estate project, in other words.[108] Since 2005, the pace of development has accelerated, and especially so since 2014 with the completion of the new Whitney Museum by Renzo Piano (2014); the Hudson Yards retail development (2019); the Shed, by the British designer Thomas Heatherwick; a multipurpose arts venue with a multi-storey sliding façade (also 2019); Pier 76 (2021), the rehabilitation of a former dock into a multi-purpose cultural space; and also in 2021, Little Island, a multi-million dollar privately funded floating park, to another design by Heatherwick.

Thomas Heatherwick, Little Island, New York City (2013). *Photograph by Richard J. Williams.*

Little Island was never part of any pre-existing plan, but it is perhaps the perfect condensation of the spirit of the reconfigured West Side Highway – a folly or bauble, infrastructure rendered as touristic fantasy. Designed with the help of the engineers Arup and the landscape architects MNLA, it sits adjacent to the highway, occupying the bay that was previously Pier 55. And it is, literally, an island, comprising 132 tulip-like concrete piers, each of subtly differing designs. The piers form an artificial forest through which the visitor enters via a narrow boardwalk. Mounted above the piers is a small but hilly park, the lowest part four-and-a-half metres above water, the highest point nineteen metres. There are 400 different kinds of trees and shrubs, a 687-seat amphitheatre for events, and a play area. Like Heatherwick's other projects, including the nearby and controversial View, it is highly sculptural, and immediately apprehensible as image from any part, perfectly instagrammable.

The history of the West Side Highway represents a profound transformation in the expressway world. The first instance of that world in New York, it was also the first to fail; its life as a ruin was almost as long as its period in existence as a functioning highway. But in its ruined period a new subject emerged – a new New Yorker at home in the tidied-up ruins of the existing city, looking on the fragments of the industrial world with interested bemusement rather than nostalgia.

Those ruins are certainly consumable now. Its piers have become architectural follies like Little Island; its rail lines, like the nearby High Line, made into luxuriant parks. The New York State Department of Transport represents the West Side Highway as fantasy nature, all trees and dappled sunlight, the highway itself scarcely visible.[109] It is a thoroughly sanitized ruinscape. Sharon Zukin described something of this kind of transformation in her classic book *Loft Living* on the conversion of New York's nineteenth-century industrial buildings for cultural purposes; the 'artistic mode of production' (AMP) superficially made the industrial world visible, celebrating its architectural form. But in making it an object of consumption, it made any return to the industrial world impossible to imagine.[110] Here infrastructure has been rendered as entertainment, public space to private concessions, and citizens to spectators, whose activities are largely pre-thought and predetermined. Out of the ruins of the West Side Highway has come one of the places that the 'new' New York is arguably most visible, which is to say a city preoccupied more than ever with the production of spectacular images, and the crowds to consume them.

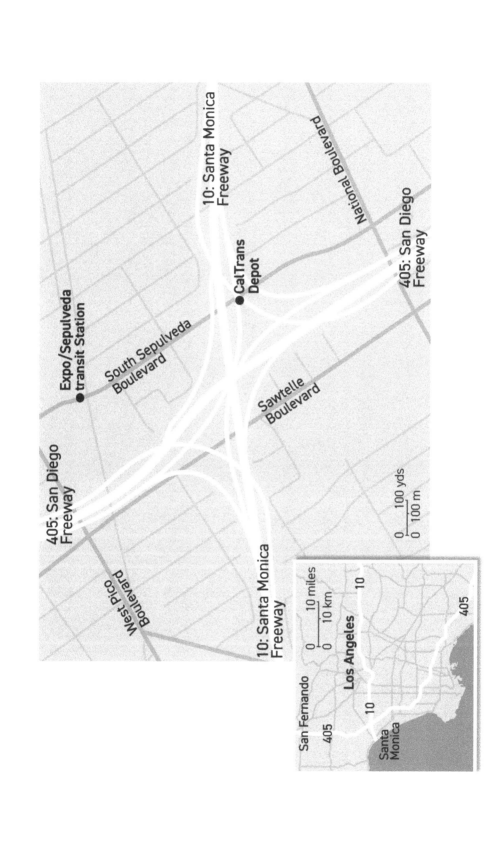

CHAPTER 3

Los Angeles: The Expressway as Art

Marylin Jorgenson Reece and Carol Schumaker with the I-405/I-10 interchange under construction. *Los Angeles Times* (6 April 1964). *Photographer unknown. Los Angeles Times Photographic Archive, UCLA Library Special Collections.*

There's an iconic picture from the *Los Angeles Times* of the Santa Monica Freeway under construction in 1964. In the foreground to the left is Marilyn Jorgenson Reece, a thirty-two-year-old engineer for the California Division of Highways, in a double-breasted white coat; beside her is a colleague, Carol Schumaker, neatly dressed in a dark suit.[1] There's a slight awkwardness about the pose, as if they've been instructed to stare at some indeterminate object to the photographer's right, but perhaps they're simply unused, like engineers in general, to celebrity. Their arms hang uncertainly by their sides; they squint, somewhat uncomfortably, into the sunlight. Just behind them are great works: a sweeping arc of concrete, perhaps half a kilometre of it, rises above them to their left, and cuts across the image in a handsome curve. The photographer is close enough to the action to show off the smoothness of its surfaces and the unearthly slimness of the cylindrical concrete piers, the economy of the balustrade. It really is finely done; you don't need to be an engineer to see that. In the distance, at the right, is the four-lane Sepulveda Boulevard with its traffic moving along as normal, and in between, the usual debris of a construction site, all rubble and dumptrucks and discarded wooden formwork. In the background, another elevated lane links the eastbound I-10 with the southbound I-405, while another punches its way under the big viaduct. In the far distance, beyond all the dust and traffic you can just make out the Santa Monica mountains to the north.

This project was Reece's – Schumaker was responsible for another, if anything more complex interchange, between the San Diego (I-405) and San Gabriel River (I-605) freeways. However, it was the 405/10 interchange that got the attention of architects and journalists because of its elegance and innovative design. Reece had worked hard on a design to enable continuous highway speeds, hence those long, gentle arcs, rising up to twenty-three metres above ground. However, the *Los Angeles Times* wasn't so preoccupied with the structure as with its designer. The interview that accompanied the picture discussed the demands of balancing a traditional family life with work. Their then unusual work schedules meant that they looked forward at weekends to 'cooking, scrubbing, gardening, herding the kids around' (according, at any rate to the interviewer).[2] Jorgenson and Schumaker were easy copy, disarmingly open about traffic problems, the latter wondering whether the regular surface streets might be better than the Santa Ana Freeway: 'After work it doesn't pay to get on it. I just get on Figeroa and avoid the whole thing.'[3] They described the work as superficially mundane, a matter of keeping the traffic flowing and the complaints from the motoring public under control. Reece: 'we feel like old friends by the time it is done.' The homespun nature of that early interview belied their remarkable achievements, Reece's in particular. An extraordinarily driven and energetic figure, Reece had succeeded in the traditionally male environment of civil engineering to become California's first licensed woman engineer.[4] Her innovative design for the 405/10 was to serve as a model for subsequent interchanges, an achievement combined with a demanding family life. In that 1964 image for the *Los Angeles Times*, she was heavily pregnant with her second daughter, Anne.[5]

Reece spoke about the 405/10 retrospectively to the *Los Angeles Times* in 1995, describing it in strongly aesthetic terms, both sculptural and experiential. It was 'very airy', she said. 'It isn't a cluttered, loopy thing. That was so you didn't have to slam on the brakes like you do on some interchanges.'[6] It opened in 1964, along with a stretch of Interstate 10, the final section, to the coast and the connection with the Pacific Coast Highway in early 1966. The whole project, from the sea downtown, a distance of sixteen miles, cost in the region of $188 million ($1.8 billion at 2025 prices). It was probably a more advanced structure than any comparable bridge designed in California, with extensive use of pre-tensioned steel to ensure the most economical use of materials (pre-tensioning also limited flexibility once construction was underway – this was an unusually precise design). It is by any standards an elegant, symmetrical form. The freeways themselves cross at near right angles at ground level, while above, on two further levels, are six gently arcing bridges, rising and falling and twisting all at the same time, their sinuous forms mirroring one another. It has an unusual lightness; the concrete arcs and piers are so slim, the ground plane so visible throughout, it's more pine forest than crypt.

Reece wasn't an artist, and interviews in print with her suggest ordinary middle-class tastes ('collecting Danish Jul plates and porcelain, gourmet cooking in the Scandinavian style, horticulture and playing the piano'[7]). This wasn't really accurate. She was in fact intensely interested in art, and knowledgeable about it, and might, had she not been so dedicated to mathematics as a teenager, gone on to study the subject at university.[8] The interest in expressway aesthetics therefore had some grounding, and she was as a result able to make a different kind of conversation possible about the expressway world, one informed by the appreciation of art, as much as engineering.

Los Angeles was rather late to the expressway party. At the end of the Second World War, Los Angeles had precisely eleven miles of expressway, all of them being the Arroyo Seco Parkway connecting downtown with Pasadena.[9] It would take another two decades before the city would become indelibly identified with its freeways (as it preferred to call its expressways because they were free, unlike the toll roads common in the eastern states). But once it did start to build, it allowed them to define an urban lifestyle in an unparalleled way.[10] There were practical reasons: the city's per capita ownership was the highest in the world, and it had constructed a lifestyle where the car had become (as the *Los Angeles Times* put it in a 1959 op-ed), 'a basic necessity – this is literally a city on wheels'.[11] There was also an aesthetic project. In Los Angeles, claims are made for the aesthetic value of the expressway that were not often made elsewhere, and the 405/10 interchange in particular is emblematic.

Expressway Aesthetics – Lynch and Halprin

Conceptually, roads already existed as art in various places. The architectural theorist Sigfried Giedion thought the parkway might be a new artform.[12] The motorcycling geographer J.B. Jackson thought something similar, arguing that, as used, the American highway constituted a significant cultural experience.[13] But the 405/10's inauguration in 1965 marks something new – a point at which the expressway-as-artform had become a respectable, mainstream idea rather than one living in the architectural avant-garde. It had become a subject of widespread academic interest. The planner Kevin Lynch's 1960 book, *The Image of the City*, is a good example. It's better known for its treatment of the pedestrian landscape, and the processes of cognitive mapping that would produce some durable words for describing urban form: 'Paths', 'Edges', 'Districts', 'Nodes', 'Landmarks', 'Element Interrelations', 'The Shifting Image' and 'Image Quality'.[14] He didn't, on the face of it, much care for the expressway world, and certainly not Los Angeles.

Lynch was based at the Massachusetts Institute of Technology, so Boston's Central Artery was a nearby reference point – it was, he wrote, a 'barrier', and 'a massive green-painted wall', widely understood as alien. His account of Los Angeles is full of navigational traumas, the experience of expressways in particular presents insurmountable difficulties, especially for the pedestrian.[15] For the driver it was often 'tense and exhausting'. Yet in spite of all this, the expressway could be generative of positive, even beautiful experiences, especially of topography. Meanwhile the kinaesthetic sensations of dropping, turning, climbing were 'like shooting rapids in a boat'.[16]

Lynch developed his expressway thinking in 1965 with his colleagues Donald Appleyard and John R. Meyer, published as a highly visual, large format study called *The View from the Road*.[17] The result of research done with a Rockefeller Foundation grant, it continued afterwards towards the completion in the Joint Center for Urban Studies run between MIT and Harvard. It's a curious and singular book, not only for its format; it is primarily retroactive, in that it primarily attempts to describe the landscape as found in the world, rather than as an ideal. In that it closely resembles Lynch's *Image of the City*; in both there is a struggle towards a form of notation that can adequately describe the modern city, as well as the experience of moving through it, at what were unprecedented speeds. Reading it retrospectively, it also somewhat resembles *Learning from Las Vegas*, published in 1972 by Robert Venturi, Denise Scott Brown and Steven Izenour, which was similarly an attempt to describe an automobile-dominated landscape, albeit one focused on its architectural forms rather the experience of moving through it in a car.[18] All of these works have a clear and striking emphasis, however: regardless of how it might have been produced, the automotive landscape deserved consideration as art. Appleyard et al. were clear about it from the beginning. 'Ugly roads', they began, 'are one price of civilization, like sewers or police. ... The authors take a different position: road-watching is a delight and the highway is – or at least might be – a work of art.'[19]

Wondering what the characteristics of this new art might be, they isolated the senses of vision and touch, and the impressions of motion and space; there were commonalities with architecture, music and cinema, dance 'or the amusement park, although rarely so violent'. These varied cultural forms, popular and otherwise, could all be instructive.[20] What then followed was an attempt to codify the highway experience through a series of constructed categories, supported by photographs and sketches: 'the elements of attraction', 'the sense of motion', 'road alignment', 'the motion of the field', 'the sense of space', 'the extension of self', 'goal approach', 'orientation', 'meaning', 'rhythm and continuity' and 'sequential form'. Each of these categories was illustrated with thumbnail sketches and photographs to explain the concept further. Sometimes the explanation is straightforward, sometimes more poetic. 'Goals', accompanied by a vertical sequence of snapshots depicting the approach to the United Nations' buildings along the East River in New York City, is borderline erotic, all 'pleasurable tension', deferral and climax. Rhythms and crescendos, sensations of tension and release, the alternate hiding and revealing of visual goals: it was all about pleasure, bodily and aesthetic.[21] 'Our highways are no mean achievement in the history of technology', they concluded. 'Will they also be remembered as works of art?'[22]

Lynch and his co-authors said little about California – they had plenty of material close by in Boston's Central Artery. Someone who did was another landscape architect, Lawrence Halprin, whose book *Freeways* was published in 1966.[23] Like Lynch and his colleagues, Halprin thought the expressway world had abruptly come into being without ever being adequately explained. Its effect could be negative – 'many … have been inept and have demeaned the cities which they were meant to serve'. But the point, again, was art, or at least its possibility, and *Freeways* was as much concerned with the freeway as a bodily experience as a structure, incorporating ideas from Halprin's wife, Ann, a prominent avant-garde choreographer.[24]

The book's photography by Steven Frisch, a California freelance with a thing for expressways, is generous and spectacular – hand-held, long exposure shots with light trails blurring into the distance, bleeding into the page. On the driving experience, Halprin wrote: 'The quality is something like swimming with fins, the water buoys you up and the slightest effort propels you forward. Here the freeway is the carrier; you push down the accelerator and away you go – fast. Planing over the land at tree-top level – the roofs of the houses below you – almost like flying.'[25] He wrote of new visual experiences afforded to the driving public – 'vast panoramic views are disclosed which were never seen before. The great vivid skylines of the city can be seen, all of a sudden, not as a static picture but as a series of constantly changing impressions which move by like the frames in a motion picture.'[26] To drive, in other words, was to participate in a film of one's own life. It was a humanistic project (as Alison Hirsch has written) about 'restoring the social of the city after disorientating change', and the possibility, however remote, that expressways might somehow enrich the places through which they passed.[27]

Halprin openly drew on Lynch, as well as his wife Ann who supplied a prototype notation for the expressway experience.[28] Based on human choreography, 'motation' was a way of accounting for the expressway experience, the position of the car in traffic, and their position in urban space; using motation explicitly theatricalized the freeway, turning its motion into mechanized, fast-moving dance; there's a parallel with Jane Jacobs here, who understood the life of her neighbourhood as performance, literally a ballet of real life going on twenty-four hours a day.[29] Halprin extends that idea to the motorized realm, in so doing showing how the expressway experience might be, at least in theory, an everyday form of performance art.

And as was clear from other photographs in the book, the expressway could also be a physical place in the city. Halprin included multiple images of the double-deck Embarcadero freeway along San Francisco's waterfront, one from the upper deck before completion when cars were allowed to pause on the seaward lane to admire the view: the expressway as park, of a kind. Even images purportedly included to criticize bad design read in more ambiguous ways. The Embarcadero's near miss with the local YMCA building – just a few metres separates them – makes an agreeably surreal picture.[30] The expressway could be a means of urban destruction, but it could also be the modern equivalent of the Roman aqueduct, or a kind of colonnade if suitably landscaped at ground level.[31]

The Expressway in Art

At the same time as Lynch and Halprin's academic investigations into the expressway world, it was becoming a subject in culture. One element caught the imagination of the journalist Tom Wolfe in his 1965 volume of collected essays, the *Kandy-Kolored Tangerine-Flake Streamline Baby*. The title essay, by turns ironic and awestruck, described the city's custom car scene, focusing on Ed 'Big Daddy' Roth, its de facto spokesman. It was, Wolfe wrote, unquestionably art – irrational, lurid, pumped full of money and occasionally very good. 'I don't mind observing', he wrote with typical provocation, 'that it is this same combination – money plus slavish devotion to form – that accounts for Versailles or St Mark's Square.'[32]

The automotive landscape became a subject in art during the 1960s, as pop-oriented artists including Roger Kuntz, Wayne Thiebaud and particularly Ed Ruscha found.[33] Making images of it is another way of getting some individual purchase on it, of owning it, of bringing it under temporary control. Ed Ruscha, moonlighting as layout artist 'Eddie Russia' for *Artforum*, found it especially rich.[34] Ruscha was, it could be said, an automotive creature; originally from Oklahoma City, on relocating to Los Angeles to study design, he drove back home up to half a dozen times a year, 2,600 miles each time.[35] Ruscha's resulting fascination with the highway landscape found its way into a series of self-published art books, the first being *Twentysix Gasoline Stations* (1963), before developing a specifically Los Angeles focus in other series including *Some Los Angeles Apartments* (1965), *Every Building on the Sunset Strip* (1966) and *Thirtyfour Parking Lots in Los Angeles* (1967). The car was a ubiquitous object in this new landscape, and its windscreen a means of framing the landscape.[36] That method seems to have produced an interest in everyday cliché: 'I seemed to be drawn by the most stereotyped concepts of LA', he said, 'cars, suntans, palm trees, swimming pools.'[37]

There were also now iconic paintings of a Standard Oil gas station, derived from one of the 1963 photographs, but reproduced in highly exaggerated perspective – the image exists in varied media, scales and colour variations. In the early 2000s for the Venice Biennale, Ruscha also made a series of large-scale paintings of anonymous industrial buildings located alongside highways, such as *The Old Trade School Building* (2005). Ruscha continued to document the everyday Los Angeles' landscape since the 1960s, donating the results to the Getty Research Institute, which at the time of writing had digitized 46,000 images in its collections.[38]

Ruscha's ongoing project means something here, less because it documents the expressway directly (route 110 appears in the top left-hand corner of the Dodger Stadium image in *Parking Lots*, but few other direct representations exist), more because of the sensibility it describes. Ruscha's images show an ongoing fascination with the automotive landscape in all its forms, the more ordinary the better. The approach is flat and unjudgemental, with no obvious hierarchy of subject, the project seemingly extendable ad infinitum in all directions. As a result, Ruscha's images have a distinctive politics, neither straightforwardly affirming the expressway world, nor criticizing it, but instead accepting it as a form of modern nature.

The 405/10 Becomes Art

Almost from its inception, the 405/10 interchange became art, of a kind. In a 1963 article in the California Highways Division's journal *Bridge Notes* on the otherwise dryly technical question of concrete strength, the engineer authors wrote 'aesthetic values were an important consideration in design', and that they were 'representative of a modern interchange'. They thought the project had drama too: 'the foreshortened view and the super-elevation as seen by the motorists, add to the appearance of mass of the structure'.[39] The 405/10 was therefore not only a technical achievement, but an image.

The Bridge Department's engineers might have recognized the 405/10's aesthetic qualities, but elsewhere it was being busily rendered as photographic art. It is an occasional subject in the work of the architectural photographer Julius Shulman, and the landscapist Ansel Adams, as Eric Avila points out – but it was the Highways Division itself that really took expressway photography seriously.[40] In the CalTrans headquarters archive in Sacramento, there is extensive photographic documentation of every state highway project. The 405/10 interchange has two files of images dating from 1962, and recording the construction and opening, with a few rather deteriorated colour images from the 1970s. There are perhaps seventy in all, the majority from the construction period. In a few images Marilyn Jorgenson Reece herself appears, alone in front of the project, or consulting plans with a colleague engineer, Thomas McKinley, the mise-en-scène a little forced. All of them give the sense of an aesthetic being worked out. It was one thing for an engineer like Jorgenson to design a project with its unprecedented loops and curves; it was another to represent it, or find a way of doing so.

The uncredited photographers had, it seems, free rein. There are numerous aerial shots of the project at various stages of construction. In those photographs from high up, it's flattened, abstracted, gestural – not unlike large-scale abstract painting in terms of composition (Clyfford Still perhaps, or Franz Kline, artists who would later find their way into local museum collections). Look through the abstraction, however, and it's a scene of ground-level devastation.[41] In one, the right of way claimed for I-10 punches through a suburban neighbourhood, oblivious to the rectilinear grid. Look at the as-built plans in CalTrans records, and it is clear what was lost – Bentley, Brookhaven, Greenfield, Sardis and Tilden Avenues cut in half and blocked off, and the same for Ivy Place, along with a square kilometre of suburban housing cleared.[42]

California Department of Transport Division of Highways, I-405/I-10 interchange, photograph 16662-6 (14 January 1966). *Photographer unknown. Caltrans Library, Sacramento.*

LOS ANGELES: THE EXPRESSWAY AS ART

At road level, the Highways Division's photographic approach was typically sculptural, downplaying function, accentuating formal drama, the singular qualities of materials and the play of light and shadow. In one 1964 image, with the basic structure complete, but the 10 roadway still to be paved, the connector roads form a dark concrete canopy, with the complete 405 northwards glimpsing out from underneath.[43] The raw brutality of the concrete stands out, stained and blemished, the natural record of its own construction process. In front of the photographer lies the dusty roadbed of the incomplete I-10, strewn with debris; it's a picture of a ruin in a way, a brutish, uncivilized object on its way to becoming – perhaps – something else. In another image, taken at dusk from January 1966, the I-405 appears looking south to LAX with intense traffic, crawling judged by the density of the cars, scarcely a metre or so between them.[44] Sawtelle Boulevard, with its ordinary suburban housing, lies off on the right, only a few metres away. This mechanized spectacle works exactly as it should, but the mood is intense. It's an uneasy image, and a great one, caught between day and night, transit and stasis, the new and existing cities; it doesn't straightforwardly represent an official view of progress, but something darker, an expression perhaps of generalized anxieties about expressway development.[45]

From the middle of the 1960s there was increasingly official recognition of Jorgenson Reece's achievements, invariably citing the 405/10's aesthetic impact. In 1965, with the intersection only just having opened, Reece was the subject of a Resolution from Los Angeles City Hall, praising her design for 'its momentous economic, social and visual impact on our community', and for Jorgenson Reece herself marking 'an important peak in the achievement of outstanding women'. It was a major contribution to the 'safety, utility and beauty of our city'.[46] Here as elsewhere, an interest in aesthetics was somehow inseparable from her gender, as if her being a woman gave permission to discuss the interchange's artistic qualities: 'Her ability and creative imagination has made a breakthrough for women in this masculine endeavour.'[47] The following year, 1966, Jorgenson Reece won the Governor's award for Design Excellence 'for outstanding aesthetic contributions to the environment', presented by California Governor Pat Brown.[48] Presented at the iconic Gamble House in Pasadena early 1967, the jury had been chaired by Nathaniel Owings, one of the founders of the architectural firm SOM, and the jury included the Argentine-American architect César Pelli.[49] Through the 405/10, Reece had helped remake the aesthetics of the expressway world, and the award was public recognition of her approach.[50]

Perhaps the writer to do the most to establish the idea of the 405/10 as art was Reyner Banham, English architectural historian, critic and general provocateur.[51] For Banham, the expressway world was definitively art. He wrote that partly to annoy the stuffy, often America-phobic English architectural establishment, but it was also evidence of his almost primal identification with technological modernity. Obsessed with Futurism in the 1950s, Banham had published a widely read manifesto of architectural Brutalism, and a well-regarded account of architectural modernism, *Theory and Design in the First Machine Age* in 1960.[52] By the end of the 1960s, he had transferred his obsessions to the United States, and Los Angeles in particular, doing four radio talks for the BBC's Third Programme in 1968 about the city and its architecture. He also learned to drive, as he famously put it, 'in order to read Los Angeles in the original'.[53] Banham declared the Los Angeles' freeway system 'one of the greater works of Man', and the 405/10 interchange in particular a work of sculptural art, referring to its structural economy and the elegance of its forms.[54]

In Banham's widely read 1971 book *Los Angeles: The Architecture of Four Ecologies*, the 405/10 appears in a Highways Division aerial photograph, showing the elegant symmetry of the plan, and in a picture attributed to the architect Julius Shulman. In that image it's an aerial, Alexander Calder-like sculpture, all apparently weightless curves, eerily depopulated.[55] In these photographs, it is a form of sculpture; Banham had more to say, however, about expressway driving as kinetic art, writing, famously, of the 405/10 interchange that it was 'the nearest thing to flight on four wheels that I know'.[56] He was, not for the first time, exaggerating, but Banham's poetry is important, a clear statement of the 405/10's aesthetic qualities.

Banham would go on to repeated LA visits and lectures, and would consider transplanting himself there at the end of the decade.[57] *Los Angeles: The Architecture of Four Ecologies* was published in 1971, and the closely related BBC film *Reyner Banham Loves Los Angeles* was shown in 1972.[58] In both the book and the film, there are well-developed reflections on freeway driving. Banham pitched himself to both the reader and viewer as a species of automotive anthropologist, interpreting minute instances of driving behaviour (a touch on the rear-view mirror here, an adjustment of the gear selector there) for symbolic import. He was anthropologically alert to myth and how it might condition everyday life. A family was said to have set up home on the freeway system, perpetually circulating in their station wagon.[59] It may not have been true, Banham went on, but it permitted him some extended speculation about the everyday life of the freeway, and what was for him its generally agreeable character.

In declaring the expressway art, Banham's intentions may have been provocative, but the category of art was in any case becoming extremely blurred. *Reyner Banham Loves Los Angeles* had plenty of evidence of its own, from visits to artists and surfboard makers, to homeless pianists working out of their camper van, to a conversation with his friend Ed Ruscha in which, it became clear, eating an ice cream sundae in an Angeleno parking lot might conceivably be a species of performance art (in 1967 the California-based artist Bruce Conner made his process of sandwich-making into a conceptual artwork for the journal *Artforum*).[60] For Banham, the 405/10 was Futurism come to life, incontrovertibly art.

That reputation continued. There are echoes of Banham in David Brodsly's quirky 1981 book, *LA Freeway: An Appreciative Essay*, in which he describes the Harbour Freeway as a peculiar modern state of nature, a mechanical beach, its traffic moving 'with an almost natural rhythm of ebb and flow', like waves on the shore.[61] And as a driver, Brodsly elaborated on the feelings of pleasure that were so important to the early discoverers of the freeway, particularly Banham. 'Driving the freeway', he wrote, 'can create a rare and distinctly urban moment of joy when the car drives well, the freeway is uncrowded and there is a good song on the radio.'[62]

For an architect, Aaron Betsky, writing in the *Los Angeles Times* in 1991, it was worth standing in the middle of the CalTrans maintenance yard to get the full effect of it as a sculptural composition: 'there it all comes together in curves that balance each other in direction and height'. He went on to praise its 'incredible cleanliness of line … column meets ramp with no transition, and ramp and rail are integrated into a single piece of concrete'. Revisiting Banham, he praised the kinetic experience that could be had while driving on it, another form of aesthetics.[63]

Jorgenson Reece was an intermittent object of interest in the media, a useful source for a quote on expressway aesthetics.[64] She was subsequently honoured after her death in 2004.[65] In 2006, the California State Senate renamed the 405/10 the Marilyn Jorgenson Reece Memorial Interchange, the citation quoting from Banham's account of it, affirming it as a 'work of art' both in terms of its form and as a kinetic experience.[66] CalTrans held a naming ceremony in June 2008 at which signage was installed displaying the new name and honouring the designer. There were speeches from the CalTrans director and the California Secretary of State. It was a significant act, not only for what it did for the memory of Jorgenson Reece, but what it did for the object of the interchange itself: naming it, labelling it, lifting it out of the everyday world, it made it something like art.[67]

Another 405/10

To experience the 405/10 as art is to see it in privileged terms ('a white, middle-class experience', in Jennifer Quick's words).[68] It is easy to overlook the human costs of its construction and ongoing existence. Eric Avila's account of the Californian expressway world describes 'deep fissures' inflicted on Los Angeles by the Federal-Aid Highway Act of 1956, 'cleaving the built environment into isolated parcels of race and class and figuratively by sparking civic wars over the freeway's threat to specific neighbourhoods and communities'.[69] From 1955, along the route of I-10, churches, groups of homeowners, the directors of a large orphanage and other community organizations all expressed opposition; hundreds of properties were said to be affected. Air pollution was a concern. Adjustments were made, although as Division of Highways' photographs show, the effects of the completed scheme on the surrounding neighbourhood were vast and irrevocable.[70]

The 405/10 intersection opened on 29 January 1965, assisted by the presence of a Goodyear blimp.[71] It almost completed the I-10, linking prosperous Santa Monica with downtown, symbolically connecting the banks with the beach. Only a few miles remained, from Bundy Avenue to the ocean. But the completion of the project did not exactly underline the city's progress, not only because of the earlier opposition to the route. By the middle of August 1965, the expressways might also

LOS ANGELES: THE EXPRESSWAY AS ART

I-405/I-10 interchange, Los Angeles. *Photograph by Richard J. Williams.*

represent a city divided on racial lines, a project to enable a wealthy white city to fly over the rest. The mostly black South Central neighbourhood of Watts was eighteen miles, and another world from the middle-class environs of 405/10 – but when it exploded in riots on the evening of 11 August, it posed existential questions of the city's growth, from which its expressways were not exempt.[72]

Enthusiasts for the expressway world were uneasy. Banham was uncomfortable with racial questions, and did not know exactly what to say about Watts, tending to downplay its significance. Its violence was 'sporadic', he wrote later, like Venice Beach, merely a 'fashionable venue for confrontations'.[73] But he also wondered whether it was Watts's isolation from the expressway world that had contributed to its poor situation. 'Whatever else has ailed Watts', writes Banham, 'its isolation from transportation contributes to every one of its misfortunes.'[74] Watts had previously been well connected by the Pacific Electric Railroad, the city's now-vanished network of suburban trains, Banham writes, but was left isolated from the development of the freeway network, literally without connection to the 101 that passes close by. The film Banham made with Julian Cooper made precisely this point.[75] Watts predictably displays its poverty, with shabby housing and stray dogs, Banham and the English film crew staying inside the car, filming behind a protective layer of metal and glass. The point, however clumsily made, was clear enough – Los Angeles's expressways represented a well-connected white metropolis laid over the top of a poorly connected black one. To see them as art – as the rest of the film did – was a privilege.

Riots were one thing; the environment was another. Exactly a month after the riots, two UCLA professors argued that freeway interchanges (such as the 405/10) might be actively injurious to human health and should be sited as far as possible from one another. It was far from the first warning of this kind, but it was a striking one. Morris Neiburger, a UCLA professor of meteorology, argued that the pollution caused by freeways might, within a century, make the earth uninhabitable; freeways were good at enabling the free movement of traffic at speed at which internal combustion motors were most efficient, but they were also good at concentrating traffic pollution, 'so when you do get a traffic jam you do get especially high doses'.[76] In the same article, the *Los Angeles Times* quoted a resident of Westwood, close to the 405/10, complaining anecdotally of a change in the local climate: 'we never get any breezes anymore … the air is always smoggy'.[77]

LA's Expressways in Ruins

David Brodsly's *LA Freeway* is a good indicator of the ambiguous later public mood towards the expressway world, written after both the 1973 oil crisis when an Organization of the Petroleum Exporting Countries (OPEC) embargo against oil exports to the United States trebled the oil price, and the subsequent 1979 crisis following the Iranian revolution. The book was written during the second crisis, the effects of which were profound on the supply of gasoline. Half of the book is a Banhamesque love-letter to the freeway, the other half filled with regret, its drivers stuck in jams ruing their life choices. 'It was not difficult', wrote Brodsly, 'during the height of the 1979 gas crisis, to forecast the end of the automobile's prodigal reign and to imagine the freeways standing vacant like some modern Versailles attesting to the sins of excess. Anyone listening to the car radio while awaiting a turn at the gas pumps heard the announcers joke about converting the freeways into bike paths, or skate paths, or tennis courts.'[78]

In cinema, Los Angeles's expressway world appears increasingly ruined. Wim Wenders' 1984 film *Paris, Texas*, about a missing wanderer's uneasy re-engagement with his family, in which the expressway plays an outsize role, a stage for much of the action. Its characters are perpetually driving on it, or about to, or lurking in its interstices.[79] But it's a melancholy space, in spite of the perpetual sunshine. The high arcs of an intersection frame an emotionally tense encounter between the male lead, played by Harry Dean Stanton, and his screen son, a place at which a critical decision – to stay or to leave – must be made. The expressway intersection is not the engineering miracle it might otherwise be, but a space of emotional possibilities, all of them consequential. It is a most unreassuring space, in other words, one that threatens to pull human relations apart as much as bring them together. The muffled roar of the freeway is a constant, pulling the characters back to the desert from where Dean Stanton emerged, or to the underworld on the Houston periphery, where his estranged wife, played by Nastassja Kinski, may or may not be. The infrastructure in this post-crisis California is enervated too, stained and cracking concrete, and battered old Volvos; not the future but a quasi-archaeological site of the past.[80]

In the latter-day, post-crises freeway world, some of the better-known images are those of the American artist Catherine Opie, who in between photographing sadomasochists and abandoned strip malls in the early 1990s, produced a series of expressway images. Made in 1994 and 1995, they employ the archaic and expensive platinum print process, where a treated sheet of photographic paper is overlaid with the negative and then exposed, producing a fine, intimately scaled contact print. Opie used a 6 × 24 cm panoramic camera giving a widescreen effect, although the pictures themselves, nearly always reproduced life size, are tiny. She considered making them monumental, but having seen the contact prints, decided against. They have a weirdly archaic quality, as if they were produced in the middle of the nineteenth century instead of the end of the twentieth.

In a long interview with Russell Ferguson, Opie described being 'on the freeway all the time'. 'I became fascinated by being stopped in traffic and watching other traffic go by on these interchanges. It became so sculptural and beautiful. It was like not being in that time and not having to deal with this traffic jam. Instead, it was about the shapes that I was beginning to see against the sky.'[81] 'I like to think about what is going to be left behind', she went on. 'I've always been interested in being in some way an archaeologist or an anthropologist. I think of all of this stuff as artifacts ... the freeways are definitely future ruins.'[82]

In image, Opie was doing what the urban historian and polemicist Mike Davis was doing in text. His *City of Quartz* (1990), a counter-reading of Los Angeles, described a metropolis already semi-ruined by its own contradictions.[83] The archaeological subtitle was 'Excavating the Future', and the cover image of the 1998 edition was the fibreglass diplodocus that could then be found in the park at the La Brea tar pits on Wilshire Boulevard, a memorial to a much earlier extinction, and a prefiguration of a future one.[84] Davis's Los Angeles was figuratively ruined before it was built, as it was even more spectacularly in the follow-up, *Ecology of Fear*, about the city's images of (self-)destruction, whether in countless disaster movies, or in reality by earthquake and fire.[85] That literal destruction occurred – in part at any rate – in the 1994 Northridge earthquake, which on 17 January 1994 caused the structural collapse of multiple freeways in the Los Angeles region – including the I-10 bridge over La Cienega Boulevard, just a few miles from the 405/10 interchange. Like a disaster move made real, the emblem of the Northridge quake was arguably the collapsed freeway, its supporting columns compressed to dust, steel reinforcing rods poking from the rubble, noodling wildly.[86]

The Homeless 405/10

One of Mike Davis's enduring interests in LA was its homeless, a key indicator of its troubled condition; how could a rich city be so unable to house its poorest? Among the more striking images of *City of Quartz* is a 'bum-proof' bus bench, consisting of three steel hoops supporting a wooden seat, semi-circular in profile, like an open cylinder. Appropriate for only the shortest of rests, and only then with the user's feet planted firmly on the ground, it was deliberately aggressive, designed to rule out the possibility of sleep. It was, Davis wrote, part of the city's ongoing 'cold war' against the homeless that also included measures to prevent access to dumpster trash, the removal of public toilets and drinking facilities and periodic schemes to deport street dwellers to an encampment on the edge of the desert.[87] The broader aim, Davis wrote, was the gentrification of downtown. Those acts of coercion at the end of the 1990s produced a superficially cleaned-up downtown, but also a movement of homeless to zones further from the public gaze.

Chief among those unsurveilled zones was the expressway underpass: it has proved an enduring site for homeless encampments, and the undercroft of the 405/10 in mid-2024 was no exception. It had an air of permanence, featuring not tents but mobile homes, as well as the usual cardboard lean-tos. The airy design of the overpasses meant plenty of light and open space, and at weekends it was quiet, with little traffic on the secondary roads. By contrast with the excessively surveilled downtown, its indifference might be a relief. In an academic survey of the use of transportation environments by the homeless, Jacob Wasserman et al. note some general advantages. While acknowledging the obvious dangers to residents and drivers, freeway environs had compensations: 'shelter from the elements under bridges, isolation from displeased housed neighbors', and when group encampments were considered, the advantages might be 'a sense of safety and security, developing community, maintaining autonomy, and ensuring stability'.[88] There might be positive reasons, in other words, for the appropriation of expressway land.

For local journalists, the persistence of homelessness in such areas became an equally persistent story. An early account of it, from 1988, when the homeless population in the city numbered just 4,000, described the advantages of living under the Riverside freeway: 'the police mostly leave people alone there and the inhabitants help one another'.[89] It was a village by comparison with later settlements, numbering just twenty, most of whom the *Los Angeles Times* interviewed. Nearing Christmas, they reported preparations among the community – a tree, some lights, plans to cook a turkey if one can be found.[90] Looking through the *Los Angeles Times*'s coverage, the story keeps returning – an endless, low-key border war, with evictions, periodic eruptions of violence, attention from the authorities, acts of random kindness, gifts of sheet plastic and beer, sometimes fires attracting the attention of police or CalTrans. In these accounts, the expressway world, in spite of itself, becomes an authentic part of the city.

In 2008, the *Los Angeles Times* ran a longer piece by Jessica Garrison, by which stage the problem had ballooned, with a reported 73,000 homeless in Los Angeles County on 'any given night'. Garrison noted LA's peculiar geography, its intermittently dense urbanism juxtaposed with wilderness, many of these encounters found on expressway land. For the homeless, the 'landscape offers many opportunities for ingenious solutions – aeries beneath bridges, riverbed encampments, ad hoc tree houses with million-dollar views – to the problem of where to sleep'.[91] Treating the expressway as a site for self-built architecture drew in Christopher Hawthorne, the *Los Angeles Times*'s architecture critic, in a 2015 article that described some inventive, if desperate, transformations of space. 'Aloof' as public space, and generally repellent to the pedestrian, freeway land was becoming something else, a 'desperate sort of community – a place to hunker down'. CalTrans did not keep statistics on the number of homeless encampments, he wrote, but (quoting the director of a legal centre used by the homeless) 'everybody senses that the number of freeway encampments has gone up'. Developers increasingly encroached on traditional homeless encampments downtown, so the homeless found themselves pushed to what Hawthorne called the 'seams', 'the unlovely and forgotten and in-between spaces. And the biggest, most prominent seam in Los Angeles is the freeway system.'[92] The system, he concluded, was being asked to do things that it had been never tasked with in the first place; designed as a means of transportation, it had been accidentally retrofitted as informal housing. Its precarious inhabitants ought, he argued, to have a say in its future.[93]

Necessity had produced self-built architecture, a topic of enduring interest for architectural modernists.[94] The following year, 2016, the *Los Angeles Times* covered one of the most inventive of all street dwellers, the so-called Mr Dice, who occupied what it described as an 'elaborate compound' under the Harbour Freeway close to the Coliseum. Artfully designed, the zebra-print decorated lodgings included de facto bedrooms (two) with double beds, a living room, and a store from which Dice sold hotdogs cooked on a scavenged grill during baseball games. So elaborate was the setup, Dice could afford to charge $25 per week rent for a camping space between the living room and guest room areas. Despite, or possibly because of a running battle with City Hall's sanitation services, Mr Dice had become a minor celebrity with a social media presence and a stream of visitors. 'I enjoy the hype like anybody else', he was reported as saying.[95]

On 11 November 2023, a Saturday, the I-10 caught fire. Flammable materials – 'pallets, hand sanitizer, cars, construction materials' – were set ablaze in a suspected arson attack, with results of such intensity that they damaged a hundred of the concrete piers holding up the roadway, and resulted in the closure of the route for several weeks while repairs were carried out.[96] It was the same stretch of the I-10 that had been so spectacularly damaged by the 1994 Northridge earthquake, and only a few kilometres from the 405/10 interchange. The fire brought numerous questions to the fore again, including homelessness, for it displaced at least sixteen people who had been living in an encampment underneath. Some blamed them for the fire; whatever the truth of the matter they are still there, despite a court order in 2020 that was supposed to rehouse all 7,000 or so homeless living on freeway land, and the actions of an energetic judge, David Carter, tasked with carrying it out.[97] The freeway, in other words, had not been returned its original condition of pure circulation; it had continued to evolve in other, uncontained directions, far exceeding the responsibilities of the original designers. It is tempting to reach for a Freudian analogy and describe it as an eruption of the expressway's unconscious; the expressway as superego threatened by whatever bubbled up from underneath.

Return to the 405/10

I visit Los Angeles again in the summer of 2024, watching Damien Chazelle's 2017 film *La La Land* for some undemanding preparation, mostly for the technical tour de force of the ten-minute opening scene. It takes place on the 105/110 interchange in South Central LA, a structure not unlike the 405/10, although with additional, almost Mannerist, loops and swirls. Filmed over two days, it depicts a jam on one of the high, arcing connectors devolving, after much frustrated honking of horns, into a choreographed sequence lasting five intense minutes; dancers burst from their vehicles, and leap precariously from one car roof to another, singing as they go; a conga-drumming trio explodes from the back of a van; the jazz musician male lead (Ryan Gosling) meanwhile stays put in his decrepit Buick Riviera, trying to nail a piano melody. All human life is there in a spectacular urban cornucopia, but precisely none of it is doing what the expressway was designed to do – it perversely exceeds anything its designers imagined.

I reach the actually existing city, and the Getty library is a temporary home as it often has been in the past. I make the daily journey in a rented Kia up the I-10 and the I-405, passing twice a day over Marilyn Jorgenson Reece's creation, now prominently bearing her name. It's never quite the experience Reyner Banham described. I suspect part of the ecstasy he wanted to pass on to his BBC radio listeners in 1968 derived from his being a newly qualified and somewhat nervy driver – he had simply driven it by himself and survived. I hit the curving connector ramp surprisingly often at 55 mph, the design limit, and it's only descending to surface level on the 405 that the traffic backs up, but never for long. This is still, on its own energy-intensive terms, a well-functioning system. The return trip is much the same, in reverse – slow on the 405, but a rapid acceleration onto the connector and then onto the I-10. For the driver, the engineering is splendid. The curves are scarcely noticeable; precisely as its designer intended, there's no need to touch the brakes. The views are tremendous. In the mornings, the sun hits the Santa Monica Mountains, and to the right, the San Gabriel range is perfectly visible sixty miles away, a seductive view. Any reconfiguration of the expressway world will need to take account of that, the ability of a well-designed object like the 405/10 to deal with such volumes of traffic and, some of the time at least, give some pleasure while using it.

There's a hint of what a different world might be a few metres to north along the surface-level Sepulveda Boulevard, and the metro E Line, a light rail line that runs parallel to Exposition Boulevard, linking downtown and Santa Monica. It's accompanied by Transit Oriented Development, which is to say chunky apartment blocks and retail clustered around the station, a different kind of urbanism, and in Los Angeles an increasingly visible one.[98] Then, underneath the 405/10, along Sepulveda is that enduring homeless encampment, and the CalTrans yard behind high wire fencing. There are the same improvised shacks and lean-tos, the same decrepit vehicles, the same air of intractability. The vans and RVs have some elaborate additions – improvised extensions and awnings made from foraged materials, whole lives' worth of possessions sprawling onto the Sepulveda sidewalk.

LOS ANGELES: THE EXPRESSWAY AS ART

I walk it a few times, trying to get a sense of it all. It's a sprawling, heterogeneous, uneasy place, very much like the city of which it is a part. The square kilometre encompassing the 405/10, in fact represents a good many of the city's typical objects, all banged up against one another: two freeways, dozens of single-family homes, a hotel, two blocks of neo-modern apartments, a metro station, half a dozen auto repair shops, a scrapyard, a self-storage facility, a judo school, CalTrans's Western parking division, those homeless encampments. The trees are fully grown now, and the greenery quite extensive. It is really quite rich in some ways and everyone gets something out of it, at least some of the time. The only thing it arguably lacks is a beach. Its complexity far exceeds the original design of the intersection, which is not at all to devalue Jorgenson Reece's remarkable work, but to say that it has over the past six decades evolved, and become an authentic part of the city on its own, imperfect, terms. There are tactics of adaptation here, ways of becoming 'at home in the expressway world' (as Eric Avila puts it), without giving in.[99] Like the Hollywood Sign, or the Watt's Towers, or Venice's vestigial canals, the 405/10 has become another of the city's unlikely sights.

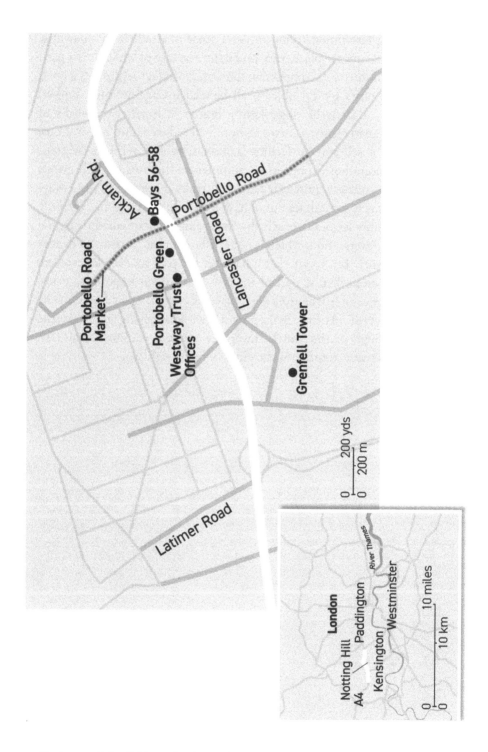

(Facing page) Scaffolding Play St. Marks, 1968. *Photograph by Adam Ritchie. Courtesy of Adam Ritchie.*

CHAPTER 4

London: The Activist Expressway

The Westway, or A40(M), is a two-and-a-half-mile stretch of elevated expressway that slices across West London.[1] Completed in 1970, it was widely reviled on opening and for long afterwards.[2] It has since become, in many ways in spite of itself, a cultural icon.[3] There's an extraordinary picture of it under construction, one of thirty or so from the period, taken by the photographer and sometime urban activist Adam Ritchie in 1968. Ritchie, just back from photographing the Pop artist Andy Warhol and his entourage in New York, depicts the Westway in embryonic form. The precise location is the section alongside Acklam Road, where nineteenth-century slum houses at that point still stood, and the picture shows the undercroft of that section, the concrete ceiling formed by the

carriageway now clearly in place, and the distinctive flat arches receding into the distance (untroubled by conflicts with nearby railways or canals at this point, the Westway's designers could employ two bridge supports here instead of one). The ground is plain gravel – there's no evidence of a landscape designer here – and it's a somewhat bleak environment, the harshness accentuated by the grainy film. But it's a far from bleak image because it's populated by twenty or so young children, the youngest of whom look to be five years old, the oldest perhaps eleven, while their parents look on. Front and centre lies a huge climbing frame improvised from scaffolding and ladders, stretching most of the thirty feet up to the carriageway above, fixed with rope swings and a tightrope. The kids are fearless; it looks like enormous fun.

Ritchie wrote 'some friends from the London Free School' (a local activist project) 'had got permission to open an adventure playground by Acklam Road out of the rubble from the demolished houses … the kids had built some amazing structures there, so I bought a saw, hammer, and a kilo of big nails and left them hidden under the rubble. I went again a few days later and the structures the kids had built were gone and other bigger, even more imaginative structures were there'.[4] As Ritchie's pictures show, the Westway meant devastation: thousands of properties demolished, hundreds of families displaced, years of filth and noise for those who remained. As the pictures also show, however, amid the ruins of modernity there were also opportunities for activists. The Westway children found the carnivalesque in the ruins, as did countless others. This chapter is about those activist possibilities, and more generally how this part of London has learned, quite successfully, to live with the Westway.

The Design: The Three Minute Motorway

The Westway as built starts in Paddington and a Victorian tangle of railway land and canals, from where it takes off across the rooftops of North Kensington, and a couple of miles of suburban grandeur, before terminating at White City where London loses its shape. Its origins can be found as early as 1910 in a scheme mooted by the London Traffic Branch of the Board of Trade.[5] However, the first clear plan for what would become the Western Avenue Extension can be found in Patrick

LONDON: THE ACTIVIST EXPRESSWAY

Costume Under Motorway, 1968. *Photograph by Adam Ritchie. Courtesy of Adam Ritchie.*

Abercrombie's 1944 plan for London's roads (there were Abercrombie plans for many, sometimes seemingly most, cities in Britain – we will see another one in Glasgow in chapter 8).[6] Abercrombie drew on the idea of the pedestrian precinct, a local, traffic-free community zone.[7] Removing through traffic from residential areas would not only improve the quality of the local environment – in theory – but it would also help define 'new, more homogeneous areas for living and working'.[8] Precincts were dependent on the existence of expressway-standard arteries directing traffic away from residential zones.

The 1944 Plan redesigned London's roads around five concentric rings, the first ('A') a tiny two-and-a-half-mile-radius loop around the central city, through to E, some fifteen files from the central point, and roughly equivalent to today's M25. You can just see the Westway in vestigial form in the 1944 Plan: it is a stump of the Birmingham artery, today's M40, set between rings A and B. The Abercrombie Plan survived, albeit very much revised to become the plan for what would become known as London's Motorway Box, the announcement of which was one of the first acts of the new Greater London Council (GLC), just a few hours after its formation in 1965.[9] The 1965 Plan envisaged some thirty-seven miles of orbital roads, encompassing an area of central London, 'the size of Leeds' according to *The Times*.[10] A good deal of it would be elevated, a novelty for Britain that had built short stretches of motorway outside of cities, but unlike New York, Los Angeles or Brussels, so far nothing inside them. It would cost £450 million, or some £7.2 billion now. Peter Hall, strongly pro-roads in the mid-1960s, had already written of their appeal in *London 2000*, guaranteeing their aesthetic contribution to the city, especially, he assured readers, at night: the elevated ringways would be a 'brilliant sight'.[11]

The Western Avenue Extension – Westway – was there in the 1965 plan, a fragment of this much larger scheme. It reads like a test piece for the larger scheme, a proof of concept, although it was still vast. It was to cost £17 million (£274 million, adjusted for inflation). Planning for it had actually been underway several years beforehand from 1959. By 1964 demolitions started, and in early 1965 a detailed plan published, with construction starting the following year. It tends to be remembered as an integral part of the Ringway project because had the whole scheme been completed, it would have linked the inner rings. But a start had been made on it earlier because it had been recommended in 1957 by Richard Nugent, a transport minister in Anthony Eden's Conservative government. It was a small 'c' conservative report, used to forestall the need for urban motorways – the short stretch of the Westway was a means of pushing the traffic problem further out of London, and avoiding doing anything else. There was therefore a structural irony to the Westway's construction as Michael Dnes writes in a history of London's failed Ringways: the Westway 'was created in response to a report that tried to avoid the construction of urban motorways'. And much later, the experience of the Westway was 'used to rule out a programme of urban motorways of which it formed no part'.[12]

Pictures of the proposed Westway soon appeared. In January 1965, newspapers including *The Times* published a dramatic perspective of the scheme, an aerial photograph looking westwards overlaid with the outline of the route and labels identifying scattered landmarks. In the foreground to the left lay Paddington Station and its murky hinterland, to the right the picturesque conservation area of Little Venice and the Grand Union canal, with the three high towers of the recently finished Warwick estate visible just beyond. Through it all swept the new road, holding close to the alignment of the Great Western railway at first, before swooping southwards around Westbourne Park to pick up the route of London Transport's Hammersmith and City Line, before terminating at White City where it merged with the existing A40 at Western Avenue. Seen like this from above, foreshortened and compressed, it's a serpentine monster. It might have followed the route of the railway to minimize land take, but its impact was vastly greater.[13] Where the railways are mostly crepuscular, buried into the earth, the road rises up and makes the landscape. A much broader, bolder intervention than the railways, it makes a new kind of city.

Its makers were the firm of John Laing, with G. Maunsell and partners the chief engineers and William Holford architectural consultant.[14] Holford, who had succeeded Abercrombie as professor of planning at the University of Liverpool, was much in demand as a consultant and had lately (1957) chaired the panel that selected Lucio Costa's design for the masterplan of Brasília. There is something of Brasília in the image, a modern city defined by the automobile.[15] The past recedes into the earth, the expressway dominates, our gaze drawn inexorably up and west, towards Heathrow and the future.

There's a simplicity about the image, and its concept. Taking the expressway, designed for 50 mph running along its whole length would reduce a tortuous hour of driving to a miraculous, free-flowing three minutes.[16] But despite any superficial similarity to the tabula rasa of Brasília, this was a forensic exercise that picked through the bones of West London, dodging historic architecture, and tempering demolitions by the use of existing rights of way, especially rail lines.[17] It all had to be done while keeping existing communications open. It was a complex human project, producing a small town in the four years of its construction – at its peak, Westway contactors numbered 1,000.[18]

The complexity is there in first-hand accounts of its creation from its engineers, running to some 140 pages in three issues of the *Proceedings of the Institution of Civil Engineers*.[19] For construction purposes the Westway fell into six sections, of varying lengths and designs. Some things remained constant. There was a desire to avoid expansion joints where possible, for smoothness, and ease of maintenance; the whole structure was to rest on huge concrete cylinders, buried deep in the London clay; drainage and servicing to be located within them; and the finished form of the roadway was to be consistent regardless of the structure underneath. As built, the structure did vary considerably, with spans varying in width according to the number of lanes, while in places the roadway was supported by a single central pier, in others two or more. There was one unusual, military, consideration. The Ministry of Defence, it was said, required the Westway to support tanks and it was designed to take their weight.[20] Were there to be Moscow-style military parades? – it was never clear.

Some of the structural complexity can be seen in the design of section one, from Wood Lane (White City) in the west to St Marks Road, at the edge of Ladbroke Grove.[21] The section, slightly less than 1,200 metres in length, included a roadway of varying height, an elevated roundabout with associated slip roads, the reconstruction of Wood Lane to the south, a bridge over London Transport's Hammersmith and City Line, and car parking underneath the main structure. Wood Lane had to be kept open throughout the construction. The designers made as much use of the air rights around existing transport corridors as possible for financial expediency, necessary as the cost of land was half that of the scheme as a whole. But that efficient approach to land meant the need for an imaginative approach to structure – in section one alone there were four distinct sections, with two different forms of columns, and a mixture of precast and in-situ concrete elements depending on the section. An onsite laboratory with £10,000 worth of equipment tested the concrete; new construction techniques had to be devised to make use of the tight site.[22]

The engineers' accounts are all about flow, of people and money and cars of course, but also flows within the structure itself – of concrete, water, lubricants, the whole thing envisaged as process. Only intermittently, however, do they give a sense of *what* it was they were constructing, and when complete, what it would be like to experience. There are odd flashes of realization – the photographs of the scheme are a parallel text of destruction. There's an intermittent sense that environmental conditions have been neglected, underfunded or fallen between jurisdictions – a letter from Holford's to the GLC's head of Architecture from 1968 says exactly that.[23]

There is some acknowledgement, too, on the post-construction discussion from 1972, when William Holford, the consultant architect, lamented some of the scheme's aesthetic shortcomings in a talk for the Institution of Civil Engineers.[24] Only 1 per cent of the budget was available for landscaping, so while the motorway was a 'blessing' for motorists, it was 'not so good for the pedestrians and householders below it'.[25] Maintenance was underestimated. The scene at ground level could be very poor: 'The costs of maintenance and organization have been underestimated. Discoloration of all surfaces over a period of three years has been far worse than was anticipated. Refuse and litter are pervasive, including quantities of broken glass.' It resembled a war zone, he continued, in a revealing note: 'Temporary split-chestnut and wire fences, protecting the growing grass, have been flattened and used as ammunition.'[26]

Outside the professional press, however, the tone was different. If the mainstream media had been broadly affirmative of the Westway in 1965 when it was announced, the mood predictably darkened once the works started. *The Times* described an apocalyptic scene along the fringes of the route: 'spectral rows of empty houses waiting to be demolished, streets full of empty houses and derelict cars ... the most visible and startling havoc'. The motorway project sliced through the inner city 'tornado-like', leaving a bleak and lawless zone in its wake. 'Worse than the bombs' in the words of one resident, referring to the devastation of the Second World War.[27]

There's something of a professional schism in the reportage. For the engineers who designed and built the project, it remained an exceptional achievement. But architects were sceptical, perhaps because they hadn't much been part of the process, which had been driven instead by politicians and traffic engineers. It was an immense piece of urbanism, one of the largest of the period, but their role was at best subservient.

The *Architectural Review* – a modernizing force, but long committed to what it called 'townscape' – didn't like it.[28] Flyovers might be 'convenient' for the motorist, but the environment at ground level could be 'grim', even in the official perspective drawings supplied by the GLC, which it illustrated in order to criticize. It was a 'farce' that minimum environmental standards had never been set for the scheme, going on to propose some small-scale mitigations including a children's play area here and there, and extending Portobello market under the Westway, both of which, in the end, happened. But there's a palpable sense of alienation from the project. It extended to the GLC's road plans altogether, which the Royal Institute of British Architects berated in 1969: driven by outmoded traffic predictions from 1961 rather than actual trends, its lack of attention to public transport would precipitate 'environmental disaster'.[29] For the *Architects' Journal*, the London of the GLC plan would be 'dirtier, untidier, with fewer people, more roads, more traffic and with its central area well on the way to the Necropolis forecast by Lewis Mumford'. ('Necropolis' was Mumford's term for a state of pathological urban decline.[30])

Towards the end of the 1960s the architectural media in general was increasingly hand-wringing and development-sceptic. The *Architectural Review*'s year-log 'Manplan' series of special issues is the signal case – no architecture, just grainy photojournalism and problems. It likely followed the tone set by the mainstream media, by that stage deeply sceptical of the architectural establishment.[31] The Westway's opening ceremony on 28 July 1970 was badly disrupted by the Golbourne Social Rights Committee, a local pressure group chaired by an Acklam Road resident George Clark. Banners behind the opening ceremony read 'Get Us Out of this Hell', 'Don't Fly over People's Lives' and 'Shut the Ramps'. Residents, reported *The Times*, slept within a 'stone's throw' of the motorway; some threatened direct action.[32]

The politicians, to an extent, listened. The Conservative leader of the GLC Desmond Plummer spent much of his speech on 28 July deploring the effect of the construction on the local environment, an extraordinary disavowal of his own project.[33] The then Minister for Transport John Peyton was conveniently busy with a cabinet meeting on the day of the opening, but agreed in principle to meet the Acklam Road residents. An agreement to rehouse them followed not long after. In early 1971 the houses were demolished and the remaining land grassed over.[34] However, the damage was done: another Westway was now inconceivable, let alone the Ringways. In a leader, *The Times* wrote acidly 'it brings Swansea several minutes closer to the Marylebone Road ... And it is a bad advertisement for the GLC's controversial programme of urban motorways.'[35] But the argument had already been made on the front page of the same issue. In the middle of the front page was a remarkable picture of the Howcroft family's home on one side of the Westway, shown on the inaugural day: a boy stares through the open window over pegged laundry, while a huge truck tears by the living room, seemingly only inches away.[36] Noise levels inside adjacent properties, *The Times* reporter noted, could reach 80 db.[37]

Rolling in the Ruins

Shortly after the official opening of the Westway, the independent leftist news magazine *New Society* published an account of the trouble brewing around it. It was a good place for it. *New Society* was interested in technology and consumer culture, and it generally liked roads. Peter Hall, wearing his journalist hat, was the magazine's de facto planning correspondent, and he had reported positively on the GLC's plans in March 1965.[38] More recently he was one of the co-authors of the intentionally provocative 'Non-Plan', a collaboration with the architecture critic Reyner Banham, the architect Cedric Price and *New Society*'s editor Paul Barker, and that envisaged an England of the near future cruising a dense network of expressways in the pursuit of pleasure.[39] Hall and Banham brought to *New Society* a sunny Californianism, epitomized by Banham's occasional car reviews. But even *New Society*'s mood had darkened by 1970, and its Westway was now defined by worried residents, racial tensions and handwringing architects. It recognized the 'astounding' engineering, but it was otherwise a different kind of automobile space to the one its readers might have been familiar with. This wasn't so much a space for drivers, but a space of activism. In terms of its media representation at any rate, the Westway was scarcely visible as a transport system; it had become a space of conflict, the wealthy versus the dispossessed, the engineers versus the people.

Westway activism found its outlet first through play. Adam Ritchie's photographs – which we started with – were the outcome of his own work as an activist. An urgent problem, as he saw it, was the lack of space for play for local children, a fraction of what was available in the vastly richer South Kensington.[40] Following the adventure playground experience, Ritchie set up the North Kensington Playspace Group (NKPG) with John O'Malley, another activist.[41] Gaining in confidence, the group broadened its scope and at the end of the 1960s renamed itself the Motorway Development Trust, a subtle rebranding suggestive of a constructive engagement with the Westway rather than outright opposition. 'Development' hinted at real estate ambitions, and the fact of including 'Motorway' in the name recognized the Westway's ongoing and inevitable existence. They produced a large map of the Westway site in 1969, fifteen feet long, which O'Malley and Ritchie used to invite contributions from local residents using sticky notes.[42]

The map seems perfectly natural now, in its finished form with residents' desires edited and collated. Instead of eight acres of secure car parking, the Trust proposed a range of community facilities – at the western end under the great elevated roundabout, a sports centre and football pitch, a nursery school, a garden centre, an art school, rehearsal rooms, a 'home repair centre', a Meals-on-Wheels kitchen, a library, a supermarket, a health centre and, right at the east end close to Acklam Road, a now permanent adventure playground. There were even stables. As activism it was unusually free of dogma. There was a tidy, nicely illustrated booklet, underlining its pragmatic approach. Traditional public space – 'a park with well-kept flowerbeds' – was out, declared 'wasteful'. In its place was the integration of functions, which might be 'social, educational and even commercial'; you might build 'an adventure playground near a supermarket'; the Portobello Road market might be extended into the scheme (it ultimately was). It was an open-minded, thoroughly eclectic approach.[43]

Running along the top of two of the pages, banner style were wide-angle shots of the Westway's path alongside the Metropolitan line looking west. Taken once the site had been cleared, but before any construction, they are pictures of remarkable devastation. Muddy pools glint in the light; nature replaces civilization. They're uncannily like the artistic images of nineteenth-century Paris amid the convulsions of Georges-Eugène Haussmann's modernization, and here, like Paris, the gaze is ambiguous, both horror and fascination, fear mixed with opportunity.[44] It is too easy to characterize the Westway activism as straight opposition. The expressway might have been unwelcome in the first place, but once the project was under way, its spaces – however awkward and unlikely – brought new possibilities the old city lacked.

The activists' media connections meant coverage in the *Evening Standard*, *The Guardian* and *The Daily Telegraph* newspapers, all of which covered the proposals approvingly. Terence Bendixson, at the time *The Guardian*'s planning correspondent, wrote of the Trust's proposals that they signified an enlightened professional approach in which the road would be properly integrated with the area it passed through – he cited Lawrence Halprin's book *Freeways* (covered in chapter 3) as a model American approach to the problem.[45] *The Telegraph* compared the proposal favourably with existing developments in Tokyo, illustrated for comparison the city's Central Station Bypass as an example of what might be achieved, the highway set atop a shopping complex.[46] For the *Standard*, it was bluntly the promise of 'Extra cash' to 'Brighten M-Ways', somewhat inaccurately giving the agency of the scheme to the Royal Borough of Kensington and Chelsea rather than the Motorway Development Trust.[47] The message was clear enough in any case – the Westway could be tamed.

A Concrete Island

Much as the activists regretted the existence of the Westway, their work showed how they could appropriate its unexpected new spaces and, albeit incrementally, make it human: the NKPG's play spaces were both actually and symbolically important, showing how an ostensibly utilitarian structure might become a space for the imagination.[48] There were some important cultural parallels. The best known, albeit probably the darkest, was J.G. Ballard's novel, *Concrete Island*, first published in 1974, by which stage the Westway was part of the everyday landscape. It was just preceded in 1973 by another autophile novel, *Crash*, controversial for its erotic themes (its protagonists find sexual thrills by crashing cars – it was subsequently made into a feature film by David Cronenberg, which Ballard much admired).[49] *Concrete Island* has flashes of the automobile eroticism of *Crash*, but Ballard's attention here is more on place, as it would subsequently be with *High-Rise* (1975) (the subject of that book closely resembles Ernö Goldfinger's Trellick Tower, then rising in the middle of Ladbroke Grove).[50]

Ballard was a rarity in public life, an intellectual who also took automobile culture seriously. He could also be unsparing about it. In 1971 the thoroughly mainstream, consumer-focused Automobile Association (one of the two main British motoring organizations) bravely commissioned an essay from him for its magazine on the future of motoring.[51] Its readers were used to travel tips and car reviews – it is hard to know what they made of Ballard's pitiless anti-humanism. 'I think that the twentieth century reaches almost its purest expression on the highway', he wrote. 'Here we see all too clearly the speed and violence of our age, its strange love affair with the machine, and conceivably with its own death and destruction.' On elevated expressways, the setting of *Concrete Island*, they were, he continued, 'the most important monuments of our urban civilization, the twentieth century's equivalent of the Pyramids'. But like the Pyramids, he asked, were they not 'after all monuments to the dead?'[52]

Ballard was thinking of car crashes, having just been in a bad one himself ('My Ford Zephyr ... had a front blowout at the foot of the Chiswick Bridge, rolled over, crossed the dual carriageway').[53] Before that near-fatal experience, he had already staged an exhibition of crashed cars at the Camden Arts Centre, and completed a draft of *Crash*. It's an obscure, but revealing passage – here Ballard takes the reader beyond the rational words of traffic engineers to what he considered an authentic understanding of the expressway, which was all sex and death.

Concrete Island's location is a heavily fictionalized Westway, imagined as it might have been had the GLC's Ringway project been realized, linked to the M4 and beyond. There are glimpses of the familiar London ('White City', 'Marylebone'), but they are not much more than signposts for long-vanished referents. This is a typically Ballardian landscape of the near future, in which the familiar has largely gone. The Westway in contemporary photographs is always, in Brutalist style, an overlay, in which the detritus of the past is clear enough along the edges of the carriageways. By contrast Ballard's Westway is disorientatingly new.[54] *Concrete Island* begins, perhaps in homage to the Futurist Manifesto, with a crash.[55] An architect in his mid-30s, Robert Maitland, hurrying from his Marylebone office in mid-afternoon, loses control of his Jaguar after a tyre blowout, crashing through temporary barriers to roll down an embankment. He comes to a halt in a triangular no-man's land between carriageways, largely invisible to the passing traffic.[56] This place, it soon becomes clear, is a prison. Incapacitated by injury, Maitland finds he can't escape, and his attempts to attract attention are fruitless. He can glimpse the world outside (red buses, distant shops) but can't reach it. Sick and exhausted, he gradually becomes accustomed to the strange life of the island and the misfits who dwell among its ruins. As it does in *Crash* and *High Rise*, technological civilization becomes savagery. Maitland stays put.

In real life Ballard was writing from his semi-detached house in suburban Shepperton, on the far reaches of West London, a good fifteen miles from the Westway. Despite his patrician style and anti-humanism, his work appealed to the contemporary London counter-culture whose epicentre lay in North Kensington, the area the Westway bisected. It was a close equivalent to the Haight-Ashbury district of San Francisco, the urban focus of the so-called 1967 Summer of Love. Like the Haight, North Kensington was a once grand area of Victorian housing, now somewhat dilapidated and colonized by hippies. It similarly had its house bands, chiefly Hawkwind and the Pink Fairies, apt to play for free, as well as its self-produced magazines. It had resident intellectuals, in this case the prolific science-fiction author Michael Moorcock, performing both as an activist and street philosopher, explaining the scene to sceptical outsiders.

London's counter-culture is one of the chapters in the American journalist Jonathan Raban's 1974 book on London, *Soft City*, bohemian and fluid, superficially squalid, but in its own way intensely global and well connected.[57] It was a scene drawn inexorably to the primitive, and that was a point of contact. For both Ballard and the counter-culture, technological modernity was never more than a veneer, and its removal was one of their chief tasks. The Westway wasn't a random object, but the key architectural figure of the counter-cultural world. The counter-culture's main protagonists lived around it, and its house magazines (*Oz* and *Frendz*) were published in earshot – the latter just a few feet away at 275 Portobello Road. The Westway represented faceless authority – 'planners!' – but it also was a space redolent with possibilities.

Ballard was friendly with Moorcock, the pair having worked together on the magazine *New Worlds*.[58] Moorcock was perhaps the counter-culture's chief intellectual and an occasional activist. He had been one of the organizers of free concerts under the Westway in 1971, occupying bays 56 to 58 just adjacent to Portobello Road.[59] Moorcock's attraction to the space was more pragmatic than Ballard's.[60] Ballard, he said later, was 'only interested in the motorway and cars, and I had no interest in it as such … I was interested in how it affected local people, he was interested in aesthetics.'[61] Moorcock worked closely with Jon Trux, editor of *Frendz*, whose offices were not only adjacent to the Westway, but located above a greasy spoon popular with musicians, the strangely named Mountain Grill (later celebrated on the title of a Hawkwind album, the ironic Grieg-referencing *Hall of the Mountain Grill*).[62]

LONDON: THE ACTIVIST EXPRESSWAY

'It was probably Trux's idea to have concerts', Moorcock said, and they built a 'decent little theatre' with murals painted by friends and associates, old railway sleepers for benches, and stalls for charity organizations, including the White Panthers and the Hare Krishnas. Power came from a variety of Portobello Road establishments, '*Frendz, New Worlds* and so on' (*New Worlds* was the SF magazine Moorcock edited from 1964 and to which Ballard contributed). 'There would have been about ten or fifteen gigs', Moorcock thought, 'usually fraught with police problems. The police, on complaints from nearby oldsters often tried to stop us, usually citing vague ordnances about our power sources.'[63] The concerts were nevertheless popular with locals and covered with benign amusement, but approvingly, by the local press.[64] Eventually, Moorcock said, the theatre mysteriously burned down: 'everything was ruined – murals, stage and so on. We suspected TORY involvement, given they were also supported by some nearby residents. It became a lost battle after that.'[65]

Moorcock's own involvement with the concerts extended to performing with Hawkwind, and it was at one of the Westway concerts that he first performed the five-minute spoken word piece 'Sonic Attack', a parody of the British government's futile advice to citizens in the case of nuclear attack. So aligned was the group with his own apocalyptic vision, he said later, that had they not existed, he might have had to invent them.[66] Their second album, *In Search of Space*, released in 1971, has photographic evidence of the Westway concerts. The front of the elaborate cardboard sleeve, designed by Barney Bubbles, is a cosmic battle flag, the inky black of the cosmos and a colourful hawk-shaped emblem, the band's name and the album title. On the inside the sleeve opens to a schematic hawk, outlined in white against a black background, and inside the hawk are photographs of the Westway concert, mostly of the audience – hairy, young, racially mixed, with two policemen looking down sternly on the scene from the top. The large central image depicts the stage, the band's wall of black amplifiers defining the middle ground, an empty demilitarized zone below that and a few audience members waiting patiently. It's all about to kick off, seemingly, both in real life and on the listener's turntable, as the picture is only revealed when the vinyl disc is lifted from the package.

That central image is curious, though – no ordinary concert hall, or even typical festival site, it's a scrappy, but evidently modern landscape.

LONDON: THE ACTIVIST EXPRESSWAY

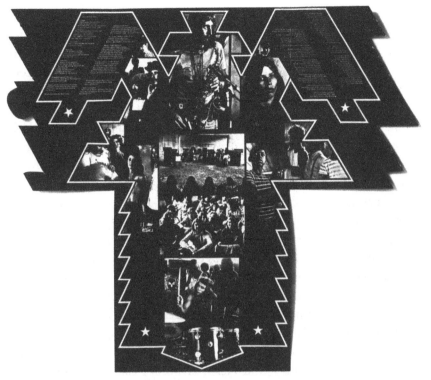

Hawkwind, *X In Search Of Space* interior gatefold, 1971. Design: © Barney Bubbles Estate. Photography: Joe Stevens, Phil Franks (United Artists, 1971). Copyright © 1969–2024 Phil Franks. All Rights Reserved.

The band set up under a flat arch in reinforced concrete, about twenty feet wide, with similar arches receding into the background (Adam Ritchie had photographed exactly the same place). The foreground is seemingly a gravel-scattered waste ground, extremely rough. It has a somewhat apocalyptic, end-of-the-world quality to it, a party at the end of the world. It's an evidently modern scene, but also a primitive one, the audience in a state of nature.

Two years after those concerts, the Westway made a cameo appearance in one of the mainstream films to emerge from the west London counter-culture, Robert Fuest's 1973 adaptation of Moorcock's dystopian SF novel *The Final Programme*. His novel, written in the mid-1960s, depicted a world ruined by war from the perspective of its anti-hero Jerry Cornelius, counter-cultural James Bond. In the film, he's depicted drunk at the wheel of his 1936 Buick Limited, careering underneath the Westway as it meets the West Cross Route. The great elevated roundabout is clearly visible, the wasteland in the middle filled with a (real life) encampment of travellers, which persists.[67] Moorcock disliked the film, with good reason, but that image remains suggestive, the expressway undercroft a picture of technological civilization in ruins.[68] The counter-cultural Westway appears, heavily fictionalized in Moorcock's own work at least once – an account of a famous police bust of a Saturday afternoon concert appears in the novel *King of the City*.[69] It also appears in another semi-fictionalized account in the work of a later Moorcock associate, the novelist Iain Sinclair – the story 'London Spirit' from the collection *Agents of Oblivion*, published in 2023.[70] The conceit of the story, Sinclair explained later, was 'a walk under the Westway summoning ghosts from Ballard's *Concrete Island*. And drawing as ever on Mike Moorcock.'[71] Sinclair did not attend the 1971 Westway concerts, but was a regular in the area from 1975 onwards, scavenging the informal fly pitches underneath the Westway for rare books that he would later sell at his stall in Camden Passage in Islington ('my luckiest find was a first edition of Lennon's *In His Own Write* signed by the four Beatles, their girlfriends – and Helen Shapiro. I sold it too soon, but a good hit at 50p.')[72]

The Westway Trust

The Westway became a carnivalesque space – a space in which a certain amount of bounded disorder was possible and sanctioned, most extensively in the form of the Notting Hill Carnival, the colossal and ongoing annual celebration of Afro-Caribbean culture.[73] Activism increasingly formalized the Westway's undercroft, producing over time an ad hoc, eclectic aesthetic and an accidental megastructure in the process.[74] It is unusual, even in London where working and living spaces are scarce and expensive: there is no other equivalent structure with such a density of uses underneath it, although the occupation of expressway space is common outside of Europe. Vena Dhupa, the CEO of the Westway Trust in 2023, said she had seen occupations of expressway structures in Latin America ('Mexico City, Bolivia, Peru') but nothing similar elsewhere in London, a fact she attributed to the persistence and energy of early activists such as Adam Ritchie ('they must have had remarkable ability to envision what is possible').[75]

Ritchie's organization, The Motorway Development Trust, spawned a separate formal entity established on 5 February 1971 with a new name – the North Kensington Amenity Trust (NKAT) – and representation on the Board from the Royal Borough of Kensington and Chelsea. A former British ambassador to Moscow, Patrick Reilly, was installed as chair. Its early history was bitter and conflict-ridden: Andrew Duncan's history of the NKAT describes its beginning, pungently, as 'a shaky start, fierce disputes, improvisation, opportunism'.[76] The activists for their part thought the Conservative-led council deeply suspect.[77] The councillors unsurprisingly found the activists 'dangerous' and 'incompetent'.[78] Its activities could be benignly straightforward all the same, for example a 1972 competition for ideas to improve the Westway's environs, pitched partly at students. Richard Rogers, later architect of the Centre Pompidou in Paris, was one of the assessors. As the NKAT grew, the MDT continued on the sidelines; now an informal organization, it anxiously watched over the NKAT and published the results in *Westway News*.

The subsequent history of the Westway was more conventional. The NKAT started to operate more like an ordinary real estate company, with a turnover of approximately £1 million by 1979. Rather later it acquired a new name, the Westway Development Trust, in 2002, before that organisation was dissolved and an entirely new entity, the Westway Trust, created, in 2010.[79] Its tortuous history is reflected in the ad hoc accretion of buildings under the expressway, comprising in 2024 an estate of twenty-three acres running the length of the structure and 160 tenants.[80] The freehold – that is the ownership of the structure and the land underneath it – belongs to Transport for London, the city's transit authority; the Trust are leaseholders. The Westway itself remains curiously visible and invisible throughout. Vena Dhupa, the Trust's CEO, said in 2023: 'I must have driven along the Westway hundreds of times. Like most Londoners I didn't really think about it.'[81] The Trust's offices, accessed from Thorpe Close off the Portobello Road, are literally built into the structure in a two-storey unit wedged below the roadway. The ceiling is the surface of the roadway, the concrete spans clearly visible. The noise is surprisingly subdued, although the structure vibrates with the passage of heavy trucks.

Acklam Road skatepark, Westway, London. *Photograph by Richard J. Williams.*

The estate varies a great deal. About a third is in community or charity use, another third let commercially, and the remainder, for sports, with a very large complex located at the Latimer Road end. It can be extremely informal: some of it is not much more than an open bay, unresolved and open to possibility. There are light industrial workshops along the westward section, upholsterers, car breakers, potters reiterating the uses traditionally made of railway arches. Food trucks cluster the Acklam Road section. A skate park occupies a bay a few hundred metres to the east, its ramps and turns echoing the giant curve of the roadway above. A significant income comes from the film/TV facility, providing a secure physical base for film crews working in London.[82] The Westway Trust's estate can also be straightforwardly corporate: in 2023 the coffee house Pret a Manger and the Sainsbury's supermarket both had branches on the Trust's estate.

The Trust promotes filming, advertising its 'dereliction', its 'edgy, urban, funky film backdrops', and locations 'rich in graffiti'.[83] It is clear enough about the negative consequences of the Westway ('this road has undoubtedly damaged this community'), running from 2024 a campaign on air quality. But as the approach to filming shows, it is pragmatic, working with the structure rather than undermining it.[84]

Perhaps the densest and most characteristic section of the Westway as currently lived is the Portobello Road market section to the west, the area temporarily occupied by the 1971 concerts organized by Moorcock and Jon Trux of *Frendz*. It was the subject of a formal planning exercise in 1978, and then remade as an architectural project in three phases by the architects Franklin Stafford Partnership in association with Buro Happold, completed in 1984.[85] It is a straightforward infill job, two storeys in concrete located directly under the expressway itself but structurally independent of it, but occupying as much of the space as possible. Ribbon windows project at first floor level, while there's aluminium facing to the units at ground level and some red engineering brick. It has an industrial look, of an indeterminate, vaguely 1930s type. Buro Happold, an engineering firm, then added a tensile structure to the north, providing shelter to thirty or so market stalls – a concession, Andrew Duncan reported later, to street traders' fears of Covent Garden-style gentrification and a takeover by 'middle class ponces'.[86] (The tent was replaced by a similar, but more modern structure by Base Structures in 2003.[87]) Inside the building there are perhaps twenty workshops, with retail façades, opening out onto an internal corridor, and the tent opens onto Portobello Green, a small park. The roadway is just visible here, with glimpses of passing traffic and a mess of signage, but despite the proximity, not much more than six metres above ground, it doesn't much intrude, perhaps because of the density of the activity at ground level. The building is one of those stylistically ambiguous structures rather characteristic of London of the period.

It has little of the straightforwardly utilitarian character of the Westway itself, which notably lacks decoration. It is reminiscent of Sant'Elia's Futurism in the fenestration, as if there's an attempt to retrofit a heroic vision of modernity the Westway never really had. The high-tech tensile roof takes it to another heroic modern site, Munich's 1972 Olympics. But what is characteristic is the variety of this quasi-subterranean estate, sometimes utilitarian and functional, sometimes arch and ironic, sometimes faux-modern. It is a bricolage. If the original expressway was a total, rationalizing vision, the later reality is eclectic. This isn't a traffic engineer's structure any more, for activism has, gradually, made over the Westway in its image. That design pragmatism was enough to win it a Civic Trust Award in 1984, presented by the Prince of Wales and marked by a plaque.[88]

The Wall of Truth

Visit the heart of the Westway on foot these days and something else is apparent. Not far west from the congestion of the Portobello Road, just a little to the south of St Mark's Road lies the Lancaster Estate, a mixed-height social housing project of 795 homes, completed by the Royal Borough of Kensington and Chelsea in 1974. A mix of houses, walk-up flats and stubby towers, it became headline news in June 2017 when one of the latter, Grenfell Tower, caught fire. The immediate cause was a faulty fridge-freezer on the fourth floor; the recently installed and highly combustible cladding, along with multiple failures in the emergency response produced a catastrophe. Seventy-two residents lost their lives.[89] It was a commonplace to link the two sites. Vena Dhupa: 'Grenfell has undoubtedly damaged this community. This community is bruised.'[90]

The stump of the tower remained a visible presence six years on: wrapped and sealed, it was a tomb. Immediately after the fire, London Transport discouraged disaster tourism from the nearby Latimer Road underground station, from whose steps a good view of the remains could be had. In any case the prevailing culture now seemed to be a conscious un-seeing of it. In the days immediately following the disaster, wrote the sociologist Paul Gilroy, it seemed 'as though the act of staring up at the tower had been expressly forbidden'. Some, he continued 'who have dwelled in the shadow of its steel and concrete carcass and inhaled the toxic residues of the blaze may even be glad it was wrapped up, hidden from sight and effectively placed in storage'.[91]

Gilroy was writing in support of perhaps the best-received Grenfell memorial to date, a twenty-four-minute film made by the artist Steve McQueen in 2019.[92] Called simply *Grenfell*, the film opens with birdsong and a somewhat hazy, early morning view of London looking east from the western periphery. The camera is airborne, borne up by a helicopter, on one of two flights made on 18 December, some six months after the fire.[93] The pilot flies in a straight line at a constant altitude for some minutes before the blackened stump of the tower emerges to the right. The Westway, horizontal and serpentine, is a clear landmark to its side, and seen together with the tower like this, it reads as an archetypal modernist composition, the expressway and the tower, the horizontal plane and the vertical accent, motion and stasis. Except here there's something badly awry: the tower is a charred stump while the Westway traffic hums obliviously. The camera circles the tower, progressively closing in, the soundtrack now becoming silence. The wreckage of the façade becomes more precise, along with a few human figures, workmen in hi-vis and hard hats, picking through the cremated remains.

There is another, informal, memorial to Grenfell under the Westway now, and its existence complicates our readings of the road: this is no longer a simple expressway, but the site of a still-unresolved human tragedy. The memorial in question is the Wall of Truth in a scrubby area of the underpass just beyond St Mark's Road, adjoining the Lancaster Estate. You can see the remains of Grenfell clearly enough from here looking south, and as you turn away from the sight, the wall provides 'first-hand accounts, facts, testimonies and statements', and angry and wide-ranging response to the slow and inconclusive public enquiry into the disaster that never really apportioned blame. 'THE TRUTH WILL NOT BE HIDDEN', the wall reads at the top.[94] But it is: this is one of the last unreconstructed bits of the underpass, one of the last of its empty sites, and it is not especially easy to find unless you are on your way to the football pitches to the west.[95]

'The true horror of the killings', wrote Gilroy, deliberately avoiding any sense that this was an accident, 'is that they present in capsule form a deeply disturbing illustration of the morbidity of institutions in contemporary Britain. Corruption, cruelty, complicity, disdain and disregard feature here as both causes and effects. All have been harnessed to the machinery of rapacious unregulated capitalism and then projected through the frames of xenophobia and racist common sense.'[96] What Gilroy says about Grenfell might be applied to the Westway too. Acklam Road had been poor and black; the Westway's path took away half the street and its residents with it, obliterating them. 'It swept out the mess of Notting Dale', wrote Gilroy, 'and the riots of 1958, ushering in a new arrangement.'[97]

What to say in conclusion about the Westway? To many commentators it seemed like an urban catastrophe when built, and initial responses to it were hostile. It's clear, too, in retrospect the extent to which it embodied a form of racialized planning, for the residents it most threatened were mostly poor and mostly black. But it came to be useful, almost as soon as it was built, too, its very unreconstructed quality carrying with it rare potential in Central London. It turned out to be ideal for the counter-culture of the early 1970s, a suitably apocalyptic setting for the counter-cultural theatrics, and later the ideal space for the Carnival. In his book *Leadville* on the A40, Edward Platt writes, 'the Westway has aged better than Western Avenue: while Western Avenue's decline has continued, the Westway has become an iconic feature of London's landscape, and the city has reknitted around its concrete carriageways. Ladbroke Grove is as fashionable now as the King's Road was in the sixties, when the demolition of North Kensington began.'[98]

The Westway remains, for the time being at least, still an automobile-focused space: 'even my car loves the Westway', Platt writes.[99] It provides a rare sensation of speed in contemporary London.[100] Like São Paulo's Minhocão, discussed in the next chapter, it keeps all kinds of contradictory things in play, very like, in fact, a traditional piece of city rather than the futuristic vision pushed out to the media in 1965. It is – to paraphrase the postmodern architects Robert Venturi and Denise Scott Brown on the archetypical American main street – 'almost all right'. They were writing in 1966 in a book called *Complexity and Contradiction in Modern Architecture*.[101] Then under threat of demolition everywhere due to new road schemes, Main Street, according to the prevailing architectural wisdom, had nothing much to offer. But the characteristics that had served Main Street well – adaptability, and legibility and resilience – might be, Venturi and Scott Brown argued, useful for the future. The Westway and structures like it are not typically praised for the characteristics Venturi and Scott Brown found in Main Street, and in many ways the Westway is the opposite of Main Street, bludgeoning through a traditional neighbourhood in an act of urban violence that set out to destroy place rather than enhance it. But the strange history of the Westway since 1970 has shown that it might perversely have some of those characteristics; once the dust of the construction site cleared, and it was for better or worse accepted, it could by activism and accident be turned into something else. Andrew Duncan wrote, it had transformed itself from a dangerous 'twilight zone' to 'one of North Kensington's main thoroughfares'.[102] Its representations in culture are innumerable. It is attracting news uses, such as a proposed new student facility for

Imperial College in 2024.[103] 'People just accept it – it's here', the Westway Trust's CEO has said. 'People aren't really thinking about a future when it has gone.'[104] Through extraordinary activism, it has become an ordinary part of the city.

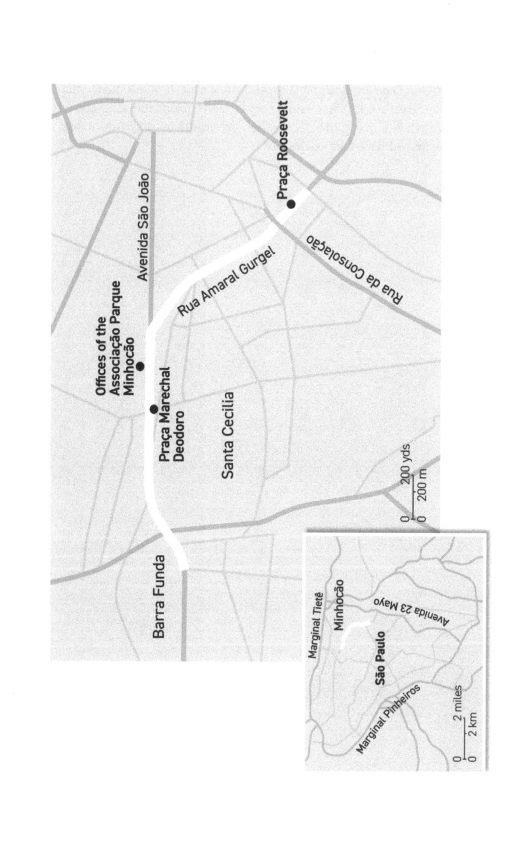

CHAPTER 5

São Paulo: The Expressway Occupied

São Paulo, 24 January 1971, mid-morning. It was hot already, the air temperature touching thirty degrees, the highest temperature so far of the summer.[1] A crowd had been gathering all morning in the treeless modernity of the Praça Roosevelt to witness the opening of the city's greatest engineering project of modern times, the Via Elevada Artur da Costa e Silva, a three-and-a-half-kilometre expressway linking the east and west parts of the central city. It had appeared, almost by magic, in fourteen months, along with the Praça, the latter being a concrete megastructure combining public square and shopping mall. A team of 3,100 labourers and engineers were responsible, the work continuing without pause day and night. The numbers were impressive: 98,000 square metres of roadway, 32,000 tonnes of cement, 100,000 tonnes of steel, 145,000 tonnes of concrete.[2] It was, it was said by the mayor of São Paulo, Paulo Maluf, the greatest work in reinforced concrete in all of Latin America.[3]

The speeches began at 10:30. Maluf started proceedings, celebrating the achievements of the builders, dismissing as 'romantics' those who wished things had stayed as they were. He was followed by the state governor, Abreu Sodré, who underlined the project's political origins: it was a project of the revolution of '64, he said, which is to say the coup that delivered military government to Brazil, with (he claimed) its emphasis on political and economic autonomy. He claimed it as a project of the same order as the Trans-Amazonian Highway, then also underway. The archbishop of São Paulo spoke briefly to bless the project, followed finally by Yolanda Costa e Silva, the widow of Artur, the military President who gave his name to the highway, but who had also expired somewhat mysteriously during its construction. 'Very emotional', according to the *Folha de São Paulo*, she unveiled the plaque commemorating the event.[4] The assembled dignitaries then took to their armoured limousines to drive the length of the highway towards Barra Funda, a journey that at the speed limit of 60 km/h would be covered in

SÃO PAULO: THE EXPRESSWAY OCCUPIED

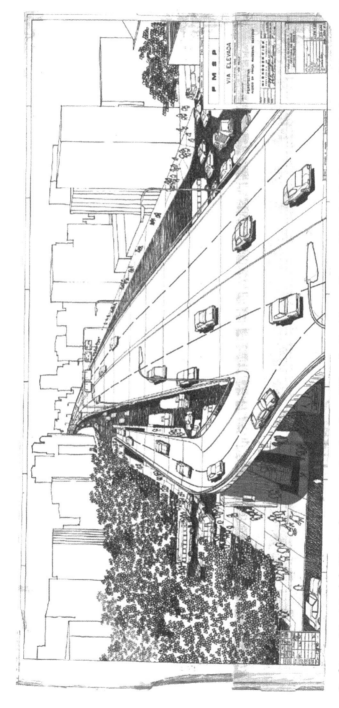

Prefeitura Municipal de São Paulo, perspective drawing of Elevado Presidente Costa e Silva, São Paulo, 1969. *Archives of the Prefeitura Municipal de São Paulo.*

three minutes. Accompanied by applause and flag-waving, it was slower that day. Thousands then took to the hot tarmac on foot, permitted to do so until 2 pm, when the first cars were allowed. That day in Brazil, it was, no question, the place to be. The *Folha de São Paulo* put it on its front page the following day, with a detailed report inside.[5]

The inauguration was a real spectacle. It was also, weirdly, an occupation. It was a day of affirmation – of Maluf's abilities as mayor, of the city on its annual founding day, of the military regime, even of God. The choreography of the event was meticulous. But the morning itself was defined by what would have been at another moment a mass trespass onto the asphalt, a surface built for cars, not people; pedestrians would normally be banished to the gloomy underworld below the roadway, along with buses and bikes. Even if sanctioned and controlled, however, this great trespass was an uncanny prefiguration of its later life.

The Minhocão (The Big Worm, as it almost immediately came to be known, after a creature from Brazilian folklore) remains an active highway during the day, but at night and at weekends it has for decades been much better known as a kind of urban beach, a space for walking, or running and cycling, sunbathing, cultural events and dog-walking – alternative forms of occupation. The occupation of the Minhocão has a long history, sometimes taking an official form, as in the 1971 opening event. It's sometimes informal, as in the case more recently of its occupation by the homeless below the main structure. Occupation is sometimes artistic, sometimes cultural, often enough political. What is notable about the Minhocão through all of these events is its basic amenability to occupation. Built to connect the east and west parts of the city by private car, it has become, however intermittent and imperfect, one of the city's great public spaces.

In contemporary Anglophone usage, the word 'occupation' is likely to call to mind the cultural and political actions of the short-lived Occupy movement that took over Manhattan's Zuccotti Park in 2011, before a series of actions worldwide.[6] Occupation in Brazil has a rather longer history, not only as a political act, but also as a centuries-old strategy for making and developing housing. In *The Myth of Marginality*, a classic 1976 account of a Rio de Janeiro favela, the anthropologist Janice Perlman describes occupation as in fact one of Brazil's dominant urban forms. In some cities, she argues, the formal city is even the exception. Its perceived 'marginality' is 'myth', she writes; *favelados* claim and occupy urban space, often, over time, regularizing what they have claimed.[7] In some cities, to occupy urban space might be the same thing as building it. Writing specifically about São Paulo, the planner and academic Raquel Rolnik has described occupation as one of the city's key survival modes, a means for ordinary citizens to deal with crisis.[8] It has occasionally taken spectacular forms, such as the occupation of the huge Prestes Maia building near Luz railway station, which housed 400 families between 2006 and 2010.[9]

At the 2023 São Paulo Bienal, the curators gave a prominent place to the Ocupação 9 de Julio, a major occupation in the centre of São Paulo that provides informal housing for upwards of 500 residents spread over ten buildings.[10] The name 9 de Julho refers to one of the central city's principal arteries, and the site of the occupation. During the Bienal, another São Paulo occupation, Ouvidor 63 (named after the narrow city centre street on which it could be found), opened its doors for a series of alternative events, as it had done alongside previous iterations.[11] The *Folha* had earlier listed both 9 de Julho and Ouvidor 63 along with three other occupations in a survey of artistic occupations worth visiting during a weekend of cultural tourism.[12]

For Nate Millington, a geographer, the Minhocão has always been connected with tactics of occupation.[13] For him it connects with a range of different kinds of occupations operating in a broad alliance – 'residents in need of housing, environmentalists committed to more and better green space and artists interested in creative engagement with the cityscape'.[14] In São Paulo, those connections include specifically the appropriation of empty downtown skyscrapers for housing, as well as open space such as the Parque Augusta (now completed, and made into a formal public park).[15] Historically he thinks the Minhocão's occupation aligns with the appropriation of the Praça da Sé, the setting for São Paulo Cathedral and the site of much political protest during the early 1980s transition from military rule – Sé, and its occupation, is a key architectural figure for the anthropologists Teresa Caldeira and James Holston, a symbol of resistance to autocracy.[16] More generally, Millington writes, the Minhocão symbolizes a 'broader pushback against a city bent to the will of financial capital'.[17] This is a capacious and liberal understanding of occupation, one capable of transcending boundaries of class and economics and uniting, if only temporarily, the liberal academic and the *favelado*.

That idea has some traction in the contemporary art world. At the 2023 edition of the São Paulo Bienal, 9 de Julho staged its own limited, and entirely licensed, occupation. Outside the entrance to the great, hangar-like, Oscar Niemeyer-designed main pavilion, the Ocupação 9 de Julho erected wooden shacks selling empanadas, along with T-shirts and baseball caps to support its activities. Inside, the occupation took over half of the first floor, for a restaurant serving lunch. The choice of Ocupação 9 de Julio for these activities was consistent with the Bienal curators' desire to break with the organization's elite origins, emphasizing work made by and for the dispossessed.[18] But in making occupation a theme, the Bienal also inadvertently reproduced the inequalities of the Brazilian city in miniature, and made them into theatre, with monumental modern architecture at the core and the informal favela on the periphery. The Minhocão, as we will see, reproduces some of the same problems, and introduces different classes of occupation, a permitted one occupying the roadway above, and another below, excluded and scarcely tolerated.

The Minhocão in History

When the Minhocão was built, São Paulo was in the middle of unprecedented population growth, nearly doubling in size each decade.[19] Its metropolitan population was a little short of 8 million in 1970, up from just under 5 million in 1960. Big growth was accompanied by big plans, and it was at this point that the city properly reconfigured itself around the private car, a process it carried out with impressive thoroughness, allied with the growth of its automotive industries – Volkswagen, Ford, Mercedes-Benz and General Motors all built plants in and around the city.[20] São Paulo's reinvention in automotive terms was typical of Brazil as a whole. The country's new capital, Brasília, planned by the urbanist Lucio Costa, assumed universal car ownership and usage, at least for its middle classes. Drawing on his own somewhat privileged upbringing in Europe, Costa had a benign view of the car, seeing it anthropomorphically as an essentially good-natured member of the family, but one in need of discipline – a sort of mechanical dog.[21]

Brazil's automobilization accelerated following the April 1964 military coup that removed the democratically elected leftist João Goulart from office, replacing him with the army chief of staff Humberto Castelo Branco. Under the new regime, Brazil boomed industrially until the mid-1970s, while it created the infrastructure desired by its large and often regime-friendly middle class. For Edouardo Vasconcellos, a Brazilian planner and academic, São Paulo's middle-class areas and its automobile infrastructure were coterminous: the middle-class city was the automobile city. 'The middle class and the automobile', he wrote, 'is the longest lasting and happiest marriage of our times.'[22] São Paulo's road projects were part of a wider infrastructural megalomania, the manifestations of which included the bridge from Rio de Janeiro to Niterói and the Transamazon Highway.[23] In São Paulo, an entire network of new highways was created alongside the Minhocão: the Marginal Pinheiros and Marginal Tietê highways alongside their respective rivers, the Avenida 23 de Mayo in the centre of the city, along with the remodelling of the Avenida 9 de Julho – not to mention the Avenida Paulista, a road of such multi-level complexity, it was a de facto megastructure.[24] The Minhocão itself was only a fragment compared to the Marginal expressways, but it caught the imagination, being so central. It also had drama. For an artistically literate driver, it really was the Futurist city come to life.[25]

The origins of the Minhocão are actually hard to pin down. The first recorded discussions about anything like it were in 1947 in the department of urbanism at the municipality of São Paulo.[26] Nine years later, a development study under the mayor and urbanist Francisco Prestes Maia produced some more detail, the *Anteprojeto de um Sistema de Transporte Rápido*. In a visionary scheme for the whole of the city, the *Anteprojeto* proposed a new road, the Segunda Perimetral to link the east and west of the central city, and the section from the Praça Roosevelt along the Rua Amaral Gurgel coincided with the present-day Minhocão – although from what it is possible to tell from the accompanying axonometric drawings, the route would be below grade level.[27] The *Anteprojeto* of 1956 was clear about one thing, however: the new São Paulo would be built around circulation and new communications technologies. Under

SÃO PAULO: THE EXPRESSWAY OCCUPIED

pressure from the car and the telephone, traditional neighbourhoods would lose their reason to exist.[28]

As far as can be ascertained however, the actually existing Minhocão was a project of Paulo Maluf, the pro-development, engineering-trained, thirty-fifth mayor of São Paulo. There was little discussion in the local news media, and the laws passed to enable its construction scarcely give any detail.[29] The contract went to Hidroservice, Brazil's (then) largest private engineering firm, the recipient of numerous government contracts. As built, the Minhocão was transformative, of the Avenida São João in particular, a popular boulevard once celebrated by the French anthropologist Claude Lévi-Strauss en route to Brazil's interior.[30] It begins at the brutalist Praça Roosevelt, from where it emerges steeply from a tunnel, then, rising briskly to the first-floor level of the surrounding buildings, it levels out, holding the line of the Rua Amaral Gurgel for a few hundred meters, before reaching a much-photographed point where the asphalt is marked 'Curva Perigosa' (Dangerous Curve). From here it bends to the left, picking up the line of the Avenida São João for two kilometres before it descends to street level at the middle-class neighbourhood of Barra Funda, where it becomes the ordinary Avenida Francisco Matarazzo.

Built in steel-reinforced concrete, it was supported on eighty piers, most of them placed centrally to make best use of the land; some beams were up to forty metres in length. The roadway level has four lanes in total, two eastbound, two westbound, while at ground level, the efficient design meant that a further four lanes of traffic could be accommodated, two in each direction, along with cycle lanes and footpaths. As infrastructure, it is rich and complex, with multiple layers, visible history and an intense, if brutal, relationship with its surroundings. Of the 800 drawings produced for the project, there were precisely no section drawings, nothing, in other words, that would have warned of its effects.[31] Underneath, Luiz Florence has written, is an urban situation 'of shade, dampness, asphyxiation, and oppression ... a mixture of unattractive pavements, uncared-for entrances to blocks of flats, poorly-preserved historic buildings'.[32] It was a 'completely new kind of nature', Florence wrote – if so, it is the nature of the monster, the King Kong or Godzilla, the oversized creature occupying the existing city.

Occupying the Minhocão: *Superfícéis Habitáveis*

Given the brutal nature of the design, it is no surprise to find stirrings of opposition in its early history, along with attempts to appropriate it in some way, to make it suitable for human occupation. One particular early case stands out: an artistic intervention in the Minhocão's undercroft called *Superfíceis Habitáveis* (Habitable Surfaces) by the artist Flávio Motta, then a professor at FAU-USP, the University of São Paulo's Faculty of Architecture. It was designed in 1971, and after approval by COGEP, the city of São Paulo's General Planning Committee, it was realized in 1974 in conjunction with another artist, Marcelo Nitsche.[33] The two made an eighteen-minute film about it, which survives in a poor-quality print, although the work itself does not.[34]

Superfíceis Habitáveis is an exceedingly simple concept. Running east to west, from Consolação to Barra Funda, Motta planned a series of painted images on the central concrete piers holding up the roadway. Painted on the eastern flanks of the piers they would be visible from a bus or a bike as a sequence, as an unfolding animation, intentionally cinematic in effect.[35] There were forty in all from east to west. They are highly abstract to begin with, flat and flag-like, the colour palette limited to primary reds and blues, plus white. A triangle in white appears first, then a flag divided in two vertically, red and white, and then reversed; a red diamond and then a white one; a white panel subsumed in horizontal steps by red over four panels. Then there is some recognizable imagery: a big white circle against a blue background step by step filling the frame, a sunrise. Then a seagull, highly schematic, but undoubtedly a bird, fluttering closer and disappearing, to be replaced by the unmistakable skyline of the Pico de Jaraguá, the 1,100 metre peak that overlooks the city from the north. Then nothing: a dark blue panel, implicitly night.

Nitsche described the project's aims in an interview for the *Estado de São Paulo* newspaper. The city was 'hostile' he wrote, responsible for 'an oppressive situation' pitting residents against one another. Art just might help ameliorate things: 'COGEP believes that through art it might be possible to soften that situation.'[36] The Motta project wasn't therefore meant as decoration, but an intervention in the social life of the city. It was certainly a form of occupying space, albeit tentative and low-key. Motta himself elaborated further in another piece for the

Estado printed the same month. The starting point, he wrote, was the work of the French modernist painter Fernand Léger, and his ambitions for the social transformation of cities through colour. Why not, Motta wrote, quoting Léger, 'a red street, another one yellow, a blue square, a white avenue, and some polychrome monuments?'[37] In relation to São Paulo, the Minhocão project was almost utopian – 'we thought about painting spaces that didn't exist. We thought about converting a part of the city into an organized sequence, almost a cinematic one.' The point went beyond decoration, to make a more humane kind of city through improved social relations in the area – something, in other words, like occupation.[38]

The film of the project remains suggestive of their artists' intentions. Early on it's a cartoon animation: an anthropomorphic VW *Fusca* (Beetle) scuttles alongside a schematic modern skyline to the ironic accompaniment of Ravel's *Boléro*; the cartoon scene morphs adroitly into a filmed one, with the real traffic and real modernist slabs of central São Paulo, before a sequence on the Minhocão project presenting, flash-card style, the complete sequence of painted columns. An extended sequence of the artist at work follows, filmed in countryside on São Paulo's periphery. Here are mountains, sky, freedom, all the things missing from the gloomy Minhocão. Then it's back to the Minhocão again for a repeat of the painted column sequence, this time with the knowledge that the painted imagery inserts nature into the smoggy concrete. The film depicts the city light-heartedly, in fragments; the artists are tricksters, shapeshifters who find ways to inhabit the city as it actually is, rather than impose a totalitarian solution. In that sense, while this is no occupation in the strict sense of the word, its attitude – tactical, temporary, contingent – suggests one.

At the same time as Motta's project, the Minhocão was becoming the most dangerous stretch of road in the entire city, accounting for no less than 20 per cent of its road traffic incidents, the majority of them at night.[39] Newspapers routinely carried lurid Minhocão stories: cars dangling off the carriageway, police chases, shootings. It was also undoubtedly noisy, rasping exhausts and blaring horns being constant sources of grief. Sealing the external window frame with an old bicycle inner tube apparently provided some relief from the racket.[40] However, it gave the lie to the modernity of the Minhocão. If this was the future of the city, when you looked more closely, it was a bodged and improvised one. By the end of 1976 a group of well-organized if sleep-deprived residents petitioned the Municipality of São Paulo to have the road closed at night. There was some debate, and by December a decision had been reached to close the Minhocão at night, the regulation coming into effect in January 1977, applying in the first instance to the hours between midnight and 5 am.[41] The locals, it might be said, were learning the art of occupation.

Further closures occurred in 1989, when the municipality extended the traffic-free period from 9:30 pm to 6:30 am, and then again in 1996 when Sundays and public holidays were included for the first time. In 2015 it was closed from 3 pm on Saturdays, and in 2018 the period was extended first to include all day Saturday, and later that year a law was passed to deactivate the highway altogether and turn it into a park.[42] The gradual deactivation of the Minhicão attracted forms of cultural occupation, including (as Kelly Yamashita has written), 'festivals of music, exhibitions, fairs, shows, open-air film projections, picnics, parties, sports activities, performances of dance, theatre and music', and other unspecified 'cultural and leisure practices'.[43]

That impression is confirmed by the 2006 Prêmio Prestes Maia, a municipal competition to find solutions to the now evergreen Minhocão problem – multiple entries envisaged the roadway punctuated by 'cultural hubs', gardens and art galleries, the winner by José Alves and Juliana Corradini being no exception.[44] One of the more striking occupations in the history of the Minhocão took place at 7 pm on 30 May 2010, on the well-known section between the Alameda Glete and the Rua Helvétia. Here, heading west, the highway makes a gentle turn to the left where it leaves the path of the Rua Amaral Gurgel and picks up, finally, the course of the Avenida São João. There's a sliproad down to street level, and eastwards, a fine axial view to São Paulo's historic financial centre. There are several fine modernist apartment buildings at this point, bang up against the highway, including a distinctive Flatiron-like wedge that shows up as a location in numerous films.[45] On 30 May, a Sunday, the road was closed as usual, but occupied by a stage with a big screen where at 7 pm there was a showing of a documentary film by Maira Bühler, Paulo Pastorelo and João Sodré, *Elevado 3.5*, made in 2007 and then about to get a general release – the outdoor screening was the atmospheric pre-release event.[46] An audience of 1,000 turned up. It was hard, Luiz Florence wrote later, to find a spot for a decent view; many more hung out of their apartment windows, straining to glimpse the screen.[47]

The event was of itself cinematic, perhaps the model for later screen occupations of the Minhocão such as Fernando Meirelles's *Blindness* (2008), in which exactly this spot on the Minhocão is the setting for an urban apocalypse in which civilized life has come to an end – the city's population, blinded by a mysterious virus, is reduced to a state of nature; the Minhocão unmistakably appears, littered with abandoned and burned-out cars. The screening, you might say, was a positive reframing of that classic dystopian scenario. It was less the end of the world, more the celebration of a possible new one.

Elevado 3.5 could not have been a more appropriate choice for the screening. A documentary of the lives of twenty inhabitants of the area around the Minhocão, it turned infrastructure into culture, as precisely did the screening. The title referred to the length, in kilometres, of the elevated section of the road. The film's precise form – a series of face-to-camera interviews in situ, with the interviewer off-screen – drew on Eduardo Coutinho's *Edifício Master*, about the inhabitants of a Copacabana apartment building.[48] Following Coutinho's model, the interviews emphasized the eccentrics – a broke gambler at the 'end of the road', a clairvoyant, a taxi driver sincerely in love with the Minhocão, a voyeur artist, a flamboyant trans woman. Among the interviewees are an ordinary couple disturbed by the Minhocão's new status; they are kept awake at weekends by the lack of traffic. Cinematic fragments cut through the film – Paulo Maluf's 1969 television announcement on the initiation of the project; an impressionistic shot of the structure from the back of a car to the accompaniment of a booming techno soundtrack; footage of the moment when each day the traffic police close the roadway and it turns into a park; extracts from Motta's film of *Superfícies Habitáveis*.

The film is largely unspectacular, keeping the city mostly in the background. It could milk the Minhocão's brutalism, but for the most part, it does not. The 2010 screening, however, turned it into theatre, with the big screen, the crowd, the literal displacement of real life with its representation. It is at this point that occupation on the high level becomes a matter of aesthetics – or perhaps it made that fact suddenly visible. Florence wrote that the 2010 screening had a 'captive audience' for whom the Minhocão was already part of weekends' life, as the location of a *bloco* during Carnaval, or as a space of leisure – these people had already occupied the Minhocão in the name of pleasure.[49] The screening was occupation as spectacle, the view of the crowd as important as the view of the screen.

The Minhocão Park Association

It is early April 2022, two months into a research visit to São Paulo. I stay close to the Minhocão and see it every day, run on it at weekends, and occasionally walk it at night; I'm constantly crossing underneath it to get to historic Centro, or crossing over it near the Praça Roosevelt. I glimpse it one evening from the summit bar at the Edificio Italia, once the city's tallest tower and still a smart place to have a drink. As the sun goes down and the city's lights come on, the Minhocão becomes more,

Minhocão, São Paulo. *Photograph by Richard J. Williams.*

not less prominent; a kilometre or so distant at this point, it becomes a river of light, the car headlights tumbling and swirling in the distance. It's an impressive sight from up here, its serpentine form clearer at dusk, the density of traffic making it stand out from its surroundings. Temporarily at least, I can appreciate something of the original scheme, why it happened, something of the original appeal, whatever its subsequent reputation.

But that, I know well enough, is a fleeting and partial impression of the Minhocão and I need to know more about contemporary plans to transform it. In particular I want to know more about the work of the Associação Parque Minhocão (Minhocão Park Association), whose work since its creation as a legal entity in 2012 has been perhaps the most systematic and sustained attempt at its occupation, at least for cultural purposes. The next morning, Athos Comolatti, a local businessman and one of the Association's founders, picks me up in his BMW. 'Have I driven on the Minhocão?' he wonders. Only in fragments, I say, a few hundred metres here and there. Right, he says – we need to do something about that. A few minutes of careful negotiation of the city's labyrinth and we pick up the Minhocão at its eastern end as it passes underneath the concrete platform of the Praça Roosevelt, a stuffy, claustrophobic underpass lined with street dwellers. I count thirty or so, the most destitute kind you see on the streets of the city, unshod, scarcely clothed, nothing. This has to be the worst of the Minhocão pitches, with its fumes and noise. But a few seconds later we're back in the light again rising sharply above street level to the main carriageway along the Rua Amaral Gurgel. It's a weekday morning, and busy with commuters, but the traffic is disciplined and brisk, the expressway, despite its dysfunctional reputation, working exactly as it should. That said, it is tight by contemporary design standards, the on- and off-ramps narrow and abrupt, the turns tight, the lanes narrow with little room for error. It's a fairground-like ride, a sort of urban log flume.

We reach the end, and the elevated section descends to street level and the quiet *bairro* of Barra Funda. We turn around and pass under the Minhocão and drive eastwards along the surface streets for a kilometre or so, where there are more homeless occupying the spaces between the concrete piers, and busy bus and cycle lanes. This is the landscape in which Flávio Motta intervened years back, although there's no sign of his work anymore; it would take an archaeologist to recover it, if it is indeed still there under layers of graffiti and advertising. We make it to a side street, the Rua General Júlio Marcondes Salgado, and park outside a big evangelical church. Here is a distinctive green-tiled building of the 1950s, triangular in form, a southern hemisphere echo of New York's Flatiron Building. We head up to the first floor where Comolatti has a flat, bought in 2012. The one above, he remarks as we go in, was used extensively in the filming of Héctor Babenco's 1985 film *Kiss of the Spider Woman*.[50] He bought his, more or less on a whim, thinking that a newly created legal entity might need physical headquarters. It wasn't, he said, much of an investment, rather a statement of purpose about the Associação.

Narrow and corridor-like, most of it overlooks the Minhocão at road level, with a spectacular and slightly alarming moment at the eastern end of the flat where it terminates in a curved glazed balcony, seemingly inches away from the traffic. It would not take much, you feel, a moment's distraction perhaps, for a car to crash though the barriers and balcony, and take out the whole flat in one move. It hasn't thankfully happened. The flat's quieter than I expected. There are some artworks, including a big photograph by Felipe Morozini, an Association stalwart.

Comolatti created the Associação Parque Minhocão (APM) in 2012 along with a lawyer, Wilson Levy, and an architect, Felipe S.S. Rodrigues. While on vacation in New York, Comolatti had visited the High Line, the repurposed rail freight line that has been a popular elevated park since 2009. He wondered if something similar might be possible in São Paulo, a piece of infrastructure made into culture.[51] It might not have exactly been an activist project, but Comolatti was attracted by the activist spirit of the site and wanted the project aligned with it. Writing later on, Nate Millington described the 'sense of ownership over the site by activists, artists and residents ... the MPA (the Association) calls attention to this spirit of (re)appropriation and occupation.'[52] In the Association's own words, 'appropriation and resignification' were key ideas.[53]

The Minhocão was an obvious candidate for the idea, already since 1996 occupied for leisure purposes at weekends. He didn't think it had been much of an investment – he thought he had lost money. There wasn't an architectural plan, either at the beginning or subsequently, to ensure relative impartiality. The Association was, however, intrigued by a speculative 1986 scheme by a maverick environmental architect

Pitanga do Amparo in which the Minhocão was an elevated boulevard with shops and cafes at road level, luxuriant palms and shrubs mitigating the harsh environment, electric trolleybuses rolling up and down the central reservation.[54] It was an occupation of a decidedly middle-class, consumer-oriented kind.

The Association's first order of business was the São Paulo Bienal of Architecture, curated by Guilherme Wisnik, a professor of architecture at USP.[55] It was an opportunity for the Association to make some 'noise'. In the small flat, with the roadway of the Minhocão just a few feet away, the association presented photographs of the High Line, restored from a disused early twentieth-century rail line, and itself a form of occupation – in its unrestored condition, like the abandoned Chelsea piers. On the wall, Rodrigues had written a short, manifesto-like text, 'O que é a Associação Parque Minhocão' ('what is the Minhocão Park Association?'), which described the 'violence' of the Minhocão, of its 'tearing apart' the urban fabric, and the way the proposed park would 'completely change the panorama of the centre of the city'.[56] Alongside the exhibition, the High Line's founders Robert Hammond and Joshua David gave a talk, widely reported in the local media.[57] Meanwhile other parts of the Bienal touched on the Minhocão's present and future, including an anti-car film *Carrópolis*.[58] The flat also showed a handful of architectural capriccios of a remade Minhocão by Ciro Miguel, a specialist in fantastic photomontages mixing contemporary Paulista urbanism with historical monuments.[59] Thanks in large part to the Association's activities, 2013 was 'Peak Minhocão'.[60]

In the most striking, and widely distributed of the images made for the APM, Ciro Miguel depicts the Minhocão at the point at which it joins the Avenida São João on its way to Barra Funda: the Association's headquarters building fills the right-hand side of the image, but turned into a hotel. In the foreground, in what is seemingly a literal illustration of the May 1968 Situationist slogan 'sous les pavés, la plage', the roadway has been scraped back to reveal a beach, dotted with women in bikinis. Just to their right, a family of cyclists emerge from behind vegetation on a cycle path. The beach extends towards Barra Funda, parasols and sunbathers stretching into the distance. With its supernaturally intense colours and cloudless sky, it has a hyperreal quality consistent with Miguel's other landscape work. Treading a line between description and

Ciro Miguel, proposal for Parque Minhocão, São Paulo, 2013. *Image courtesy Ciro Miguel.*

absurdity, like early pop collages, it makes everyday life into a theatre of the absurd, but one in which we are all in on the joke. It was an Association commission, and Miguel acted under their instructions, adding and emphasizing elements where he was required.[61] Its playful surrealism is nevertheless consistent with his work of the time, and what the APM needed at this stage, a playful provocation without too much commitment.

Miguel's beach image, undoubtedly one of the more iconic images produced in this period, is an image of an occupation. The cars have been displaced, and the roadway populated – but it is a highly selective occupation, which if we were to take it literally says that only the young, the beautiful, are admitted.[62] That is unfair to the origins of the image, and its playful intentions; it isn't meant to represent a programme of any kind, merely one of a number of suggestions of what might be. Nevertheless, its understanding of 'occupation' is a notably hedonistic one. The Association's apartment building has become a beach hotel, identified by a sign on its roof. Its occupiers are on vacation, and occupation an agreeable game rather than an economic necessity, and life is fundamentally unserious. Occupation of the Minhocão increasingly meant turning it into a beach, literally so in early 2014 when it briefly hosted an Olympic-length swimming pool.[63] In 2017 the idea piqued the interest of Jaime Lerner's major architectural practice who produced speculative images of their version of the park in 2017, even more archly surreal than Ciro Miguel's.[64] Occupation in these images meant hedonism.

There was opposition to the Association. In fact as Felipe Rodrigues wrote in 2017, there had always been some kind of opposition to the Minhocão's occupation – it was always a threat to someone, always, since 1971, a problem to be discovered. In 1996, in his second term in office as mayor, Minhocão progenitor Paulo Maluf tried, without success, to reverse its closure to cars at night and at weekends.[65] Progress towards a park had been intermittent and never assured. Once the Association had been formed, a counter-movement appeared, the Movimento Desmonte do Minhocão (Movement for the Demolition of the Minhocão), aimed – despite the environmental cost of the disposal of 300,000 tonnes of steel and concrete – at demolishing the structure and reinstating the original street. Aligned with the political right, according to Rodrigues it wanted to reinstate a version of São Paulo dating from 1930, 'when the city had a population of one million'.[66] The Movimento was hostile to any kind of occupation of the Minhocão whether a cycleway, or a road race, or any kind of cultural event – in short, 'they did not want to see people on the street'.[67]

There were other forms of opposition. The Association's invocation of the High Line brought out numerous objections on the grounds of gentrification, the New York example being the focus of some of that city's most intense real estate speculation; the accidental and indeterminate landscape of the Minhocão might have sheltered a population that would otherwise have been unable to inhabit the central city.[68] According to some research, it was an unusually rich area culturally, and its complex and auto-generated cultural ecosystem might be threatened by the Association's support for a permanent park. Here different forms of occupation banged up uncomfortably against one another. On the one hand, the Association liked to be adjacent to activism and creativity; on the other, some of those activists perceived the Association as a threat, at best a benign organization, at worst a vehicle for real estate development.[69]

Rodrigues titled his summary of the Association's activities with some irony 'Razões do Parque Minhocão' (Roots of the Minhocão

Park) – irony because it referred to a classic 1936 essay by the urbanist Lucio Costa.[70] One of the great essays on architectural modernism, Costa's 'Razões da Nova Arquitetura' (Roots of the New Architecture) is a historical justification for the inevitability of the modern style. It is almost the exact opposite of Rodrigues's essay, the grand versus the low-key. Where Costa invoked historical inevitability, Rodrigues offered tactical decisions in the present; where Costa proposed architecture, Rodrigues suggested occupation.[71]

After the Bienal, the Association commissioned a poll that – they claimed – showed some shift in public attitudes to the Minhocão. Seven per cent wanted it demolished, 23 per cent wanted it as park, and 53 per cent for it to stay as it was, that is to say, intermittently occupied.[72] There were other outcomes. Their activism helped produce a 2014 municipal law enshrining the gradual deactivation of the expressway and the creation of a park in its place.[73] A further law in 2016 gave the name of the Parque Minhocão to the expressway during its periodic closures, and then in 2018 a law was passed – although later rescinded – for the creation of a permanent park of the same name.[74] The Association agitated for and got guardrails to enable the continuation of public events.[75] The Parque Minhocão itself closed during the Covid-19 pandemic between 2020 and 2022, re-emerging with new furniture, washrooms, and a visibly LGBTQI-friendly identity. What did Comolatti and the Association want further ahead? It could be a long, decades-long process to achieve anything like a permanent park, he thought. What mattered was the continuation of the process.[76]

The Other Occupation: Below the Minhocão

Brazil, writes Alex Hochuli, is economically 'Belindia', which is to say a rich, highly urbanized country (a metaphorical Belgium) supported by a poor, mainly rural one (a metaphorical India). Its middle class, particularly visible in São Paulo, lives well, in some ways better than its European equivalents – but its wealth depends on the existence of, and proximity to, a vastly poorer nation to do its manual work.[77] Brazil's cities tend to reproduce this disparity in miniature. A famous aerial photograph from the early 2000s by the São Paulo-based photographer Tuca Vieira depicts a luxury high-rise in upmarket Morumbí, its spectacular splayed balconies each sporting a swimming pool. But the left half of the image is occupied by Paraisópolis, an adjacent *favela* of self-built shacks, separated from the flats by a concrete wall. When reproduced outside of Brazil, it is typically used to illustrate an argument about urban inequality.[78] But it more accurately describes co-dependency: the favela is there because the flats are, and the residents of the flats need the *favelados'* cheap labour. It is, in other words, Belindia in miniature.

Arguably the same situation can be found at the Minhocão. If the weekend Parque Minhocão was in effect occupation by the rich, below the Parque Minhocão is occupation by the poor: the division, as it often is in Brazilian cities, is by altitude: the rich above in their secure high rises, the poor on the street below. As part of the rich occupation, you typically enter the Minhocão just to the west of the Praça Roosevelt, passing through the security fence with guards, entering a short section of on-ramp before joining the expressway proper. There, clearly visible through the fencing, is another world; campfires burn, tents rustle, children play. It would be picturesque if the destitution wasn't so self-evident, the majority of the hundred or so down here entirely without shelter apart from blankets provided by the municipality. In 2022 the situation at Praça Marechal Deodouro, about halfway along the Minhocão, was dire, with perhaps 200 or so sleeping rough, a few in tents or shelters improvised from plastic sheeting or cardboard, the majority without. This was also certainly an occupation, but of an altogether different kind, shelter of last resort.

The Minhocão is the Brazilian city in miniature, a condensed representation of the past half century of architecture and politics. In its relation to the question of homelessness, it is no different, condensing a national state of affairs. Rachel Rolnik outlines its contours in *O Planejamento da Desigualdade* (The Planning of Inequality) published in 2022: at the national scale, an economy shifting decisively from the production of goods to services, but failing to produce employment to replace the lost (and relatively secure) jobs done by hand; the growth of temporary and insecure labour; the growth of the informal sector; the explosion in informal housing, from 1 per cent of São Paulo's population in 1973 to more than 11 per cent in 2010, and more now; the uneven rise in violent crime; the depletion of population of the historic centre of the city, down 30 per cent or so from its peak.[79] At the same time,

Rolnik notes the growth of real estate markets in São Paulo, and the mushrooming of new kinds of development eroding the functions of the historic centre – shopping malls and gated communities, automobile-focused and perfectly secure; an inward-looking and defensive private realm against the uncertainties of the public one.[80]

Homelessness seemed to be getting worse. In December 2023 the *Folha de São Paulo* reported new statistics that showed a growth of 935 per cent in the number of homeless persons since 2013, a situation it attributed to successive economic shocks during the past decade, including that of the Covid-19 pandemic. Purchasing power in general had markedly declined, repossessions were up.[81] They were perfect conditions for the growth of the Minhocão's homeless. It was a striking enough phenomenon to interest the BBC, which reported a 31 per cent rise in São Paulo's official homeless population since the pandemic, indicative, it thought, of structural economic adjustment, rather than natural fluctuation.[82] Santa Cecilia, one of the two neighbourhoods through which the Minhocão passes, was reported by the public–private research organization Nosso São Paulo in 2023 to have the highest number of street dwellers of any of the city's neighbourhoods, officially 5,000.[83]

The reportage of the Minhocão's homeless situation could be picturesque (confirming Hochuli's thesis of a Brazilian middle class almost uniquely accepting of life's paradoxes).[84] In 2017, *BBC Brasil* told the story of a thirty-three-year-old veteran of the street, Wladimir del Vecchio, whose immaculate home could be found pitched up against one of the central piers of the Minhocão, near the Marechal Deodouro metro. Everything was scavenged from the street, or 'recycled', as he described: a bed, fully made up; a chest of drawers, a bookshelf ('with lots of books'), a carpet, utensils, plants, a clock, precisely reproducing the compact and stylish domestic interiors popularized by the Swedish home furnishings store IKEA. Del Vecchio had something of a talent for design. A faux-naïf mermaid painted on the concrete pier was an existing graffito, but he had artfully made it part of the overall scheme. In the BBC's video interview, del Vecchio stressed the orderly and hygienic nature of both his dwelling and his life, the model of the deserving poor. But his circumstances were also bad: years addicted to crack and alcohol, estranged from his family, and most recently evicted from his pitch by the municipal authorities on a regular clean-up campaign. He tried and failed to get a regular job, but seemed destined to remain under the Minhocão.[85]

The Catholic newspaper *O Jornal de São Paulo* provided a more complex account of the Minhocão's homelessness in 2022. Reporting on the increase in the homeless population in the area, it noted the endemic violence and noise making for a hostile environment, but also that its inhabitants chose the location for good reasons – the structure provided an important, if imperfect, shelter from the rain, as well as a consistent source of free food and casual jobs (*bicos*, typically selling cardboard): these things compensated for the municipality's occasional zealousness in cleaning the area, along with the ever-present noise and violence.[86]

But the upper and lower worlds remained chillingly separate: at weekends, security guards actively forbade street dwellers from entering the road deck, even for semi-legal business such as selling sweets (the rules of the Parque Minhocão forbid street trading, making this, for Brazil, an unusually sterile form of public space). Like any system of exclusion, the borders are intermittently challenged. In 2022, a so-called Cracolândia (Crack-land) emerged around the Rua Helvétia, and crack dealers fired shots at pedestrians on the upper level, angry at being observed. Not long after that, a demonstration took place on the upper level against the lack of security ('Santa Cecília asks for Help' read the banner).[87] It would be a mistake to assume that the demonstrators on the upper level represented the Parque Minhocão, and equally that the homeless represented Cracolândia. But the case represents the existence of different forms of occupation of the Minhocão representing different and mutually exclusive worlds.

One small gesture at bridging those worlds involved the artist Felipe Morozini, earlier interviewed for the documentary *Elevado 3.5*. In that film he's depicted making voyeuristic photographs of his neighbours, observed sunbathing or going about their everyday business. Morozini's later work consists in large-scale text murals depicting a simple phrase, installed in prominent public spaces. It is not unlike a southern hemisphere Barbara Kruger. Around the Minhocão, three works are well known: *Eu Era Outro Lugar* (I Was Another Place) installed at ground level at the Rua Helvétia, and two others close by, *Eu Sabia Que Você Existia* (I Knew You Existed), *Eu Me Vejo em Você* (I See Myself in You) and most recently *Você Me Faz Melhor* (You Make Me Better). In

2023, one of these, *Eu Sabia Que Você Existia*, was temporarily altered to address the homeless question, in conjunction with an art agency, SP Invisível. The original work has two adjacent parts: the left-hand panel has the text in black script on a while background, the right-hand panel the tones reversed, alluding to the city's acute racial divisions without being exactly specific. The temporary revision of the work, called *Eu Sabia Que Você Existia (Parte II)* shown on three nights beginning on 20 April, projected photographic portraits of street dwellers over the top of the text, naming them ('Charles', 'Tamara', 'Pricilia') along with the phrase 'em situação de rua' ('homeless').[88] Morozini wrote, 'the process of getting to know these characters and capturing their portraits seeks to remind everyone about who the people behind their scars are, using art to dialogue, embrace and transform this situation'.[89] It is hard to judge the success of Morozini's intervention. Perhaps it is enough that it is a reminder of the Minhocão's contradictions, a reminder that its pleasures are not available to everyone.

The apparently settled condition of the upper part of the Minhocão is not quite what it appears. Much has been done since the formation of the Associação Parque Minhocão in 2013 to consolidate its weekend use as a space of leisure, and as a niche tourist attraction – fencing along the side of the roadway, the accumulation of temporary beach furniture, the proliferation of murals on buildings alongside the highway made possible by the municipality's Museu de Arte de Rua programme.[90] It seems also to have the power of capital behind it now, with numerous real estate projects ongoing, focused on the development of well-serviced small studio and one-bedroom apartments, and pitched at the young and affluent.[91] The Parque Minhocão exists enough of the time to give developers the confidence to build. They have developed a new typology, too, addressing the aspirational condition of the new Minhocão rather than the past; many contemporary developments are now raised up above the level of the roadway on top of several storeys of car parking, ameliorating, if not entirely solving, the problem of the proximity of apartments to the passing traffic. A good example is the Condomínio Edifício Cosmopolitan Higienópolis (optimistically named – it is not actually in the upper-middle-class neighbourhood of Higienópolis, but down-at-heel Santa Cecília). Designed by local practice MCAA Arquitetos, and marketed from 2014, the complex comprises 311 small units in a tower set back from the expressway; the lower storeys of the complex form an environmental barrier, comprising sports facilities and parking. It breaks up the street line and creates a private enclave, but it is also a solution of a kind; other complexes have since followed.[92] Athos Comolatti thought the market pragmatic, operating as if the park already existed, which, in some respects it does.[93]

The transition to a more permanent park is not clear. The Parque Minhocão remains a functioning highway during the week, and a law passed in 2018 mandating its 'gradual deactivation' and transformation into a permanent park was rescinded the following year on the technicality that it had not been ratified by the legislature as a whole, only by the executive.[94] There have also been periodic attempts by the municipality to restrict the number of hours it is open to pedestrians.[95] It remains, in other words, a space in some dispute. It could be argued that its performative occupation of space has more of a politics than might initially appear; perhaps it is a way of imagining a different kind of city to the defensive, inner-directed one Rolnik has described so succinctly with its enclosed shopping malls and gated condominiums; a way of imagining a more public city.[96] Whatever the imperfections of the Minhocão project, it has shown more clearly, and with more imagination than any of the other projects in this book, how it is possible to come to an accommodation with the expressway world, even to embrace it in its contradictions. As a location for cultural occupations, it has only grown. In April 2024, a two-week festival, Cine Minhocão, showed sixty short films from twenty countries close to the Largo do Arouche cross-street.[97] But the performative occupation of the Minhocão every weekend, seductive as it is, reiterates rather than challenges the contradictions of the existing city. To put it another way, the well-ordered, and highly aestheticized occupation of the upper level is dependent on the suppression of the occupation below. Both, perversely, need each other – but, reiterating the exclusionary urbanism of the surrounding city – they must be kept separate. Both in a way are nevertheless true occupations, whatever their difference. Temporary, contingent, constantly negotiated and fought for, they ultimately now define the Minhocão. The Minhocão now, at least in terms of culture, is the sum of its various occupations.

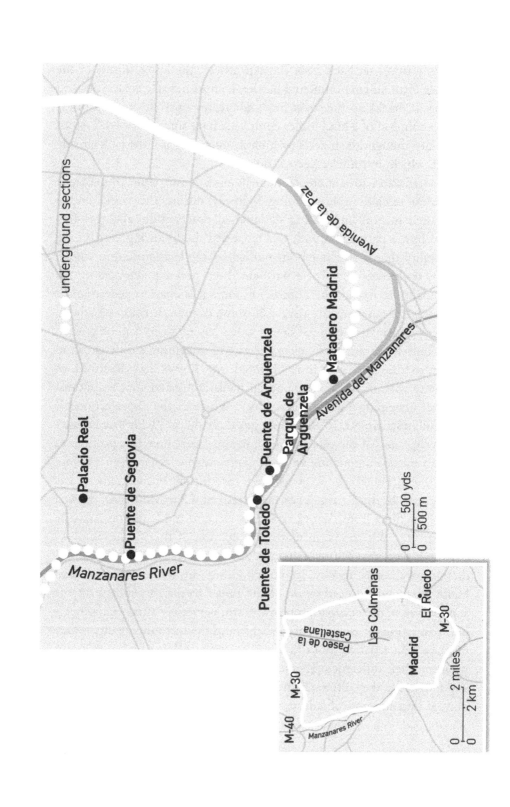

CHAPTER 6

Madrid: The Expressway as Public Space

Madrid Rio from the Puente de Toledo, Madrid. *Photograph by Richard J. Williams.*

It's an intensely bright February morning in Madrid and I am standing in the middle of an eighteenth-century baroque bridge, the Puente de Toledo crossing the shallow and fast-flowing Manzanares; to the east is a formal avenue lined with trees arches leading to the Puerta de Toledo, the old city gate and once the western boundary of the city. Designed by Pedro de Ribera, Philip V's architect, the Puente opened in 1732, although its origins lie much earlier. Its eight piers bulge splendidly, fat and assertive. In the centre there are two intricately carved statues facing each other, the patron saint of Spanish farmers, Isidore, on one side and his wife, Maria Torribia, on the other. At river level is some Versailles-like formal landscaping. Close-cropped, geometrical lawns carved by granite

MADRID: THE EXPRESSWAY AS PUBLIC SPACE

paths are planted with delicate shrubs and trees: lavender, wild rose, Japanese privet, box, two species of pine. Here in the early morning, there are a few lone figures about, silhouetted in the sunshine, but it's uncannily still, a space of discipline and quiet.

I remember it quite differently. The last time I was here was some time in the early 1990s when I had a sales job in the city; I'm behind the wheel of one of the company cars, a Renault 21, a big but underpowered saloon, and generally inadequate to the task of navigating the M-30 expressway. The Puente de Toledo is one of the pressure points of the old M-30, where the expressway squeezed down to two lanes each side of the Manzanares, threading itself improbably through the existing piers. It leaves the bridge superficially unchanged, but it absorbs it entirely into the expressway world, leaving it a strange fragment, a sign of a long-vanished world, cut off from pedestrian life by asphalt and traffic. It's the middle of the day and the traffic is thick but fast as we pass under the bridge, everything belting towards the Vincente Calderón Stadium, the home of Atlético de Madrid. I've driven it countless times already. If the piers of the bridge are close, I still can't quite believe quite how close the stadium is to the roadway; we practically touch it, as we do the dense blocks of flats, bang up against the road at this point. It's an experience of some intensity. It feels like a Futurist city, if a decidedly murky one (the car windscreen is also filthy). I will drive it most days over the next three years, and it began to seem more like a natural feature than anything else, a vast, defining piece of geography, like a river or mountain range, albeit man-made.

The M-30 still exists, but it's now buried underground, invisible, replaced by parkland, and here on the Puente de Toledo in the sunshine it's entirely undetectable. It is an extraordinary transformation, the expressway world tuned into quiet, polite public space. This chapter is about the transformation of the M-30 over time into a species of public space, and the politics of that transformation in a city that has undergone remarkable and under-reported economic and population growth.[1] It's a megaproject that in scale exceeds both Boston's Big Dig and Seoul's Cheonggyecheon (see chapter 7), and it was realized with unusual efficiency. Around public space there is a temptation to see it in progressive terms: public space as the opposite of private space, the corrective to the market, the space of accommodation of the other. It seems to represent the European liberal consensus on public spaces at the end of the twentieth century, most clearly represented in the work of the architect Richard Rogers, or the *Architectural Review*, or most of all, the reconstruction of Barcelona under Oriol Bohigas and Mayor Pasqual Maragall.[2]

It constituted a liberal ideology: of centres rather than peripheries, of unity rather than fragmentation, of rehabilitation rather than demolition, and of continuity with the past rather than its outright rejection. It sublimated public space to the point at which it was coterminous with the city. As Bohigas said, when he accepted the RIBA Gold Medal on behalf of the city in 1999 – the first time the prestigious award had been made to a city rather than an individual architect – the city *was* its public space and vice versa.[3] Although its political comfort zone was liberal or left, it tended to reassert traditional city forms and institutional order, with private and public interests held in in an agreeable balance.[4] For Anglophone observers, for whom the political circumstances were unusually ill-disposed towards the very idea of public space, Spain had enormous appeal. It seemed to build public spaces with speed and conviction, and fill them with life. Madrid, although less discussed than the Catalan metropolis, seemed to be able to do it as well as anywhere.

The M-30 reconstruction was a public space project comparable with innumerable other Spanish public space projects of the same time. If admired by progressive architectural critics, it is also not at all clear how much it was itself a progressive project.[5] Carried out by a right-of-centre administration in the face of substantial leftist opposition, its achievements, which are many and substantial, must be tempered by its obviously gentrifying effect; one needs to ask in whose name it was all done. It was also in many ways architecturally conservative, restoring and enhancing historic, sometimes Royal monuments. The section of the project around the Puente de Toledo, which is substantial, is a neo-Versailles in its landscaping. Undeniably impressive in both its conception and execution, it also reasserts an image of a polite, ordered, and socially conservative city, the exact opposite of the expressway landscape it replaced.

The View from the SEAT 600

To make sense of the M-30, however, we need to begin at the beginning. If there is an object that can be said to define the context of the M-30, it

MADRID: THE EXPRESSWAY AS PUBLIC SPACE

Las Colmenas housing and the M-30, Madrid. *Photograph by Richard J. Williams.*

might be said to be a car, the SEAT 600 to be precise. If you are looking at the M-30 as a driver for the first time, very likely you are looking at it from the cramped and noisy cabin of a 600, over a simple metal dashboard through its tiny windscreen. If you reach 100 kilometres per hour, you are lucky – and you will have taken a long time to get there. But you are in a car, perhaps your own car for the first time, and you have unprecedented freedom to explore Spain's vast interior. It's not just the car, but a rapidly improving network of major roads; it is an automotive system of increasing scale and sophistication. Produced from 1957 in a factory on the outskirts of Barcelona, the 600 was a licensed version of the Italian Fiat 600, in production in Italy two years earlier. It wasn't the only car popular in Spain at the time, for large numbers of Citroën 2CV and Renault 4 were also sold, but it was the first indigenous car to be produced in serious volume, and it became a cultural icon, the central figure in, for example, the 1958 comedy film *Ya Tenemos Coche* ('Now We Have a Car').[6] It is crude by contemporary standards, but immensely popular at the time, and socially transformative. It remained in production until the early 1970s.

The 600 was a product more generally of Spain's booming 1960s car economy. From 79,000 vehicles per year in 1963, Spain produced 274,000 in 1967, a figure that only steadily increased from that point on.[7] From the opening of the M-30 in 1974, through the transition from autocracy to democracy, through to membership of the European Economic Community (EEC) and then the European Union (EU), Spain's automotive economy went global – very like its equivalent in Brazil or Korea, which in some respects it resembled. Spain did not just build cars; it built roads, everywhere and it turned its six ancient radial highways into expressways. It built or expanded car factories in Barcelona (VW group including SEAT, Ford, Nissan), Valladolid (Renault), Vigo (Peugeot Citroën), Zaragoza (General Motors) and Villaverde on the outskirts of Madrid (Peugeot Citroën again), taking its car production to record levels, and making Spain the fourth largest European producer by 1990.[8]

Spain's new highways led to the production of suburbs, of bewildering architectural typologies. Sometimes the suburbs were high-rise enclaves, like the Ciudad de los Periodistas ('city of journalists'), at Madrid's northern edge; sometimes they were variations on Anglo-American row houses with fussy postmodern details; sometimes they were low-density enclaves of Californian bungalows. Spain built schools to service them, and shopping centres, and hypermarkets, and endless ribbon development, and industrial estates, often very large, and often the nucleus of more or less entirely new settlements. Development was both rapid and uneven. Where the cities ran out into the surrounding countryside, there could be arresting contrasts: a shepherd driving his flock though a cluster of skyscraper towers, or a superbly engineered boulevard, complete with streetlamps, coming abruptly to a halt in a pile of dirt. All Spain's cities had these things, but Madrid, unconstrained by natural features or existing settlements of any size, simply had more of them. It was creating an entirely new, and somewhat under-reported city, a sprawling polynucleic metropolis traversed by expressways, a Los Angeles of the central plain.

That transformation took place largely under General Franco's authoritarian political regime. Initially a military theocracy, the regime liberalized its economy in 1959, opening it to foreign investment, and at government level importing wholesale the apparently successful French model of organization, even down to the titles of institutions and arms of government.[9] It helped create a vast, cheap labour force, and a docile one too, given the regime's prohibition on organized labour. The resulting boom was prolonged and transformative: between 1960 and 1975 Spanish gross national product doubled, with annual growth in this period averaging 7 per cent, among comparable countries second only to Japan.[10] The demographic transformations that both accompanied the boom, and contributed to it, were no less striking. In one account, in the quarter century following 1950, 6 million Spaniards moved from the land to the cities, 20 per cent of the national population, and one of the biggest peacetime migrations in European history.[11] At the same time, more than two million Spaniards migrated to other parts of Europe, France and Germany in particular, and also quite commonly, Switzerland.

Spanish cities grew remarkably, at the same time their equivalents in northern Europe and North America were tending to shrink. As the sociologist (and much later, Spanish Minister for Universities) Manuel Castells described in 1983, between 1960 and 1970 alone, Madrid grew from 2.4 to 3.6 million inhabitants, a rate of 50 per cent, comparable with the growth of industrial cities in the nineteenth century.[12] The accommodation of that growth was chaotic: big shanty towns on the urban periphery, wild property speculation near the centre, the explosion of poorly serviced high-rise suburbs. Castells, a Marxist, was critical, especially of its expressways such as the M-30, for which, he wrote, 'large sectors of the city were destroyed'.[13] Castells thought this new Madrid fundamentally inhumane, the result of a dictatorial government in league with property speculators, whose motives were fundamentally profit. Shabbily constructed housing, the elevation of the profit motive, a decayed public realm crisscrossed by expressways: for Anglophone readers, Castells's 1970s Madrid oddly prefigures Mike Davis's Los Angeles of *City of Quartz*, the ur-city of disaster-capitalism.[14] Perhaps – but 1970s Madrid is also another of this book's Big Man cities, all populism, authoritarian capital and roads.

Castells had good reasons to be critical. Franco-period Madrid did, however, produce plans that both anticipated the city's colossal growth and attempted to put a shape to it. The M-30 appears as early as 1943 in the so-called Plan Bidagor, after the urbanist Pedro Bidagor Lasarte who wrote it: it is there, perfectly clear as an urban connector, running north–south in parallel with the ceremonial Paseo de la Castellana, distributing traffic to the great national arterial highways to the Pais Vasco (N I), Barcelona (N II), Valencia (N III) and Andalucia (N IV – the Roman numerals are intentional).[15] At a detailed level, the Plan Bidagor indicated that the city's main watercourses, particularly the Manzanares to the west, but also the ancient Abroñigal to the east, might be the basis of the new roads – they might literally be built over the top of the rivers (exactly as we will see in Seoul in chapter 7).[16]

The vestigial M-30 is there again in the 1963 metropolitan plan for the city, where for the first time it forms a loop around the historic city, and also for the first time it details two further metropolitan loop roads that would in time become the M-40 and M-50.[17] And in 1968 there was a Plan Especial de la Avenida de la Paz, a 'special plan' for the eastern part of the M-30, describing a series of works alongside the expressway, plans for housing and industrial development, the creation of a whole new section of city.[18] That year, the government, still at that point headed by General Franco, issued a decree concerning the 'ordering and urbanization' of the Avenida de la Paz, describing a series of extraordinary legal mechanisms that would allow the extension of the city to be built. The decree was clear about the ambition – the urbanization of arterial roads was a 'topic of maximum importance' in urban design in general; in terms of Madrid, it was the 'most important work for the expansion of the capital'.[19]

It was a project of national importance, for which the government had special powers. But if the state led, it was – like Baron Haussman's nineteenth-century remodelling of Paris – done with the full co-operation of private developers, who wasted no time in selling the Avenida de la Paz as a desirable place to live. From 1969 onwards, the pro-government daily *ABC* carried numerous advertisements pitching apartments with all the modern conveniences – swimming pools, landscaped grounds, balconies and views of the coming M-30.[20] In the developer imagination the expressway was a positive asset, a symbol of modernity to be shown off to visitors from the terrace. You could park your SEAT underground, and reach all parts of the national road network in minutes. Andalucia or Valencia would be, at least in theory, in easy reach, as well as more distant destinations from Barajas Airport, potentially now only minutes away.

The censored press reported it approvingly, although images of the destruction wrought by the works often sat uneasily with the reportage. An image from 1968 published in *ABC* shows a park on the edge of the about-to-be-reformed Avenida de la Paz, the huge slabs of Las Colmenas rising vertiginously from the steep banks leading to the avenue. A vast moonscape dotted with agoraphobes, it makes for a compelling photographic image – but it's also the opposite of the restorative oasis described in the text.[21]

The new road ran within a few feet of recently constructed apartments, and opposition was vocal.[22] There was considerable opposition to the project during its construction, along the Manzanares section in particular, But the M-30 was opened in its entirety as planned on 12 November 1974. The front cover of the *ABC* showed Franco's Prime Minister, Carlos Arias Navarro, and dignitaries including the mayor of Madrid cutting a ribbon in the colours of the Spanish flag.[23] Thirty-six-and-a-half kilometres of expressway came into use that day, comprising the Autopista de la Paz to the east running parallel to the city's central spine, the Paseo de la Castellana, and to the west and north, the Autopista del Manzanares, after the river whose trajectory it loosely followed. It was huge. Navarro called it 'the great urbanistic work of our generation'.[24] His motorcade then did the whole trip, from the then northern tip at the Puente del Rey to the junction with the Calle Maria de Molina on the north-eastern side of the city, having inspected all the intersections along the way. Ordinary motorists were allowed on after three in the afternoon, and *ABC* reminded its readers of the unfamiliar rules in case they wanted to follow suit: the prohibition of slow traffic and of parking anywhere on the highway. A clear success, it signalled the 'urgent' (of course!) need to complete the third belt around the city, linking the east and west parts of the M-30 via the north – and perhaps even the need for a fourth belt around the city, like Saturn's rings at a still greater distance from the core.[25]

Against the M-30

The *ABC* rarely criticized the government directly, but it had a necessary safety valve for local complaints, the column 'Madrid al Dia' ('Up to date Madrid'). Only a few weeks after the inauguration of the M-30, it posted a summary of complaints from residents in the south of the city. The M-30 hadn't been good for them. In place of the 'beauty' they might once have found opening their blinds of a morning, there were now only 'closed views', a reference to the intrusive safety barriers that had been installed at ground level to prevent cars escaping at high speed from the expressway.[26] But there was worse, it reported: the loss of light and space, the poor finishes of the project, the accumulation of rubbish, the gathering of street gangs, the commonplace theft of cars. Match days at the Estadio Vicente Calderón, home of Atlético de Madrid, were a pedestrian nightmare. It was all an archetypical modern hell. The new road cut old connections across the Manzanares, in practice isolating inner and outer cities from each other. According to the architects responsible for the later rehabilitation of the area, it became 'practically impossible for pedestrians to cross from one side of the river to the other'. It was the material form of an 'extraordinary urban conflict'.[27] It is surprising to read this now given the controlled nature of the press and the fawning coverage of any official event – but it makes clear perhaps the uneasy nature of the coalition holding Spain together, a mix of economic liberalism and social repression, simultaneously looking outward to foreign capital and economic growth and inward to social control. Given the scale of the changes to the city and its accompanying social life, conflict of some kind was inevitable.

In 1976, with the old regime in terminal decline (Franco died at the end of 1975) COAM, the Colégio Oficial de Arquitectos de Madrid, staged an extraordinarily critical exhibition on the eastern part of the M-30, the Avenida de la Paz.[28] It depicted the project as the end product of a 'system of violence' dedicated to capital accumulation.[29] Rather than depict the project as a finished object, it rendered it instead as a landscape of gigantic flows: 'materials, people, demolitions, movements, trades, machines, property titles, money, credit, files, allegations, visits, inaugurations, bankruptcies, auctions, expropriations, beneficiaries, demonstrations, protests, evictions, works'. These flows, it went on, constituted 'an opaque and blind machine', determining 'in their tiniest details' all human relations.[30] The violence was real enough too: the dislocation of perhaps 20,000 people and the demolition of hundreds of properties, and the use of force to overcome resistance, especially in the notorious example of the barrio San Pascual in 1969.[31] The exhibition commissioned a bitterly acerbic comic strip on the project, depicting a brutal, semi-militarized chaos of building sites and squatter huts. The legend read: 'once more progress has acted, transforming what was a desolate and inhospitable landscape into an incredible world of fabulous abundance'.[32]

Infrastructure Becomes Culture Again

The M-30 became, as all roads inevitably do, culture. It was a space in which drivers could and inevitably did get lost, as in a cute story published in *Arquitectura* in 1982 by one of the journal's editors, Gabriel Ruiz Cabrero. 'Las Dos Holandesas' ('The Two Dutch Girls') tells the story of the tourists of the title, looking without success for the exit to the Carretera de Andalucía on their journey south to the sun; thrown by the complexities of the M-30, they find themselves repeatedly passing the Ventas bullring, a major landmark; after a while they begin to accept their fate, celebrating the appearance of the bullring with a joint and a beer each time it makes an appearance. Eventually they give up, by which time the M-30 itself has become the object of their vacation rather than the southern beaches. They park up by the side of the M-30, finally on holiday. It's a joke of course, one that plays up on Madrileños' own rich local knowledge: to go 'adventuring' on the M-30, they know that getting lost is easy, and accidents common, the result of its fragmentary design. It was a 'zigzagging route that disappears down multiple holes', along with 'violent turns, total lack of protection for pedestrians and drivers … a provisional quality that goes back years'.[33] But it is also a place whose 'improvisations' and 'urbanistic abuses' have by accident produced real urban spectacle (illustrated by a photograph of the setting of Las Colmenas, the exact place Almodóvar explored two years later).[34] And more seriously, the M-30 in 1982, writes Cabrero, is one of the few places where one might have an image of a 'bright, modern and fast' city, a 'powerful urban aesthetic' in its own right. But perhaps most important, it's the very imperfections of the M-30 that have value, permitting – even making inevitable – the urban detour that by accident more than design reveals parts of the city that would otherwise remain invisible.

That secret M-30 is nicely visible in the closing sequence to Pedro Almodóvar's 1984 film, *Qué He Hecho Yo Para Merecer Esto?* (What Have I Done to Deserve This?). For a minute – it seems much longer – the film fixes on a view of Madrid's immense Las Colmenas ('beehives') housing complex that has been the claustrophobic location of the previous 90 minutes; a slab block with myriad balconies fills the entire frame, foreshortened, making its bulk if anything more unfathomable. The camera zooms out progressively, first to include the adjacent block, then to most of the complex, and then finally to its location by the side of the M-30 expressway, at this point twelve lanes wide. The camera lingers there for a few seconds, lingering as if hypnotized by the scene, the traffic moving fast and without interruption, exactly as designed. It's not the first time we've seen this view – it appears briefly before, at the fifty-five-minute mark as a transition between scenes, a break from the cramped interiors that characterize most of the film.

We've had plenty of other references to it, however. The film's second scene, in which we meet Antonio (Ángel de Andrés López), the abusive husband of Gloria (Carmen Maura), takes place on the M-30 as he drives his cab, regaling his back-seat passenger with his experiences as a forger in Germany some fifteen years previously. Antonio's life outside the confines of the flat is, more or less, the M-30, even for leisure; late in the film in a crucial sequence, he makes to leave the flat to meet a former lover from Germany. 'I'll drive her on the M-30. She'll like that', he declares. We've had several shots of the scrappy verges of the M-30, and the concrete plaza overlooking the roadway where Maura's teenage boys play football, and sell drugs. The motorway conditions the soundscape inside the family's tiny flat, a constant, background roar. But that closing shot is something else – it's what Almodóvar leaves us with as the final impression after an eventful ninety minutes of prostitution, paedophilia, drug abuse and matricide. It's not a pretty sight: the blocks themselves, ten of them put up by the firm Banús in the 1950s, are strewn with laundry, and fitted with balcony screens of every imaginable design, while at ground level parked cars clog every gap. It's a picture of a peculiarly modern kind of disorder, a long way from any architect's perspective drawing. The landscaping is perfunctory; where the buildings hit the ground, it's dusty and bleak, the ground level occupied by some down-at-heel-looking stores.

Conventionally speaking there is nothing to like about the M-30 at this point. And yet the scene, with its jaunty accordion music rising in the background, suggests, despite everything, some kind of accommodation with the expressway world. Gloria, the principal character, has literally got away with murder, which happens to be the right result in this peculiar moral universe; the prodigal son has returned; the mother-in-law has gone back to the village for which she was yearning; the police have been made to look like the idiots that they are. The M-30 and its environs represent a perverse cosmic order, now, after a period of uncertainty, restored. Infrastructure, yet again, is shown to be transformed into culture.

Calle 30 to Madrid Rio

At this point in Madrid's history, there are discursive parallels with Los Angeles, a city, to put it another way, that remade itself through its expressways, and increasingly defined itself in those terms – Almodóvar got there early. The city's polycentric, expressway-led tendencies became more exaggerated through the 1990s. In 1998, an architect, José María Ezquiaga, described the new landscape in detail, with a mixture of horror and fascination. The old city with its clearly demarcated core and periphery was 'disappearing for good ... new ways of organizing the territory are emerging, thanks to high-capacity transport connections, new computer and telecommunications technology and the growing mobility and flexibility of economic activity'.[35] A 'vast low-density periphery' defined the new city, its expressways 'colonizers of new territory'. Architecture had started to become secondary: a city of 'voids between fragments of unconnected residential schemes; gaps between urbanized zones, abandoned farmland'.[36] Traditional public spaces fell

Dominique Perrault, Puente de Arganzuela, Madrid Rio (2011). *Photograph by Richard J. Williams.*

increasingly into decay, while its new periphery had no replacement. In this excitable account at least, Madrid was almost the exact opposite of Barcelona, with its much-vaunted revival of traditional public spaces.[37] (In reality, Barcelona sprawled as much as anywhere. No matter – it was a good story.)[38]

If Madrid had Angeleno tendencies, they included – rather like Frank Gehry's early work – rhetorically defensive architecture exploiting the hostility of the environment for aesthetic effect.[39] Unlikely complexes sprouted along the M-30 leaning into the hostile environment, quoting the ubiquitous nearby industrial sheds. Presenting a blank face to the highway, the overall effect of these often highly regarded buildings was to reinforce – even exaggerate – the hostile qualities of the environment rather than ameliorate them. A project by Iñaki Abalos and Juan Herreros from 1993 is a metallic shed rendered in grey, a building that looked exactly like a secure storage facility; it was in fact, social housing. 'In contrast to other architecture that has chosen to hide itself from the M-30', wrote the architects, 'this work emphasizes the public nature of the motorway.'[40] It was an acknowledgement of, and an accommodation with, the brutal surroundings. Francisco Javier Sáenz de Oíza had earlier taken a similar approach in his gigantic, snail-like housing complex of 1986, popularly known as El Ruedo (the ring, or arena). An M-30 landmark, its forbidding terracotta exterior is a defensive wall, the interior a protected enclave. It looks positively carceral, except the design programme derives from the need to keep the M-30 out, rather than the inmates in.[41] The expressway world became a somewhat perverse source of inspiration and excitement.

But the latter history of the M-30 is something else entirely, a reaction to this incipient Californication of the city, to sprawl and dispersal. Over an eight-year period, 2003–11, the city reconfigured a ten-kilometre stretch of the expressway by burying it underground, and then building a park over the top, a thorough reinvention of the traditional city. Among the projects discussed in this book, this one ranks with Cheonggyecheon as the largest and most technically elaborate. It is also on various levels ideological, about the reassertion of the traditional, pedestrian-oriented public space against the private car, about the recovery of connections between the city and the natural landscape, and between the inner and outer cities. The impulses were at some level conservationist and the rhetoric restorative. It drew on and elaborated the contemporary liberal consensus on public space. Peter Rowe, public space advocate and Cheonggyecheon expert, was involved.[42] Madrid's concept of public space was both liberal and globalist.

Its origins, however, were in a monstrous highway improvement scheme, of the same order as the original M-30. It had, undoubtedly, its Robert Moses figure, Alberto Ruiz-Gallardón, born in 1958. Trained in law, he had a brief career as a prosecutor in Málaga before entering politics for the right-wing Alianza Popular, historically the successor to Franco's Falange party, subsequently rebranded as the centre-right Partido Popular (PP). Gallardón was elected as a senator for the Alianza Popular to the Spanish parliament in 1987, but his first significant leadership role was outside of parliament, as president of the autonomous region of the Communidad de Madrid, a position to which he was elected in 1995 aged thirty-eight, and that he held until 2003, at which point he became Mayor of Madrid for two four-year terms, leaving office in 2011. He subsequently became Minister of Justice in the PP government of Mariano Rajoy, resigning and leaving politics in 2014.[43] He was, according to the architect of Madrid Rio, Ginés Garrido, a 'proud' individual, 'very sure of himself', 'capable of taking risks', 'somewhat arrogant'.[44]

As president of the Communidad de Madrid, he took a particular interest in infrastructure projects, assembling a group of engineers specialized in tunnelling, and he led on the development and implementation of improvements to the Cercanías suburban train network. Key projects included work to extend the network to Móstoles in the south-west of the city, and Alcalá de Henares, thirty kilometres to the north-east. During this period, he also led on a significant expansion of Madrid's already extensive metro.[45] For Garrido, Ruiz-Gallardón's expertise gained at the Communidad de Madrid was critical to his success later on: he had a disciplined team of sympathetic engineers, and they had experience of large-scale project management.[46]

When Ruiz-Gallardón was elected Mayor of Madrid in 2003, he brought the engineers with him. He asked what they thought was the most serious problem of circulation in Madrid and they replied without hesitation, the M-30.[47] Built piecemeal, it was compromised by existing streets and historic structures such as the Toledo and Segovia bridges, and its intersections were notoriously tight. Partly a national highway, partly a symbolic boulevard, partly an urban connector, it also had an identity problem.

For the engineers with their railway experience, the solution was obvious – tunnels. Reminiscent of the process of building the new capital of Brasília in the late 1950s, or Cheonggyechon's restoration in the early 2000s, the work had to be completed within four-year electoral cycles – the first phase, in other words, between 2003 and 2007.[48] The project got a name, Calle 30 ('30 Street'), officially denoting the legal transfer of responsibility for the highway from the Ministry of Transport to the city of Madrid, perhaps a deliberate misnomer. It humanized a project that actually meant the expansion of the expressway, albeit underground.[49] (There was no betting here, as there was in Seoul, on the so-called Braess effect, the seemingly paradoxical reduction of road capacity leading to a reduction in traffic demand.[50])

Ruiz-Gallardón nevertheless clearly understood the rhetorical value of public space, even if Calle 30 in the first instance had none of it, just tunnels. On announcing the project, he spoke airily of a 'city of uses' based around public space rather than the dominance of private car.[51] He acknowledged comparisons some had made between his proposals and the creation of other great urban public spaces, such as London's Covent Garden, and Paris's Centre Pompidou. 'I reject both of them', he said boldly, 'for lack of ambition.'[52] Speaking a few days before the election on 25 May, Ruiz-Gallardón underlined the ultimate ambition of the project. It would give birth, he said, 'to the greatest urban park of the twenty-first century' (he left the audience to decide whether he referred to Madrid, or the world).[53]

Calle 30 had opposition, lots of it. As the architects of the subsequent Madrid Rio project put it in a brutal summary, it was 'one of the most criticized public works in the history of Madrid'. Its costs were never made clear, and its management ('with almost no public participation') they thought questionable. For the cost of the project, such as it was known, it might have been possible to refurbish '50,000 dwellings in the city centre' or build '1000 kilometres of interurban highway'. Nor did it, of itself, solve any great traffic problem, merely, in their view, shifting it underground.[54] The mainstream left agreed. The Socialist (PSOE) and the United Left (IU) parties regarded it as a project designed to increase the amount of traffic in the centre of the city, as well as one that benefitted an already privileged, which was to say, car-driving population.[55] A 'pharonic' project according to the PSOE candidate Trinidad Jiménez, it would bring the M-30 to a state of 'collapse' during its construction and, when built, bring more traffic into the city, against prevailing European urban trends. On top of that, Jiménez argued, it would bankrupt the city – Madrid would be paying off the construction debt for twenty years.[56] The centre-left *El País* newspaper consistently opposed the project for those reasons. Other newspapers were friendlier, although still sceptical.[57]

Perhaps there was a residual fear in these criticisms of Franco-era *desarollismo* – whatever Ruiz-Gallardón said about public space, it was a megaproject on the same scale as the Avenida de la Paz, with some of the same characteristics. Critics on the left might also have been aware of some other possibly troubling human connections with the past too – Ruiz-Gallardón's wife, Maria del Mar Utrera, was the daughter of Franco's sometime Secretary of Labour.

Ruiz-Gallardón countered the criticisms with *desarollista* rhetoric. To do as the PSOE had proposed and turn the M-30 into an ordinary urban boulevard, deliberately restricting traffic, would be a competitive disaster. It would result in a 'historic collapse' to which 'no European city would consent'. More than that, he said, ramping the rhetoric: a single traffic light on the M-30 would 'cost jobs ... and a city in collapse can't address the future'. It was, in other words, *desarollismo* revisited – a vast programme of works done in the name of the public, but also quite clearly at this point representing the interests of capital; in sum, the people needed their public space, and the 'scar' ('cicatriz') of the old M-30 needed removal, but at all costs capital needed to continue to flow.[58] The mysterious Braess effect had no purchase here, unlike in Seoul.[59]

The first phase of Calle 30 was as vast as its critics feared. As reported by *El Pais*, it involved 700,000 cubic metres of concrete, 75,000 tons of steel and 186,000 square metres of roofing slabs.[60] Between 2003 and 2007 the team designed and built all the tunnels on the Manzanares side of the project, six kilometres of the ten-kilometre route, and did some improvements to the eastern side of the M-30 as well.[61] It was also a remarkable exercise in project management, if compared with Boston's equivalent exercise, which took more than twenty years instead of four and cost three times as much (the comparisons are less favourable with Cheonggyecheon, although that project saved billions by simply getting rid of the traffic).[62]

What Calle 30, did not do, however, was the imaginative labour for what might come next. The engineers had no time to think of anything else, under pressure to deliver the project by the date of the next mayoral elections, 2007. They had no interest in anything that might add complexity or expense, or otherwise threaten the delivery of the project (and Ruiz-Gallardón's re-election).[63] Windy political rhetoric aside, there was no plan, in the first instance, for anything else.

What to do with the land freed by Calle 30 was the subject of a two-phase design competition held by the Ayuntamiento de Madrid (city hall) in 2005.[64] The first phase invited local firms to compete; the second, in November, invited international firms to compete to work with the winning locals, a selection that included Peter Eisenman from the US, Foster + Partners from the UK, the Netherlands' Office for

Metropolitan Architecture and also West 8, and Dominique Perrault from France.[65] The jury, which included the Harvard academic, public space advocate, and Cheonggyecheon expert Peter Rowe, selected the small Madrid practice Burgos & Garrido, and the Rotterdam-based West 8 to work with them, the consortium naming itself MRio.[66]

Burgos & Garrido had already been working on what was in effect a test piece for the larger project, the design of the park over the top of the tunnelled section of the Avenida de Portugal, at the edge of the Casa de Campo, later subsumed into the Madrid Rio project.[67] Their approach was the most 'realistic', according to Christian Dobrick of West 8, a pragmatic reworking of the existing landscape rather than an attempt to remake it altogether. They understood the site and its complexities. It was not a 'blank site ... but one full of pre-existing conditions'.[68] The terrain the architects had to work with was extremely difficult. In reality it wasn't a 'void', Garrido said, 'but a gigantic building site ... with all kinds of services and cables beneath the surface ... you couldn't understand anything'. The first job was therefore to 'gather all the information from the engineering teams so we had a complete map of what was there, and work out what was going to be the future of this space because nobody had thought about it'.[69] The topography was complex. The engineers were unhappy with the plans to construct a park over the top of the tunnels, arguing that nothing of the kind had been done before on the same scale (Boston is a fraction of the size).[70] Ruiz-Gallardón nevertheless had confidence. It was, in retrospect, a means of turning contested highway engineering into a civic legacy, an astute piece of political management.

If Calle 30 was engineering, Madrid Rio was public space. As a public space project, it was straightforwardly liberal and ameliorative, aimed at healing urban wounds, infrastructural and implicitly political.[71] The overarching principles were restorative and therapeutic: to connect the city with the surrounding natural landscape, to connect the inner and outer *barrios* of the city, cut off from each other by the construction of the M-30, and to integrate the Casa de Campo and the Royal city better with the dense central areas.[72] It was the familiar language of liberal urbanism.

As built, Madrid Rio has three distinct forms of public space. At Arganzuela, the *barrio* to the south, the design is informal, even picturesque, with an approximation of the wild landscape surrounding the city. Here the Manzanares is at its most unruly, and where banks of vegetation mid-stream are most prominent. The middle part of the project, from Arganzuela to the Puente de Toledo, is the so-called Salon de Pinos ('Pines Salon'), a linear park dominated by densely planted local pine trees, a domesticated representation of both the alpine landscape to the north of the city, and the cultivated semi-wilderness of the Casa de Campo to the west. There was a connection with the high mountains of the Sierra de Guadarrama, especially La Pedriza, a zone of weird granite outcrops, to which Burgos & Garrido's competition entry made special reference.[73] The most northerly part of the project, from the Puente de Toledo, is the most formal, a severe and restrained setting for the Palacio Real. It reasserted the traditional city and, by implication, behaviour – in place of the old *terrain vague* of the expressway and the football stadium, where anything could, and might, happen, here was a quiet, disciplined, affluent-looking place, the very picture of urban order. It embodies a strange contradiction. The Franco regime, obsessed to a fault with social order, created the chaos of the M-30; the restoration of order took place – Ruiz-Gallardón's own politics notwithstanding – in a vastly more liberal polity.

The Madrid Rio project took from 2007 to 2013 to complete, with the bulk of the work done by 2011 (a late stage, the rehabilitation of the former Estadio Vicente Calderón was still to be completed at the time of writing). The project cost perhaps €400 million in total, although for reasons of political expediency it was divided into seventy-nine small contracts, from a little over €300,000 to nearly €40 million.[74] An entirely publicly funded project, 65 per cent of the overall cost was met by the city, and 25 per cent from assorted departments of the Spanish government. The remaining 10 per cent came from the European Union.[75]

The Parque Arganzuela, by far the biggest park of Madrid Rio, opened officially in April 2011.[76] The critical reception seems in retrospect almost entirely positive, a function in part of the speed at which it had all been done and the scale; for *The New York Times*'s architecture critic Michael Kimmelman, Madrid's success in building infrastructure only highlighted New York's failure to do the same.[77] It won over some sceptics. Writing after the completion of the whole project, the Spanish architect Eduardo Mangado said that at the time he thought Calle 30 'mistaken and illiterate', a 'topographic and cultural sin', whose name,

Calle 30, was a deliberate obfuscation, a means of smuggling a highway expansion into the centre of the city.[78] But he was converted by Madrid Rio, which had been rapidly adopted on opening by 'citizens, neighbours, and others not so close'; he praised the quality of the professional work, by the 'architects, landscape designers, gardeners, engineers, builders, Portuguese tilers, children's playground craftsmen'. All had produced an 'intelligent reading of the site, and of the Madrid geography in general'. The pragmatism cultivated by the designers was clear: a welcome contrast with the parks in which 'corten steel, lifting bridges, lighting and concrete invade everything, overwhelming ... the essential condition of the park'. Here, in contrast, the primary material was 'the tree'.[79] Madrid Rio won academic plaudits too, receiving the Veronica Rudge Green Prize from the Harvard Design School in 2015; previous winners included the Cheonggyecheon Restoration in 2010.[80]

Walking Madrid Rio

To drive the length of Madrid Rio underground is to experience a ten minute engineering spectacle, one of contemporary Europe's greatest. Its tunnels are generous and beautifully surfaced, the traffic immaculately managed, the interchanges sublime. It is in every way an expansion of the original expressway, structurally and conceptually, exactly as its critics feared. To walk it above ground could not be more different, taking the pedestrian through a full repertoire of contemporary European public spaces, all to an extent familiar, but composed in an elegant sequence. Brilliantly realized, even exemplary, it has rendered formerly uncertain parts of the city now safely consumable. Areas formerly characterized by sex work have become safe for families; slaughterhouses have become art galleries. The wealth of the central city appears to flow across the Manzanares where it once stopped. House prices, they say, have gone up.[81] Here, as everywhere, the project of public space is also a project of gentrification.

From the south, the way begins at the junction of the M-30 and N-IV Carretera de Andalucía, not technically Madrid Rio because the M-30 lies above ground here, unreformed – but it is a reminder of the expressway world as it was. A scrubby, fragmented area crossed by elevated highways, the N-IV stretching into the distance to the south and Andalucía, the M-30 to the north-east. It's a huge, largely flat landscape against which the infrastructure looks strangely fragile. To the north-west, the topography of central Madrid is clear, especially the ridge of Gran Via holding its 1930s skyscrapers in play with the Palácio Real. In the other direction AVE high-speed trains hurtle backwards and forwards to Seville. At ground level, the Manzanares is apparently at its most natural here, thick with vegetation, the occasional heron stalking fish. It is here that the road infrastructure is most visible, but here the landscape is also, paradoxically, at its wildest.

The path leads west from here, hugging the Manzanares with eight lanes of the grade level M-30 to the left, and a loose grid of slab blocks built in the 1980s aligned lengthways with the road, precisely the fragmentary, car-oriented development that characterized the area for decades. There's a crumbling Doric column at one point, a strange survival from the 1926 reconfiguration of the Manzanares. The columns, originally built every 300 metres along the banks in the city, were actually disguised ventilation shafts, built to carry noxious gases safely away from the filthy river.[82] All eight lanes of the M-30 abruptly drop into a tunnel and the landscape takes on a slower, more bucolic character. The old Matadero (slaughterhouse) complex comes into view on the right, low-rise, brick and terracotta marked with signs labelling the animals to be processed in each quarter ('cerdos', 'vacas', etc). Polished and immaculate now, it has become an arts complex, several of the pavilions designed by Burgos & Garrido.[83]

The right bank broadens to a generous Parque de la Arganzuela, oriented around leisure and exercise, a place for activity. There are a couple of bridges shaped like upturned canoes, cast in concrete, the clearly visible marks of the formwork suggestive of the materials out of which real canoes might have been made. And then at the end of this section is a giant bridge designed by Dominique Perrault whose proposal had come second in the competition. A consolation prize, it takes the form of a huge tubular spiral, broken in the middle, linking the *barrios* of Arganzuela and Comillas. I AM A BRIDGE it screams, a little too anxious to heal the perceived divisions of the city. Garrido didn't much care for it when it was built – it was too big an object he thought, too conventionally iconic, although as the trees have matured it has become less obtrusive.[84]

MADRID: THE EXPRESSWAY AS PUBLIC SPACE

From here the park becomes progressively more formal as it passes first the Puente de Toledo with its long axial views back to the old city to the Puerta de Toledo, and then the section where the old M-30 swept around the Estadio Vicente Calderón. At this point the park is defined by the Salon de Pinos, as the name suggests the principal design element being a formally planted garden of local pine trees. 'Salon' is a traditional usage for landscaped promenades, suggesting a formal, indoor space. The design is certainly controlled and contained, the opposite of wild; the architects described its character as 'sober, silent, and tough'. It is a profound job of sanitization for an area that until 2017 was dominated by the Estadio Vicente Calderón.[85] The M-30 is an occasional presence as it emerges from a tunnel near the Puente de Toledo, but the area is otherwise quiet. The formality is more apparent in the upper reaches, the park becoming an enhanced setting for the Palacio Real, as if a much older way of life has been reasserted. If there is an emblematic figure for the transformation, it is perhaps the reconfigured Puente de Toledo and its environs where we started. A complete refiguring of the eighteenth century, it achieves a degree of politeness and order that, realistically, the original can never have had.

The planting is impeccable, and the standard of maintenance nearly fifteen years after the original opening impressive. It is an immaculate place, as refined as any European urban setting. At the same time something inevitably has been lost, as it is in any comprehensive transformation. The new park is a carefully controlled environment, activity pre-thought and curated. You get a clearer sense of this when you return to the section of the M-30 that remains so far unburied, in the barrio of Ventas, near the Bullring and where Almodóvar shot his film *Que He Hecho Yo Para Merecer Esto*? What appealed to Almodóvar was precisely the sense that the M-30 created a scrubby edgeland, unsurveilled and uncontrolled, and implicitly permissive. Anything might be bought and sold here, anyone might be welcome, the strangest creatures (a luminous green lizard!) might be found wandering the pavement.

No utopia, Almodóvar's city nevertheless had a freedom about it mostly absent from the Madrid Rio project. It remains a little like that now, although the housing of Las Colmenas is in perfectly good shape, appreciably richer and better organized than it appears in the film. Madrid Rio has replaced traffic with pine trees, and it is hard to argue in the long term that this should not be any other way, given the high physical quality of the environment that has been created. But this is also a more ordered environment than the one it replaced, more docile and disciplined. Under Alberto Ruiz-Gallardón's leadership, the city became distinctly more ordered and richer in its central areas, and at the same time further removed culturally and ideologically from the Madrid that Almodóvar depicted. That may be a cause for regret or celebration or a mixture of the two. The Madrid Rio project has not been neutral in this process, its spectacular public space being both the image and the enabler of a disciplined and gentrified new Madrid. Meanwhile the traffic flows below in its brilliant tunnels, the expressway world's future here assured.

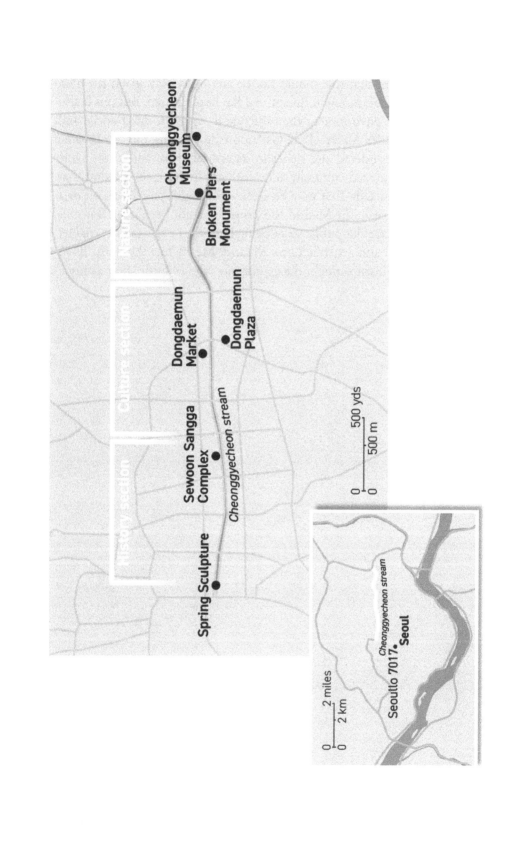

CHAPTER 7

Seoul: The Return of Nature

Cheonggyecheon restoration, Seoul (2003–5). *Photograph by Richard J. Williams.*

At ground level, it is the embodiment of the picturesque: three immense concrete columns in progressive states of decay. The most complete one, furthest away from you, stands perhaps fifteen metres from the ground, a great, heroic 'T', its arms cantilevered from the central point. The middle column has lost chunks of its arms, and sprouts tufts of grass, busy with pigeons. Closest is the most decayed column, little more than a stump, its rusted steel reinforcing rods poking through the grass. Weather-beaten but defiant, they are magnificent ruins. At ground level, there's a reedy, fast-flowing stream, thick with carp. A family of ducks play in the shallows, sparrows take dust baths along the meandering path by the stream, a white egret imperiously looks on. There are the odd few people in this early part of the day, enjoying the cool of the morning before the autumn heat builds. But the message of this place is that of all ruins, wherever they are, which is the ultimate futility of human endeavour in the face of all-powerful Nature.

Unusually for Seoul, the columns are original. This a city that was practically razed to the ground in the Korean War, and occupied at least five times by military force. A place formed by destruction, few physical signs of the past survive. These columns do, but almost everything else about the scene is an elaborate fiction. It's the Cheonggyecheon stream in the centre of Seoul, South Korea, a city of 25 million, probably the world's second largest. And everything about the scene is a construction. The river occupies the site of an existing stream, but so decayed was its hydrology that its water must be pumped ten kilometres from the Han river downstream, and purified before becoming the supernaturally clear Cheonggyecheon. The river is also incomplete, the restored section less than half of the whole; the rest is completely disconnected, and more or less completely dead. The visible Cheonggyecheon is, in effect, a giant fountain. The three columns are what remains of the four-lane elevated Samil (later Cheonggye) Elevated Highway, opened to traffic in 1971 and subsequently demolished. It might look like the return of Nature, but this is a megastructure of the same order as the original highway.

The Cheonggyecheon is in this book because it represents both a possible answer to the expressway question, and also an important fantasy. It is by far the most complete radical project here because the existing road was simply erased, on the understanding that the traffic would largely go somewhere else, a belief that turned out to be largely correct.[1] And as fantasy, it is important because it represents in image the most complete return to Nature. An example of how the expressway world can be reformed given the political will and the capital, its appeal outside Korea has been immense; it invariably appears as an example of what can be achieved.

That, as we will see, has become particularly important to Seoul's projection of itself to the world in recent years. The 4th Seoul Architecture Biennale, held in 2023, had the recovery of nature as its organizing principle. To underline the point, its central site was not a building at all, but a field, mostly of wild flowers, at Songhyeon Green, close to the reconstructed Gyeongbokgung Palace. 'Our ancestors have designed Seoul in accordance to the flow of nature', said the Biennale director Byoung Soo Cho. 'Its harmony with nature was unrivalled. If we can recover this harmony, Seoul can become one of the most habitable cities in the world.'[2] The Biennale's theme, posted everywhere, was 'city of mountain ranges, waterways and wind breezes'.[3] 'Hanyang was an eco-friendly city', claimed the Biennale catalogue somewhat anachronistically. 'To the north Bugaksan and Bukhansan mountains protected the city against the cold winds of winter. To the south was a wide, open space with a river running through which welcomed the summer breeze',[4] the space being Songhyeon.[5] Things had been lost in the Westernization of the twentieth century ('Westernization' here implicitly included Japan): 'we overly adapted to that culture and lost our unique sense of land'.[6] This gave the exhibition a melancholy cast, especially at Songhyeon. But there was optimism too, symbolized by the Cheonggyecheon restoration, a few minutes' walk from the exhibition sites, and a key Biennial reference point.

The Cheonggyecheon project represents, on the one hand, a peculiarly local set of conditions. It makes two big historical corrections, consistent with contemporary Korean practice more broadly: of the Japanese colonial period and the authoritarian regime of Park Chung-hee, the former army general who presided over Korea from 1962 until his assassination in 1979. But it also represents the liberal desire for the correction of the expressway world. It's an unusually complete enactment of that desire, because the expressway – with the exception of those columns – has not disappeared underground, or been rerouted, or been turned into a park. It has simply gone. Because of the thoroughness with which the Koreans carried out the job, the critical reception of Cheonggyecheon has been extraordinarily positive, and extraordinary things are believed about it.

Cheonggyecheon represents for many what can, and what should, be done. Like Brazil's Minhocão, however, and Madrid Rio, its politics are not quite what they may seem. Beloved of progressive architects outside of Korea, such as Brazil's Jaime Lerner, whose book *Acupunctura Urbana* has a chapter on it, Cheonggyecheon was a project of the populist right, and a mayor fixated on his election as president.[7] It was a power play in other words, and a successful one, as well as one in which democracy and ecology both took a battering. Whatever the undoubted popular success of the project, this is a megaproject that has more in common with the original highway constriction than it does any putative restoration. It is tempting to read Cheonggyecheon as a correction of autocracy, or at least of its visible symbols; it is in some ways legible as its continuation by other means.

Cheonggyecheon: History Lessons

Visit Cheonggyecheon now, and right at the start, where the pumped and purified water first emerges as a waterfall, there is a history lesson on a steel plaque, the text engraved in both Korean and English. There's another, more elaborate, history lesson at the opposite end, in the form of the Cheonggyecheon Museum by Junglim Architects, a big, car-park-like structure opened in 2005.[8] Over four ramped floors, it describes the first civilization of the river, in the form of a set of improvements carried out in 1411 by King Taejong, who built high embankments to control flooding, widened channels, as well as the Gwangtong bridge a kilometre or so from the start. Its history then jumps to the eighteenth century and the reign of King Jeongjo, depicted here as a proto-modern, enlightened king. His works on the stream in 1760 included an intense period of dredging to improve flow, the works carried out by 200,000 men over fifty-seven days.[9]

For the museum, the twentieth century by contrast is a period of decay, the river becoming polluted and stagnant, lined with slums. For the Japanese colonial regime that ran Korea between 1910 and 1945, the stream marked a clear demarcation between (rich) colonial Japanese and (poor) Korean parts of the city, the Japanese to the north, the Koreans to the south. The Japanese covered a portion of the stream between 1937 and 1942 for reasons of public health. After the end of the Korean War (1950–3), Seoul's population fell to just half a million, and the banks of the Cheonggyecheon filled with wooden shacks housing returning Seoulites, along with some North Korean refugees.

Works to complete the covering of the river entirely started in 1958, including a six-lane road over the top, and were carried out by the mid-1960s, by which time Cheonggyecheon had developed a new identity that still, partially, persists: the location of innumerable small workshops where it was said almost anything could be made, up to and including an army tank.[10] It was the nucleus of South Korea's post-war economic boom. It was also a tough place: here in 1970 a young garment worker, Tae il-Chun, notoriously burned himself to death in protest at punitive labour conditions and, by extension, Korea's industrialization.[11]

One political figure defines this period of Korean history, President Park Chung-hee, one of this book's authoritarian populists. Number two in the Korean military, staunch anti-communist and development-obsessed, he initiated and consolidated a period of astonishing economic growth accompanied by political repression, the so-called 'miracle on the Han'.[12] His government restructured the economy around heavy industry and exports, in the process consolidating the power of the large family conglomerate, or *chaebol*. Of those firms, Samsung and Lucky Goldstar (later LG) already existed; the Hyundai heavy engineering firm came into being in this period.[13] It was a period of intense infrastructural development too. President Park built Expressway no. 1, or the Seoul–Busan motorway in two years 1968–70, 400 kilometres in length, by any standards a remarkable achievement.[14]

In the capital, similarly ambitious infrastructural works were promised in the capital by a technocratic mayor, 'Bulldozer' Kim Hyun-ok, elected in 1966.[15] His project was the much shorter, but still complex Samil Elevated Highway, a four-lane expressway threading 5.6 kilometres through the centre of Seoul, right along the path of the now mostly buried Cheonggyecheon. Built in reinforced concrete, and supported by single-column, centrally placed piers, it allowed just enough room to allow traffic also to flow along the existing surface-level highway. On 22 March 1969, President Park himself opened the first section, the four kilometres from Myeong-dong to Sinseol-dong, identifying the redevelopment of Seoul's inner city with the project of national modernization – it was one of the great images of that project.[16] It was planned for 60,000 vehicles to use it daily and, to encourage more drivers to use it rather than the congested surface streets, tolls were waived.[17]

Photographs of its construction show an entirely new kind of city, on a new scale, laid over the top of a congested mess of one-storey shacks. It was also of a piece developmentally with President Park's project for the country's industrial development. Under his leadership, Korea's motor industry boomed following the Automobile Industry Protection Policy, a straightforward import substitution tool, resulting in the establishment of seven major companies between 1962 and 1968.[18] Here, on the Samil Elevated Highway, was the urban space where the products of that boom could be experienced to their full effect; it was a picture of a new, consumer-oriented world.

The Samil Highway was an object of some fascination, not only in the sympathetic media where it was portrayed as evidence of Korea's rapid progress, but also in art.[19] It featured strongly in a striking, Dziga Vertov-like avant-garde film made by the artist Kim Ku-lim in 1969, *The Meaning of 1/24 Second*.[20] Kim, born in 1936, had been based briefly in New York in the 1950s where he had been a member of the New York Art Students League, and where he became alert to avant-garde depictions of urban life. Picturing contemporary Seoul in tumult, the film consists of hundreds of tiny film fragments – snapshots of modern industry (a workshop, a factory), the public realm (buses, crowds, traffic) or modern domestic life (a shower head, cigarette smoke, spectacle frames). Running insistently through the film, connecting up the city symbolically and actually, is the newly opened Samil Highway (it opened in March and the film was shown for the first time on 21 July – it really was new).[21] It appears momentarily from below, but Kim depicts much more of it from above, from the side window of a moving car. Tiny shacks, one-storey workshops, and new constructions flash by. It was, yet again, a Futurist vision of a world in motion, 'a dizzying succession of imagery intended to evoke the dramatic acceleration of urban growth'.[22]

At some level Kim was enthralled. On another level, he clearly meant his film as a critique: the 2023 show of Korean art including Kim's film described the period as 'trauma', and 'dark', defined by censorship and repression.[23] For Shin Chung-hoon, the piece was simultaneously a serious critique of the 'boredom' of modern life, a mechanized existence without meaning or direction, and a spectacular multimedia event, involving performance and sculpture as well as film.[24] Kim and other contemporary Korean artists, Shin wrote, had a 'deep interest ... in new architectural events that arise in Seoul ... this new urban condition became both challenges and opportunities to the then Korean artists as well as the public'.[25] It was, perhaps, Seoul's contemporary equivalent of the Eiffel Tower for Parisian Impressionists, for good or ill, an inescapable symbol of modernity.

Kim Swoo-Geun, Sewoon Sangaa, Seoul (1967). *Photograph by Richard J. Williams.*

At its opening in 1969, the Samil Highway was, as contemporary news photographs show, the defining element in the contemporary downtown landscape; to all intents and purposes it *was* the landscape. The one building to match it in scale was Sewoon Sangga, a true megastructure built between 1967 and 1971, and that also featured momentarily in Kim's film.[26] A kilometre in length, crossing the highway from south to north at a mid-point between City Hall and the Dongdaemun market, it occupied an area the Japanese had cleared as a fire break during the Second World War. Designed by Kim Swoo-geun, an architect friendly to President Park's government, it consists of three distinct zones. At street level it has vehicle access, servicing and light industry, its lower level to a large extent continuing the small scale, retail and manufacturing traditions of the surrounding area. Above this lies a generous open-air pedestrian mall running the full length of the complex. Above that are apartment blocks of varying heights, the tallest rising to fifteen storeys above the podium, with some variations in the massing.[27]

Still largely intact despite some demolition and reconfiguring in the 2010s, it resembles an ocean liner embedded in the city.[28] As originally designed, it combines several functions in the same complex (work, leisure, production, residence, retail) but keeps them separate from one another – above all, it is circulation that is differentiated, motor traffic kept apart from pedestrians. There may have been no direct vehicular access to Sewoon Sangga from the Samil Highway, but this was unquestionably an automobile-oriented building, built on the same scale as the highway, touching it and acknowledging it in its design, and in its organization, built for the city's many new drivers. In a remarkable documentary film by artist Seo Hyun-Suk, *The Lost Voyage* (2018), Sewoon Sangga is the main character – substantial in its impact on the Seoul landscape, it is shown to have evolved, even as it decayed, into a rich neighbourhood, loved and feared in equal measure.[29]

Sewoon Sangga plus the Samil Highway comprised a new model of urban landscape for Seoul. At the Cheonggyecheon Museum, there's an appealingly homespun diorama of it depicted in cross-section, its cars and pedestrians frozen in motion. In the background, grainy news photographs depict the construction, and presidential opening. Occupying the same sequence, and same space as the dioramas of the fourteenth and eighteenth centuries, this one consigns the expressway world already to history.

Towards a Newer Cheonggyecheon

The creation myths of the Cheonggyecheon restoration are partly structural. Engineers found the highway to be structurally unsound in 1991, major remedial works were carried out over a two-kilometre section from 1994, and in 1997 its traffic was restricted to light vehicles.[30] The authorities were no doubt conscious of the consequences of doing nothing, for in the recent past there had lately been two deadly engineering failures in Seoul. A major crossing of the Han, the Seongsu Bridge, collapsed into the river in 1994, killing thirty-two, while only a year later, in 1995, the Sampoong Department Store's structural columns gave way, bringing down the whole building and killing more than 500, the greatest peacetime disaster in South Korea's history.[31] The collapses, it was said, were the result of the ferocious pace of economic transition and an associated lack of attention to safety.[32] It was a good moment to consider alternative ways of doing things.

There were more poetic creation myths. Two Yonsei University academics who routinely drove the Highway together to work, Noh Soo-hung, a professor of environmental engineering, and Lee Hee-duk, a professor of history, apparently speculated about its demolition and the restoration of the Cheonggyecheon below. That conversation led to the formation of a research group in 2000, the Cheonggyecheon Revival Academy, and a symposium in September that year, hosted by the novelist Park Kyung-ni at her Toji Cultural Center in Wonju, where she also lived; 200 experts from a range of fields attended.[33] Park, plus Lee and Noh, formed the core of the Academy. The symposium reflected international trends on the 'daylighting' of buried urban watercourses, as well as the revival of urban waterfronts in diverse global cities.[34] Restoring the Cheonggyecheon simultaneously made it into the architectural mainstream – the Korean Pavilion at the 2000 Venice Architecture Biennale was a pitch for the 're-establishment of the old city as a fundamentally pedestrian, riverside city, uncovering Cheonggyecheon at its core'.[35]

The Toji symposium represented Park's longstanding ecological interests, and her desire to recover balanced, pre-industrial modes of existence. Her best-known work, the historical family epic *Land*, was a celebration of the simple life, in some respects an ecological manifesto.[36] In a much-cited interview with Kwon Tae-son for the left-wing newspaper *Hankyoreh* on New Year's Day in 2002, Park, then aged seventy-six, set out an anti-capitalist, anti-globalist, ecological vision for Cheonggyecheon. She wanted it returned to its pre-industrial condition.[37] 'We have turned it into a trash can', she complained; Seoulites were 'trapped in cement spaces'; the only solution was a 'break with capitalism and materialism'. What would a restored Cheonggyecheon look like? Not unlike a Korean version of William Morris's *News From Nowhere*, it turned out: 'I would build harmonious two- to three-storey buildings with very Korean characteristics on the banks of the Cheonggyecheon, and plant various types of trees along the stream to create a forest so that even otters and raccoons can live there.'[38] It was (as Jeon and Kang put it later in summary) no less than 'an eco-centric society in which humans and nature would co-exist in harmony'.[39] If this condition had existed at all, it had not done so for at least six centuries, given the history of human interventions in the stream; it certainly predated King

Jeongjo's celebrated eighteenth-century reforms. Park Kyung-ni's ideas were nevertheless crucial in helping secure support for the demolition of the Samil Highway and restoration of the river: the interview closed with an exhortation for 'the next mayor of Seoul' to take up the challenge; 'he will become a figure to forever remain in our history'.[40]

That mayor turned out to be Lee Myung-bak. Lee, a monstrously ambitious former Hyundai CEO, and member of the Korean National Assembly, made the restored Cheonggyecheon the central issue in his mayoral campaign in 2002.[41] Standing for the populist, right-of-centre Hannara Party (the GNP, or Grand National Party), Lee – it was said – chose Cheonggyecheon to appeal to the poorer north of his Jongno constituency in the city, rather than the south, where his party already had substantial support.[42] There were easier ways to get votes. More likely it represented his desire – ultimately successful – to achieve the presidency, which he did with an unprecedented majority in 2010.

Ironically Lee had been a highway engineer in the 1970s, responsible for the delivery of Expressway Number 1 in 1970, among other projects, aged just twenty-nine.[43] In other words, he had been part of the exact world that had delivered the expressway he was now proposing to demolish. Both he and his sometime predecessor Kim Hyun-ok – the progenitor of the Samil Highway – went by the popular epithet 'bulldozer', no accident. Lee won the mayoralty against his left-wing opponent Kim Min-suk, promising restoration, and initially it was a scheme with wide popular support. The political rhetoric emphasized restoration, drawing on Park's ecological vision. Once elected, Lee's approach became straightforwardly technocratic. Using his Hyundai experience, he brought the Cheonggyecheon project under direct mayoral control, assembling a committee of engineers and project managers focused on delivering the project on budget in a compressed timeframe. Its priorities were not in the first instance ecological. Safety and sewage treatment were, along with slum clearance, to facilitate large-scale commercial development, and the promotion of history and culture; this was an infrastructure project aimed at raising the capital value of the Cheonggyecheon area.[44]

The desire to recover history and culture suggested an understanding of culture as a financial asset, in line with the then emerging international discourse on the creative city. Cultural assets might become more visible; infrastructure itself might become a cultural asset.[45] And the desire to clean up a slum area – in this case the industrial zone around Dongdaemun, which specialized in the manufacture of machine tools – was straightforward gentrification. Both motives would be difficult to pursue with the highway still in place; the demolition project therefore was a device to enable a familiar transformation of a city from one organized around industrial labour to one organized around services. For Peter Rowe, a Harvard architecture professor who has written on it more extensively than anyone in the Anglophone world, Cheonggyecheon was a 'threshold event', marking the transition from production-oriented development to one more oriented around lifestyle.[46]

Whatever Cheonggyecheon was, it was certainly big. The deconstruction process of the Samil Highway – celebrated in a series of dioramas and images at the Cheonggyecheon Museum – was heroic, its Stakhanovite crews working twenty-four hours a day for eighteen months.[47] The dismantling of the highway produced images uncannily similar to those of its initial construction, to the point that it is hard to distinguish one from the other: construction or destruction, it no longer seems to matter. The speed of the project won Lee international recognition even before completion, at the 2004 Venice Biennale and elsewhere.[48]

The hydrological works were equally vast, requiring the construction of an entirely new infrastructure. The stream was historically inconsistent in flow, alternating between flood and drought, and prone to being stagnant and smelly. If this was to be a daylighting project, there was not much of a stream to daylight. The solution was an entirely new river, and an associated pumping station by the Han, transferring 120,000 tons of water daily to the start of the river near City Hall, emerging purified and regulated as a waterfall, flowing back down to the Han.[49] The pumping station runs twenty-four hours a day; without it, the Cheonggyecheon would not flow.

In spite of the remarkable challenges, Lee brought the whole project to completion in under three years, and at a cost of US$280 million, staggeringly good value by comparison with Madrid's M-30 reconstruction (US$5.8 billion) or Boston's Big Dig (US$21 billion). The official inauguration took place on 1 October 2005.[50] In his speech, Mayor Lee claimed that Cheonggyecheon had 'returned to nature', with 'clear water, bright sunshine, a cool breeze, [and] pussy willows'.[51]

The Cheonggyecheon restoration was, and is, impressive. At Cheonggyecheon Plaza and for the two kilometres east towards Dongdaemun, its official theme, one of three, is 'history' and has a formal quality, dominated by hard landscaping. It is set off at the start by a monumental public sculpture in the shape of a spiral shell, called *Spring*, by the US-based artists Claes Oldenburg and Coosje Van Bruggen. At this point, the high embankment displays an immense ceramic tableau depicting King Jeongjo's procession from Changdoek Palace to Hwaseong in 1795 (mysteriously, Jeongjo himself is represented only by his horse at the centre of the action). It is another of the creation myths: Jeongjo, the enlightened king briskly reforming the stream a stand-in for Mayor Lee – the visitor is left in little doubt.[52]

The 'history' phase of the Cheonggyecheon breaks down around Dongdaemun, and it becomes, officially, 'culture'. Here is a frenzied commercial area thick with markets and clothes stores, and still some industry. There are still areas specializing in the production of nails, or neon lighting, or socks. Here Sewoon Sangga still looms, momentarily shading the stream. Just to the south sits the blobby cultural complex of Dongdaemun Design Plaza, designed by the British-Iraqi architect Zaha Hadid and opened in 2013.[53] Cheonggyecheon here has a hybrid quality, the surrounding buildings are lower, the sky brighter, and the vegetation thickens. It is welcome relief from the frenetic commerce at street level.

Moving further east towards the Han, the landscaping becomes decidedly informal as the river makes some gentle turns before it disappears under the high piers of the Yongdugyo Bridge carrying the Seoul City Route 30 highway. Here is, officially, 'nature', and this section of the project is one of the most contradictory – on the one hand, the part where the expressway world reasserts itself, the view overhead a spectacular tangle of high-speed roads, and at ground level, big, multi-lane avenues thick with traffic. It is the Miracle on the Han period Seoul at its most intense. But, on the other hand, at river level, it is here that the idea of restoration is most convincing, where the stream appears most natural, and where by the water the human world seems most in abeyance. The columns, artfully arranged in a state of progressive deterioration, tell the story of nature's progressive takeover. Rhetorically, it is the strongest part of the project, the part where the image of the post-automobile city most convincingly appears; it's also the place where

Cheonggyecheon restoration, Seoul (2003–5). *Photograph by Richard J. Williams.*

the layers of history are most visible. It is, in spite of the trucks rumbling thirty metres above your head, also a strangely contemplative space, with humans and nature in some kind of momentary equilibrium.

Cheoggyecheon: Critical Voices

Cheonggyecheon was an immediate popular success, visitor numbers exceeding those on New York's High Line within a month or so of opening. The international critical reception was almost supernaturally positive: something huge had been achieved quickly and at apparently low cost, the kind of project that in the Anglo-American world in particular tends to remain fantasy. Unusually for an infrastructure project, it was widely reported in the mainstream media. For *The New York Times*, reporting in 2007, Cheonggyecheon had already been 'wildly successful', and compared it with Central Park. More than a landscape project, it was evidence of a new national concern for 'quality of life'.[54] The Spanish architects Francisco Burgos and Ginés Garrido admired it as a model for their contemporaneous Madrid Rio project: 'in terms of

157

popular acceptance the project can be considered a complete success'.[55] Like that project later on, it won an award from the Harvard Graduate School of Design, the Veronica Rudge Green Prize in urban design, accompanied by a well-footnoted, if gushy, catalogue that celebrated the 'sheer optimism and audacity of the project, its speedy realization and profound contribution to public life'.[56] For Peter Rowe, Cheonggyecheon represented a 'paradigm shift in Korean urbanization', from urbanism as development to what he called 'actively promoting public good'.[57] Cheonggyecheon here and in numerous other accounts was therefore not only a development project, but a moral one.

Bold claims were made for the Cheonggyecheon's effects on the city's ecology. The restored river, it was said, was 'a new kind of hybridized public work: a catalytic agent that spawns new forms of ecological and social life in the city'.[58] Official statistics described a transformed biome: twenty-seven species of fish, up from four, thirty-four species of birds where there had been just six previously, no less than 206 species of insect, up from a mere fifteen. These miraculous figures were widely repeated.[59] Its effects on health and wellbeing were apparently no less impressive. Jenny Roe and Layla McCay wrote in 2021 that 'the project has increased opportunities for active living, helped reduce the urban heat-island effect, added to the downtown quality of life and helped humanize what was an industrial eyesore'.[60] Atmospheric pollution, it was said, dropped 35 per cent, and noise by 18 per cent.[61] Cooling winds increased their speed, temperatures dropped 10 per cent in the vicinity, and more Seoulites took to their subways. There was no end to the positive effects.[62]

But Cheonggyecheon is also more complex than it initially appears. Seen from outside Korea, Mayor Lee's brusque efficiency was a thing of wonder, especially from the point of view of Boston, labouring so long and so expensively over its Big Dig. Inside Korea, however, perceptions could be different. It was, for Cho Myung-rae writing later, a profoundly undemocratic project, meant 'to aestheticize the rule of power via human-nature relations'. Perhaps alluding to the enlightened despotism of the eighteenth-century King Jeongjo, Cho wrote, 'people paid their loyalty to the king for his wise rule'.[63] Ecology, to put it another way, was a cover for authority.

Criticism of the project was visible first in the question of the displacement of industrial workers in the Dongdaemun area. Park

Chung-hee's regime saw the establishment of thousands of machine tool workshops in the district, and the creation of a large industrial working-class. Densely inhabited and worked, it represented the hardships involved at a particular stage of Korea's economic development, but also a distinctive culture. At the start of the Cheonggyecheon restoration, there were thought to be 60,000 businesses in the area, along with 300 street vendors, and 220,000 merchants. Several thousand businesses were relocated to Garden Five, a high-rise development in the south of Seoul, or the Dongdaemun stadium area. The project involved significant displacements, with many Cheonggyecheon traders unhappy with the new arrangements, or unwilling to move.[64] The project, with its slum clearances was, in some accounts, a species of class war, justified by modernization.[65] A Citizens' Committee was set up in 2002 to deal with issues arising from the construction works, including displacement, but Lee dissolved it when it began to question the masterplan.[66] This was the official line, reiterated and reinforced, conflict brushed aside. As Mayor Lee put it in 2004, 'I persuaded them using democratic methods ... Trust arose in the process, and I was able to guide an agreement.'[67] The reality was undoubtedly messier.[68]

Democracy was shaky in other areas too. *Spring*, the monumental sculpture at the western end of the project, was Mayor Lee's decision, after some consultation – one suspects not much – with the National Museum of Modern and Contemporary Art. Oldenburg and van Bruggen were blue chip artists, massively experienced in public art commissions, and their work straightforward signifier of the global. Their choice was impeccable given the Cheonggyecheon's economic logic, but it enraged local artists who felt excluded from the selection process. 'Time will tell', van Bruggen said blandly in response.[69]

Ecology was, unsurprisingly, another area of conflict. In 2000, there were superficially aligned visions of a Venice Biennale pitch and Park Kyung-ni's early interventions, but they quickly separated. Venice, and subsequently Cheonggyecheon, 'restoration' was the post-industrial aestheticized waterfront, the very picture of the service-oriented modern economy. It was a global vision, in which the Cheonggyecheon might equally have been the post-industrial Thames, or the Hudson. Park's vision, by contrast, was inward-looking, anti-global and positively pre-industrial, imagining the restoration of a world that predated human intervention. The schism, Cho has pointed out, had an inevitability about it, as Seoul had no obvious, even existing, model for any kind of urban restoration. The very concept had to be invented.[70] It was an argument between two unresolvable positions, Park's 'deep ecologism' versus 'instrumental environmentalism'; the former facilitated the latter, but the latter ultimately won out. The project as built *looked* ecological but was actually 'simulated nature' that turned half the Cheonggyecheon river into a fountain and made the rest invisible.[71]

Having inspired the restoration project, Park Kyung-ni became a critic. By 2004, just nine months into the construction phase, she thought her ecological vision almost entirely sidelined. In an interview conducted at her Toji Cultural Center with the *Hankyoreh*, Park found landscape architecture to have already replaced restoration. Having read through the chapters of the Seoul Metropolitan Government's Project blueprint, she complained bitterly about the space given over to landscaping, sewage, roads and bridges – for her, restoration meant leaving nature to its own devices.[72] She went on to complain about the political imperative to complete the scheme within the four years of the mayor's term: 'The Cheonggyecheon is a river that will flow for hundreds of years', she wrote. Why the rush, except for reasons of political expediency? In short, the restoration project was 'development' rather than restoration.

There was also a nationalistic element, as so often in Korea. 'Landscape', the term Park so disparaged, she thought an alien, specifically Japanese, import. Koreans, she asserted, 'have always sought harmony with nature'.[73] Nothing in the interview suggested Park much understood the hydrology of the actually existing Cheonggyecheon, and the fact that there was no longer a river to restore, however much that might be desirable. As a rhetorical position it was nevertheless important, not only for Seoul, but for potential future cases of highway removal everywhere. What might start as an ecological project might quicky become its opposite; Cheonggyecheon restoration was really the creation of infrastructure of the same order as the original expressway, less an 'environmentally friendly civic jewel', as Jeon and Kang wrote in 2019, than a 'humongous fish tank dependent upon an artificial water supply'.[74] They note, with some amusement, the appearance in recent years of a movement to 're-restore' the Cheonggyecheon, in other words to peel back the layers of the restoration project to reveal whatever might be left of the original stream.

For Lee Hyun Kyung, a historian, the concept of 'difficult heritage' is essential in modern Korea. She refers specifically to the problem of dealing with the remnants of the Japanese colonial past – most spectacularly the Government General Building, a neoclassical behemoth housing the colonial headquarters in South Korea, built, in the most brutal power move, on the site of the fourteenth-century Gyeongbokgung Palace.[75] Dealing with the 'difficult', Lee argues, has often meant erasure. In the case of the Government General Building, it meant demolition in 1996, and the now mostly complete reconstruction of the palace; of the Japanese occupation in this location, or the adjacent Songhyeon Green, there is scarcely a sign. The palace is a modern fiction, albeit an impressive one. Cheonggyecheon might be thought of in precisely the same terms, as 'difficult heritage' in the first instance, doubly so with the Park dictatorship laid over the colonial period, and like Gyeongbokgung, the solution has been erasure, and the substitution of historical fantasy. The implications extend far beyond Seoul, for the desire to erase the expressway world is global. But what we replace it with and for whom are not straightforward questions.

The erasure of the Samil Highway removed a key symbol of the Park government, and of developmentalism in general.[76] It also erased an authentic part of the city. In the documentary *Cheonggyecheon Medley* (2011), directed by Kelvin Kyung Kun Park, it appears again as an authentic place, tough but self-regulating with a culture threatened by new (which is to say, post-highway) development.[77] In a poignant moment in *Cheonggyecheon Medley*, displaced metalworkers visit their new premises in Garden Five. Fifteen kilometres south, on the other side of the Han from the tiny workshops of Cheonggyecheon, it is an entirely different proposition. An antiseptic high rise with secure entry and air conditioning, it is capacious and modern, and has everything these businesses require. But culturally it's alien; a welcoming party falls completely flat, and the pervading mood is loss.

Seoullo 7017

A mile due south from Cheonggyecheon through Seoul's old Central Business District is Seoullo 7017, a project that is now almost as

SEOUL: THE RETURN OF NATURE

MVRDV, Seoullo 7017, Seoul (2017). *Photograph by Richard J. Williams.*

well known, and often spoken of in the same terms. The awkward name amalgamates 'Seoul Street' and the dates of the original highway's completion (1970) and its opening as a park (2017). Where Cheonggyecheon takes the visitor beneath the formal city in a trench with high embankments, Seoullo 7017 lifts them seventeen metres up above it, onto the road deck of the decommissioned Seoul Station Overpass. Unlike Cheonggyecheon, the elevated structure still exists in its entirety, linking Sowol and Toegye streets across the fourteen tracks of Seoul Station, the city's mainline rail terminus. But instead of cars, the road bed now carries a meandering path, threaded between circular concrete planters housing 24,000 trees of 240 species, arranged in fifty botanical family groups, along with a paddling pool, children's trampolines and poles carrying CCTV cameras. Early in the morning gangs of gardeners feed the plants. The architects, the Dutch firm MVRDV, who won the design competition in 2014, had high ambitions for the project, hoping that it would act as a literal nursery for the city, a 'botanical garden for Seoul' in the words of Winy Maas, the firm's combative director.[78] The Seoul Metropolitan government, who commissioned it in the first place, made grand claims about history and culture and the benefits of walking.[79]

As ever in Seoul, history was awkward. The station building was, along with City Hall and the Government General Building, one of the most recognizable buildings of the Japanese occupation, put up in 1925 to a neo-baroque design by Tsukamoto Yashui. The highway, four lanes wide, seventeen metres high, and a kilometre in length, sliced across the old station building's northern façade. It was a project of Mayor Kim Hyun-ok during Park Chung-hee's regime, which is to say the same political team responsible for the Samil Highway in 1969. Another symbol of modernity, it was also useful, linking the clothing markets of Dongdaemun with rest of the city. It opened on 16 August 1970, a year and a half after the Samil Highway opening.[80] It might have only been a kilometre in length, but it was another project of national significance, a symbol of automotive modernization at the commercial centre of Seoul.

The later story of the Seoul Station Overpass has further similarities with Cheonggyecheon. Engineers found it structurally unsound in 2012 and recommended demolition or remodelling by the end of 2015.[81] But the then mayor, Park Won-soon, was keen on a defining project during his term in office, and a pocket version of the Cheonggyecheon restoration emerged as a candidate. Mayors Park and Lee were very different characters: Park, a student activist had once been expelled from Seoul National University for participating in a protest against President Park Chung-hee; he subsequently made a career as a human rights lawyer.[82] He seemed, however, to be set on a similar political path to his predecessor – a big infrastructural project as mayor, and then, with luck, the presidency.[83] Park formally announced the project at a press conference in 2014 on New York's High Line, along with an architectural competition – the choice of the High Line (which has made an appearance already in chapters 2 and 5) was significant, signifying a clear direction for the project, and a global turn.[84] The *Korea Times* put a picture of the closed viaduct on its front page, filled with pedestrians in anticipation of the project. Work started in 2015 and was completed two years later at a cost of US$50 million, another bargain by international standards.[85]

Opened on 20 May 2017, its opening ceremony included an address by the then European Union ambassador to Korea, Michael Reiterer. Its opening formed part of 'Eurovillage! A Green Bridge to Europe', an event that promoted both the EU's brand in Korea and World Environment Day, as well as (perhaps optimistically, given South Korea's rather better progress in the area) Europe's electric car industry.[86] An unintentionally sinister public artwork made for the project displayed 30,000 pairs of shoes, to symbolize, it was said, the transformation of the Overpass to a pedestrian space.

By most measures, the opening was wildly successful. It was estimated that 250,000 visited on the first weekend, and five million in the first six months.[87] Rents shot up in the surrounding area, good news for landlords. The international reception was, as it had been for Cheonggyecheon, glowing. For the design magazine *Icon*, it marked Seoul's 'redemption' from the car.[88] Rowan Moore, writing for *The Guardian* praised it as the more convincing of the world's 'High Line Wannabees', a legible symbol of the city's desired transformation from the car to the pedestrian.[89] *Time* magazine listed it as one of the 'World's Greatest Places' in 2018, praising its spectacular illumination at night.[90] *The Washington Post* thought it evidence of transformational thinking in a metropolis of 25 million.[91] For Tony Robinson and Ji Minsun, in one of the project's more considered academic assessments of the project, it was 'a space of healthy greenery, carbon uptake and air purification in the streets of the old industrial city'.[92]

There were some rough edges. In an interview with the *Architectural Review*, Winy Maas of MVRDV admitted that it had been a 'rush job', and that the concrete surface applied to the structure to make the new pedestrian route had cracked, as no prototyping had been possible.[93] Ten days after the official opening, there was suicide, a Kazakh who scaled 1.4 metre security glass to jump to his death.[94] Two years after opening, the English language *Korea Times* noted the failure of the extensive planting to mitigate the summer air temperatures ('the air felt stuffier than on the shaded sidewalks below. Tourists and office workers from nearby buildings squeezed themselves into sparse patches of shade') and a drop in visitor numbers after the enthusiasm during the first year.[95] The same article quoted a professor of landscape at Seoul National University, Hann Pae-Jeong on the project's failures: 'It's become a good example of what hastily done urban spaces look like – born from the fad-like nostalgia for recycling, sentimentalism capitalizing on the positive image of green spaces, populist politics and spatial designs drawn up without discussion or consultation.'[96]

Visit Seoullo 7017 now and there is something in that assessment. It has the feel of a student architectural project, or a temporary Biennale pavilion, a sketch for something larger that might be built in the future rather than the project itself. The overpass structure couldn't carry the weight of continuous planting, so circular planters were used instead. But it gives it a somewhat unresolved and contingent character, more like a plant sale than a landscape design. It needs a lot of maintenance and servicing, unsurprising given its location high above Seoul Station. It also needs a lot of rules for visitors. The fragility of its surfaces requires that almost everything apart from the quiet appreciation of the plants is forbidden, and CCTV every few metres ensures compliance. Fussy, over-determined and over-surveilled, it has more in common with the art museum than a traditional public space. Perversely it provides a first-class view of the intense traffic below, to which it has by some accounts worsened.[97] In relation to the immensity of the Seoul Station area, and the city in general, it's a small gesture, far from the large-scale restructuring of the landscape found at Cheonggyecheon. We can no longer find out what its principal author, mayor Park Won-soon felt about it: after major sexual harassment accusations by a former secretary, he died by suicide at the age of sixty-four.[98]

Ecological Theatre

They differ in scale, but both Cheonggyecheon and Seoullo 7017 are species of ecological theatre. Their success has proved the public appetite for such spaces, and it has also confirmed the public's willingness to subject itself to control (especially true perhaps of South Korea, but true everywhere to an extent). Cheonggyecheon is strikingly disciplined given the rhetoric about the restoration of nature. Even on the surface it is nothing of the sort. It is hard to imagine a more controlled space outside of an airport or prison: notices at every access point establish rules for approved behaviour (no bicycles, pets, fishing, littering, drinking, swimming or drones), notices of emergency exits in the case of floods, notices explaining every moment in the stream's history, notices informing how many calories the visitor has burned walking since the last notice.

That control of the present environment extends to the control of the past. The erasure of the expressway world is almost total, the ruins of the remaining columns an artful staging of what can now not feasibly return. There is no way back for that world, in the same way that in the nineteenth-century cities of the northern hemisphere, there can be no return to industry now that the buildings that housed it have become museums.[99] It has become a similar orthodoxy, so much so that a further fourteen highway removal projects have been carried out in Seoul since Cheonggyecheon, contributing to the Seoul Metropolitan Government's broader aim to make private car ownership 'obsolete by 2030', by means not only of highway removal, but 'road diets ..., constraining downtown parking, creating efficient bus-only lanes, and expanding ride-share programs, subway lines, and bicycle lanes'.[100] (It should be said that South Korea remains an automotive superpower, the fifth largest by volume in the world, ahead of any European country.[101]) Cheonggyecheon is as complete an erasure of the expressway world as this book encounters; that erasure has undoubted benefits in terms of air and water quality, and for visitors general peace of mind in a frenetic metropolis.

Cheonggyecheon is also symbolic of a transformation towards a service-oriented economy that has firmly and irrevocably displaced industrial workers from the centre of the city, raised the price of accommodation, and created a prolonged and complex housing crisis. That crisis has, in its current phase at any rate, been accompanied by sharp population decline – 700,000 between 2012 and 2022, or close to 10 per cent of the city's core population, comparable with the rates of decline in Western industrial cities after the Second World War with their planned and market-driven processes of dispersal.[102] But Seoul's decline is the result of something more sinister – South Korea's birth rate at the time of writing is the world's lowest, lower even than Japan's. Seoul, where half the country's population lives, cannot, if current trends continue, reproduce itself.[103] The successful, Oscar-winning film *Parasite* (Bong Joon-ho, 2019) depicts a city rendered unliveable by a rapacious housing market. The city of the new Cheonggyecheon is, despite appearances to the contrary, rapidly shrinking. Its deliberate ruination of its expressway world, you might say, has started to happen at precisely the moment when it could, when the city has reached its peak and is headed for decline. It will, maybe soon, no longer have so much use for those expressways because there won't be as many drivers who need to use them. Cheonggyecheon, in other words, isn't necessarily the prefiguration of a progressive future as its authors intended, but of a smaller, emptier, older city.

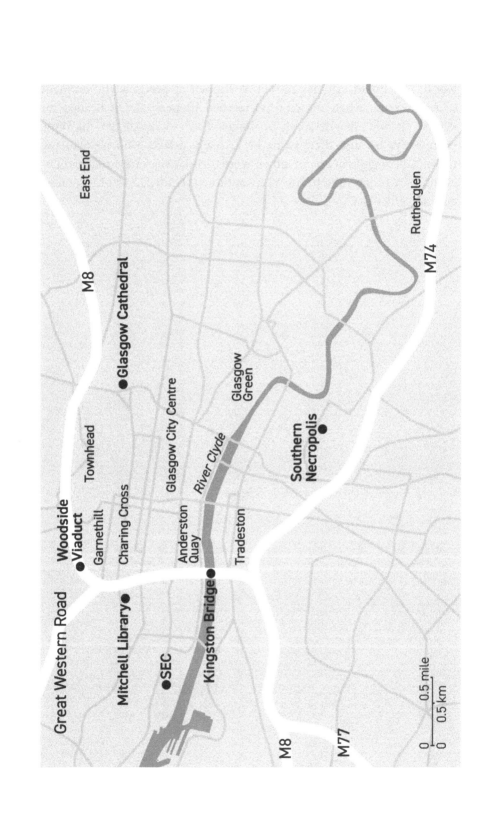

CHAPTER 8

Glasgow: Living with the Expressway

M8 at Charing Cross, Glasgow. *Photograph by Richard J. Williams.*

I am standing again at perhaps the most intense part of Scotland's M8 motorway. Perhaps 80 per cent of Scotland's population of five million lives along this road, and where I am now is, demographically speaking, probably the densest part of the country. This is Charing Cross in Glasgow at precisely the point where the M8 crosses through the city centre, dividing the nineteenth-century commercial core with its bulky Victorian offices and grid plan from the middle-class, mostly residential West End. The road has just done a dog-leg manoeuvre, its ten lanes skirting the city centre to the north at Townhead, abruptly turning south here before the crossing of the River Clyde on the gigantic Kingston Bridge. It is not pretty, this part of town, but it is grand, one of few parts of British cities built on an American scale. For some, Glasgow represents a uniquely fearful urban experience, and it has historically been a driver of anti-urban sentiment in both culture and politics – the M8 is easily assimilable into that way of thinking.[1] For one contemporary architecture critic and Glasgow native, the M8 is evidence of the 'shipwreck' he thinks the contemporary city has become.[2] In the feature film *Red Road*, made in 2008, the M8 is all squalor and decay and feral sex.[3]

We have been here before, both metaphorically and in real life, for this place was where we started the book; it was our first image of an expressway, a stand-in for expressways everywhere with its threats and opportunities and still, occasionally, under the right traffic conditions, the promise of free movement. To return to it is in some ways perverse, for there are many things that Glasgow and the M8 are not. The city proper, with a core population of a little over 600,000 is not Los Angeles or London or Seoul.[4] If it has Victorian grandeur and regional scale, it is not now a big city, or really a global one, although it still has ambitions in that direction – it hosted the United Nations annual meeting on climate change, COP26, in late 2021.[5] Once the so-called second city of the British Empire, it was an industrial superpower until the middle of the twentieth century, having built at one point a fifth of the world's tonnage of ships. It was a political colossus once too. City Chambers is as grand a municipal seat of power as you will find anywhere. As the heart of the Strathclyde region until the early 1990s, it was said to have such a large political hinterland that it had its own foreign policy. But it was an eviscerated polity at the time of writing, well-intentioned but weak. There is no Robert Moses here. Its cultural capital was in trouble too. The city's globally famous 1909 School of Art, designed by Charles Rennie Mackintosh, was mostly destroyed in a fire in 2018, leaving its future uncertain along with the city block to which it belongs.[6]

In terms of its expressways, Glasgow's history is also one of uncertainty and decline. The ambition of its plans after the Second World War exceeded anything elsewhere in the UK. It was a genuine 'motorway city' as a 2024 BBC radio programme put it.[7] Its recent history is, by contrast with its heroic past, mostly one of inaction. No tunnels have been dug for it, nothing torn down, no new parks have been created, no flowers have been planted on the carriageways, or bicycle lanes marked to signal – after COP26 – a post-automobile future. In 2011, as Madrid formally opened a park, built over the top of the now-buried M-30 expressway,

Glasgow was seemingly doing the exact opposite, threading Britain's last urban expressway, the M74 extension, five mostly elevated miles through its inner-city.[8]

There are pragmatic reasons for returning to Glasgow. For the Edinburgh-based author of this book, it was just there down the road, an everyday point of comparison with Seoul or Madrid. But it also represented a different reality of the expressway world. It would have been easy to write a story of exceptions: megaprojects, or mega-disasters, and some of the chapters do indeed describe those things. The cases of Seoul or Madrid are, in most senses, exceptional in terms of their scale, ambition and politics. Madrid's transformation of the M-30 is inconceivable without an unusually able and ambitious mayor, Seoul's Cheonggyecheon project likewise. Most cities are not, however, like these ones; most cities, most of the time, cannot access the funds or the leadership to do transformational change; most cities, arguably, are like Glasgow in 2024, stretched by the effects of the Covid pandemic, the Ukraine war, and energy price spikes. I return to Glasgow for the reason that it could be said to represent most cities, and it would be good to know what most cities will do with their expressway worlds. Glasgow has some exceptional qualities, but it will be for many readers also a representative city – a nineteenth-century industrial metropolis with much in common with those on the eastern seaboard of the United States or northern Europe. Its 1960s enthusiasm for the expressway world is theirs too.

Like their expressway worlds, Glasgow's expressway world has been more complex than it might initially appear, a landscape of resistances and occasional occupations, of political theatre and spectacle – and latterly, some rich consideration of what a future, post-expressway city might be, from the municipality, consultants, and especially activists.[9] The city's expressways have also been the subject of much repair work by Transport Scotland, the authority responsible for them. Detailed and unglamorous, this necessary work is mostly experienced as disruption, both on the part of motorists who find their exit ramps inconveniently blocked, and pedestrians whose routes underneath the expressway have become a mess of temporary barriers and plastic cones.[10] It would not be true to say that nothing has happened as regards the M8 and the future of Glasgow's expressways. It is rather that what has happened has been tactical and incremental, in terms of one of the key themes of the book, a learning to live *with* the expressway rather than an abrupt transformation of it.

The Promise of the Highway Plan

We begin on that somewhat bleak section of M8 at Charing Cross, and it is hard to find much that is positive to say about it, much less of the rest of the scheme. It was this section in particular that caught the (negative) imagination, for it is here that the impact on the existing, largely nineteenth-century city, is most visible. Walking from the end of Sauchiehall Street in the city centre across to the West End feels like walking off a cliff. The dense Victorian city falls away, with a seven-metre drop to the expressway, a huge hole that, when dug in 1969, took a chunk of the past with it, including local landmarks such as the Grand Hotel.[11] It is rare to find accounts of the Charing Cross section of the M8 that are not also accounts of regret and loss for monuments like this, and – in spite of its sometimes unsavoury reputation – the Victorian city altogether. Peter Kelly, an urbanist responsible for the anti-motorway Replace the M8 campaign from 2022, notes a pathology of loss in the area, a pervasive nostalgia for the Victorian city, and a neo-therapeutic desire to heal it, to recover its completeness.[12]

Whatever the mood around the M8 may be now, we need to make sense of how it happened in the first place. Its story begins with the First Planning Report to the Highways and Planning Committee of the Corporation of Glasgow, published in 1945, generally known as the Bruce Report after Robert Bruce, the city's chief engineer and the report's principal author.[13] It is remembered for two startling proposals: first, the demolition of almost all of the existing city centre, up to and including the Corporation's own City Chambers in George Square, and second, an entirely new system of roads, based on a hierarchy of uses and with an expressway-standard inner ring at its core.

A blueprint for an entirely new kind of settlement, Glasgow's was fuelled by pathological anxieties about Victorian squalor, mixed with others about road safety and likely congestion ('astonishing').[14] Projections of doom required 'drastic measures', wrote Bruce.[15] That meant roads for 'the exclusive use of fast moving mechanically propelled vehicles ... dual carriageways separated by a central reservation ... it follows that pedestrians have no access to such roads'.[16] The inner ring road proposed by the report had some differences with what was later proposed, such as eight huge roundabouts, spaced evenly around the city to allow access to the surface streets. But otherwise the plan substantially prefigured what the Corporation later envisaged, essentially a ten-mile square box, its sides roughly aligned with the points of the compass.

The Bruce Plan was followed by the Clyde Valley Regional Plan of 1946.[17] Written by Patrick Abercrombie and Robert Matthew and eventually published in 1949, it argued for the city's radical decentralization. Victorian Glasgow was too dense –'here in an incredibly small area, some fifteen miles by ten miles live and work more than two million people crowded together at densities hardly touched anywhere else in Great Britain ... six generations of immigrants have flooded the land to saturation point'.[18] They proposed to shrink the city by an incredible half million, down to 650,000 through the development of towns throughout the Valley region, and 'the repopulation of Scotland as a whole'.[19] The report juxtaposed photographs of barrack-like Victorian tenements with images of open space and leisure: sailboats bobbing on the Clyde estuary, an ascent of the Cobbler (a popular local hill), endless beaches and parks. There would be at least five 'holiday towns', mostly near Loch Lomond. A regional vision of parks and pleasure, connected by expressways to every point, the city centre reduced to a node in a network, it was a Celtic California.[20]

The 1965 Highway Plan

The key document for understanding the Inner Ring Road is, without question, the Corporation's 1965 Highway Plan, written by the consultants Scott Wilson Kirkpatrick (SWK) and Partners, with William Holford and Partners as consultants (Holford had pedigree, as a judge for Brasília and consultant on London's Ringways).[21] For James McCafferty of SWK, writing later, it not only involved inventing a new urban typology ('where no standards existed, we invented them') but also a new scale of infrastructural ambition for Scotland ('we were involved in the greatest project in Scotland').[22] SWK assumed the automobile would be transformative. Acknowledging its threat ('noisy, smelly and dangerous'), they recognized its world-changing potential, and Scotland's potential to lead on it: 'we believe this mobility does enlarge the life of the ordinary citizen to a greater degree than any other single innovation of the 20th century'.[23]

By contemporary standards, SWK's work was strikingly urbanophobic, regarding urban depopulation as both inevitable and desirable. 'Many of the residential areas of Glasgow which were developed at very high densities during the last century have reached the end of their useful life', they wrote in 1962, a pattern 'experienced by almost every major city both here and in America.'[24] In place of the sooty tenement city, they proposed a low-density parkland dotted with towers, expressways the defining element.[25] In their images, the old city has mostly gone, at Charing Cross the Edwardian baroque of the Mitchell Library is there clearly enough on the left, high up above the roadway, but everything else is new. It's not unpleasant, at least in this sketch. Trees line the road on both sides, traffic flows, and everything is agreeably decluttered. From the same series, a perspective drawing of Townhead to the north-east of the city centre shows some human life. Down in the underpass beneath the elevated ramps over Castle Street, satchel-bearing children make their way to school, women chat, while trees politely screen the traffic.[26]

Whatever the results, the plan had some concern for the look of the city. Changes were inevitable but could be presented as positive additions to the city's landscape; they even help citizens appreciate the past ('more open space and in some ways a quieter and more suitable setting could be provided for the cathedral').[27] At Charing Cross, they wanted to preserve the sightlines of the existing city, hence using a depressed road design rather than an elevated bridge.[28] There was a bucolic vision throughout – the landscaping of the road would create a kind of parkland throughout, screening cars from humans. 'Every effort', the report's authors wrote, 'should be made to preserve an adequate landscaped belt and where possible to give a "face lift" to existing development so that driving the new roads will give a new image of Glasgow.'[29] The council commissioned a distinguished town planner, Lord Esher, to write a positive account of the M8's effect on architectural conservation. In Garnethill, said Esher, perhaps straining a point, 'the dramatic hill-top siting of this small residential and educational enclave with its shabby old houses and cobbled streets has been accentuated by the chasm of the Ring Road'.[30]

It is not clear what local residents thought. But in theory at least, the expressway world reconciled modernization and conservation.[31]

SWK's key recommendation was an Inner Ring Road, about fifteen kilometres in length, very much like the Bruce Report's, but with the addition of a new and dramatic bridge over the Clyde, high enough to allow the passage of ocean-going vessels (mostly unglamorous dredgers). It would be built over ten years, 1965–75, for £163 million (£2.7 billion in 2025 terms).[32] The traffic, a lot of it anyway, was going shopping: as its reports increasingly showed, the Corporation envisaged a new generation of hyper-mobile, consumption-oriented Glaswegians, roaming from one out-of-town store to another.[33]

From a contemporary perspective, the Charing Cross section of the M8 is an open wound, a scar, a site of trauma. Its pathology is always bodily, reconstructive surgery never far from the imagination. And aspects of those early plans propose violence on the urban body that would be inconceivable now. It is hard to summon up the urbanophobia that Bruce must have required to consider the erasure of the entire central city. At the same time, many of the impulses in the early plans are enduring and familiar: to mitigate the effects of car traffic and to render it safe, to make the city greener and more spacious, and to improve the setting of the city's historic buildings. Whatever its concrete results, SWK's expressway world was largely well-intentioned. They didn't, I think, understand what they were doing as urban violence at all; any violence was already embodied in the material form of the Victorian city, which their work hoped to mitigate.

The Plan Meets Reality

The Secretary of State for Scotland ceremonially opened the western and northern flanks of the Inner Ring Road on 4 February 1972. A short souvenir booklet reproduced delicate line drawings of the completed scheme, along with details of its structural complexities.[34] Inauguration was met by protests from a group of students from the nearby Glasgow School of Art. A banner, displayed prominently over the motorway for the benefit of the Secretary of State, read 'this scar will never heal'.[35] An editorial in the *Glasgow Herald* on the same day described the expressway's 'massacre' of the city. 'Not only has Charing Cross, one of the most attractive landmarks of the city been destroyed but the residents of Garnethill and the St George's Road area now find themselves living in a shambles more closely resembling a ghost town than a community.'[36] In the *Architects' Journal* Charles McKean and J.M. McKean wrote that Glasgow planning was 'characterised by a ruthlessness of purpose unmatched in the UK'. Charing Cross was 'now in such a serious state of shock that it could die'.[37] They thought the Esher report a stitch-up: 'fundamentally it could blend into official Glasgow policy without much curdling'.[38] The *Glasgow Herald*, up to that point generally supportive of the Corporation's enthusiasms, increasingly thought roads an existential question: 'We must think increasingly about ways of combatting the interminable intrusions of the motor car and consider what kind of cities we want to live in.'[39]

The city opened the west flank of the Inner Ring Road in 1972, but it significantly did not proceed to further stages. As McKean and McKean pointed out with alarm in 1971, the eastern flank might leave the city's cathedral literally cut off 'from the city to which it gave birth'. Worse, it might go right through Glasgow Green, 'annihilating Britain's oldest civic park'.[40] James McCafferty of SWK thought the plans essentially dead by 1973, a combination of weakening economic circumstances, waning political enthusiasm, and the consequences of a new Land Compensation Act, which awarded compensation rights to property owners should values fall due to road construction.[41] Any remaining energy for the project vanished in 1996 with the abolition of the Strathclyde regional authority.[42] 'Motorway', in Glasgow and elsewhere wrote McCafferty, 'became a pejorative word.'[43] Glasgow's expressway world was, it seemed, dead.

Carhenge

Or not quite: it's February 1995 and four old cars have just been driven into a southside construction site by anti-road activists from Brighton and Oxford, joining five cars already there, from where it is not quite clear.[44] Three-foot deep graves have been prepared for all of them in a rough semi-circle, and all nine have, with some effort, been manhandled into them, nose down.[45] When half-buried, they poke out of the ground like menhirs, creating a 'carhenge'. Painted in slogans – 'Pollution', 'No

M77', 'Rust in Peace' – they're set alight and a party ensues with wood fires, music and drinking. *The Herald* quoted one activist, Jake Hunter, on the purpose of the event: 'This is the first car on the M77. We're trying to make sure it's the last.'[46] It had the look and feel of a religious ritual, an improvised mashup of faux-pagan rites, or some version of them. Paul Routledge, an activist and academic who was one of the participants, described the scene: 'We revel in the burial of the car …. Once the cars are buried, petrol is poured over them and they are set alight. Voices of celebration fill the air, accented with Glaswegian, London English, Australian, Swedish, American. People dance in the fire-light, their shadows casting arabesques of celebration upon the road: we dance fire, we become fire, our movements are those of flames.'[47]

This time the target was not the M8. Carhenge targeted another leftover of the 1965 Highways plan, the extension to the M77 running from the southern end of the Kingston Bridge and then south-west towards the seaside town of Ayr. It took a long time to build. There was a controversy over the land, the proposed route taking it through Pollok Country Park on Glasgow's south side, gifted to the city in 1967 and the home of an important art museum, the Burrell Collection. Pollok was also historically poor, and had, ironically, the city's lowest levels of car ownership. A public enquiry took place in 1988, concluding the road should, on balance, be built; preliminary construction started in 1992, and it was opened in December 1996.[48]

The 1995 Carhenge action might have appeared spontaneous but it was calculated, 'a stunt to get media attention'.[49] For Alistair McIntosh, an activist aligned with the action, it had a straightforward message: 'you can have your great car economy' (he referred to Margaret Thatcher's phrase from 1989) 'but this is what the planet thinks of it'.[50] As an image, Carhenge closely resembled a celebrated piece of American public art, *Cadillac Ranch*, commissioned by Stanley Marsh in 1974 from the radical architects Ant Farm, and installed in Amarillo, Texas. (Marsh had a track record of eco-art commissions, responsible, among other things, for the American land artist Robert Smithson's last work, *Amarillo Ramp*.) *Cadillac Ranch* took the form of ten Cadillac cars, built from 1949 to 1963, buried nose first in a line outside Amarillo. It is now a popular attraction. If Carhenge referenced *Cadillac Ranch*, it also had ironic echoes of Stonehenge too, not only the neolithic moment, but also the Free Festival held by the stones until 1985, and so well within the memory – and possibly experience – of some of the M77 activists.

Paul Routledge's position was ambiguous, simultaneously academic chronicler and activist. As the former, his accounts of the action range from the anecdotal to the analytical; in the latter mode, he described the action as 'imagineering resistance', borrowing a corporate term more associated with the Disney corporation to describe the preoccupation of the activists with image; it was, he wrote, 'the most visually dramatic symbol of the campaign' and, later, evidence of a 'theatrical politics' of a new, and in his terms 'postmodern' kind.[51] 'Media images', he wrote, 'are increasingly seen by environmental groups as an essential aspect of organization, a tool for changing attitudes, raising public awareness and relaying the views of the movement to a wider public.'[52] Carhenge was just the most spectacular of a series of media events in the efficient campaign led by the messianic, 'Birdman of Pollok', Colin McLeod.

McLeod's activities included a week-long occupation of a tree on the M77 construction site (hence 'Birdman'). He staged a similar occupation of a contractor's crane, and the establishment of the so-called Pollok Free State, a putative independent republic complete with passports and a 'university'. McLeod also involved local schoolchildren in the M77 actions, specifically students at Bellarmine Secondary School whose building the project threatened; they staged a well-organized strike.[53] Modelled on earlier occupations such as Wanstonia along the site of the M11 extension in East London, the Pollok Free State and the M77 resistance in general was Scotland's first anti-motorway action, although not the last.[54] 'The more we get on TV the better', the activist Jake Hunter was quoted as saying, the media coverage a meaningful result in itself.[55]

Judged in purely transactional terms, the campaign had limits. 'On that particular metric', Routledge said later, 'the movement failed – it didn't stop the road.' But, he continued, success might be judged in other ways. In material terms '50-odd trees' were saved from felling by the campaign, 'an environmental plus'. The Pollok Free State created a network of relationships lasting decades that led to other activist projects, more or less related to the anti-road protest, relationships of quite a varied nature ('some people met and had kids together!'). 'I don't think movements begin or end or succeed or fail in neat ways', he argued; this was a process more than an event. In terms of the effect on roadbuilding policy, it had an impact, adding perhaps £1 million to the overall cost of the scheme and ensuring that future schemes priced in the disruption caused by anti-roads activism. It was 'direct action as a market force'.[56] The M77 activism he thought contributed directly to the end of the central government's roadbuilding programme, as well as the lively ecosystem of anti-roads actions, including Reclaim the Streets, which staged numerous media-friendly anti-road actions during the 1990s.[57] Its significance lies less in its concrete results than as a cultural phenomenon, and in the way it complicated the field in which it operated. Carhenge and the Pollok Free State became integral to the history of the M77, part of its identity; Glasgow's expressway world was, at least imaginatively, changed.

After Pollok

After Pollok and the M77, the comprehensive expressway plan may have been dead, but Glasgow, uniquely among UK cities, continued to build fragments. The M74 extension followed, completed in June 2011, cutting through the southern suburbs from Tradeston to Rutherglen to the Kingston Bridge and the now complete M77. Mostly elevated, the M74 was built while Boston and Madrid were burying their equivalents, and Seoul had demolished its own. A public enquiry failed to stop progress, in spite of lively opposition.[58] The expressway was facilitated, according to some, by a neo-emergency 'state of exceptionalism' produced in the run-up to Glasgow's hosting of the Commonwealth Games in 2014, a state that made strange things possible.[59] (The same condition produced the fortunately abortive plan to blow up five of the six towers of the Red Road public housing complex as part of the Games' opening ceremony.[60])

When the M74 extension did finally open, the Glasgow *Herald* mischievously reported tailbacks and chaos, as if it had created the set of problems it had come into being to solve.[61] *Prospect*, a local architecture journal, covered infrastructure projects sympathetically, but even it was sceptical, perhaps because of the trouble its photographer had getting past the site's security guards. It was all, it concluded, 'decidedly 1974'.[62] Indeed in many ways it was – the final, decades-delayed, form of the southern flank of the Inner Ring Road, ostensibly cancelled in the 1970s but here re-emergent, like a re-created dinosaur.

Glasgow hosted COP26, the annual United Nations meeting on climate change in late 2021, the event itself a spectacle of road chaos, security arrangements at the venue (the SECC, to the west of the city centre) producing two weeks of delays and diversions, at the same time as the start of repair works to the M8's Woodside Viaduct. Glasgow's expressway world lay temporarily in ruins. A good moment for a rethink, Peter Kelly, an urbanist, set up Replace the M8. It wasn't, he said, 'a charity, or organisation of any kind … just a group of people with occasional conversations', mainly on a Twitter account. There was a 'passion for tunnelling' among followers, he noted, but the discussions were varied.[63] It did not develop proposals itself, but the solutions it promoted with interest at various points on its channels ranged from structural caps across the chasm at Charing Cross, turning the road into a slower, speed-restricted boulevard, to complete deactivation with through traffic routed around the south on the M74 extension.[64]

There were public events, a panel discussion and a small related exhibition of architectural drawings.[65] Student architects proposed hedonistic uses of the undercroft: clubs, cafes and so on.[66] There was sympathetic media coverage: *Bella Caledonia* called M8 reform an 'act of restorative justice', associating it with its advocacy of Scottish independence.[67] Kelly was open-minded as to the exact solution to the M8 problem, but was keen on what he called a 'high-capacity boulevard' open to multiple modes – trams, were Glasgow ever to get them, cyclists, walkers, even some cars. The Kingston Bridge he wanted removed, to improve 'severance', seagoing traffic long having disappeared. The M74, now it existed, might be useful, taking traffic away from the central city.[68]

Among politicians intrigued by the M8 were Christy Mearns, a Green councillor and depute leader of the council; Paul Sweeney, a Labour member of the Scottish Parliament; and Angus Millar, an SNP councillor and convenor of the city's Transport committee, whose central city ward the M8 bisected. Millar spoke of feelings of 'malaise' and 'antipathy' towards it.[69] But it had not been possible until recently to think of alternative solutions. His interventions, summarized in a submission to the petition to the Scottish Parliament, were a mixture of potential short-term mitigation to deal with the M8's immediate effects, looking at the possibility of improving lighting and access, and longer term strategy towards some form of deactivation: tactics first and then strategy.[70] He led an unsuccessful Glasgow City Council bid for UK government Levelling Up funding in 2022 (a short-lived scheme to support regeneration projects in poorer areas of the UK), a project that would have provided funds for some mitigation of the M8's environmental impact. But Millar was upbeat: the idea of the cap was now in the public realm, along with a more strategic debate about 're-engineering' the M8, including imagining the possibility of deactivation, with, he hoped, the co-operation of the public body responsible for it, Transport Scotland.[71] But this initiative ran into familiar, endemic British local government problems – no money, and little ability to raise capital from taxation or other sources to pay for it, even in devolved, ostensibly public-spirited, Scotland.

I met Millar in early 2023 in City Chambers, Glasgow City Council's headquarters. It was instructive. The huge neo-Renaissance palace is the material representation of a nineteenth-century global city at the height of its powers, and seemingly more or less empty. It seemed half-empty, another example perhaps of the 'shipwreck' city, as well as a council struggling with a £770 million equal pay claim.[72] Millar and other advocates for change at the council were reduced to symbolic tinkering, such as reducing speed limits along the central sections of the M8 to 30 mph (50 km/h), if anything, given the traffic flows, an increase in speed.[73] Good for presenting an image of the city as a 'progressive environmental beacon' post-COP26 (as Dominic Hinde, an environmental journalist has put it), not so good in terms of effecting material change.[74]

Walking Glasgow's Expressways

It is easy to feel despondent about the state of contemporary Glasgow, especially when contrasted with its ambitious 1960s self. So I decide to go for a walk. A tour of Glasgow's Inner Ring Road, or what survives of it, is an impromptu homage to Iain Sinclair's *London Orbital*, although his journey took months and mine can be done in a day.[75] It starts unexpectedly well, with bright May sunshine on arrival at Queen Street, and it is a pleasure to pick the route north across the centre of the city – first of all, across the wreckage of Sauchiehall Street, a place in transition

M74 at Tradeston, Glasgow. *Photograph by Richard J. Williams*

from an old-style retail economy to something new, then edging north past Cowcaddens subway station and the slabs and slim towers of the 1960s Dundasvale Estate, before reaching the Woodside Viaduct of the M8 at Townhead. It is only ten minutes on foot from Queen Street, but it already seems to represent some kind of edge, for the city proper stops here, and beyond, underneath the viaduct, the city falls away into something much lower in density, not conventionally urban, and visibly poorer. I think of Ian Spring's book *Phantom Village*, and the way he described the Glasgow and its expressways; how thoroughly he thought their separation of the centre of the city from everything else.[76] The viaduct itself is a mess of hoardings and barriers while Transport Scotland carry out structural repairs. I head west after that towards the junction with the Great Western Road, holding the line of the expressway as closely as possible, but it's not an easy task, zigzagging this way and that. The expressway nevertheless remains constantly in sight and in earshot.

There's a grubby, but quite elegant pedestrian bridge in concrete curving across the M8 where it makes its right-angle turn south. I pause for a moment and realize I'm looking at the same view represented in the spidery pencil drawing on the cover of the 1972 souvenir booklet from the opening.[77] The real-life view is tougher than the drawing, of course, but it is recognizably the same place, and in its way, impressive

– multi-layered, vast in scale, dynamic, a proper piece of modern city. I turn due south, passing The Locale, a pub occupying one of the remaining Victorian fragments on the right, a Tesco Metro and a Bank of India before descending below the level of the road to the M8's epic undercroft. Here, the expressway ascends to become the Kingston Bridge, while simultaneously the land slopes down towards the river, and in between a colossal space opens up, twenty metres at its maximum height. An architect might build something in these spaces, but this one is too big. There are some electric vehicle (EV) charging points and a few lonely parking spaces, neither much used. The traffic thumps overhead, the trucks thudding over the expansion joints. It's huge, noisy and cold despite the warmth of the early summer sun – not a place to linger.

At the Clyde, I dodge left briefly along Anderston Quay to pick up the low-level Commerce Street bridge to cross the river, turning right again on the south side to find the confluence of the M8 and the M74. One of the city's biggest single engineering structures, it's hard to comprehend as a single entity; it's more like a landscape than a building. It abuts the Grade B-listed Co-operative Wholesale Society building, a rambling Victorian behemoth designed by Bruce and Hay and opened in 1897; the CWS have themselves long gone. I skirt its edge, and turn around the back to the east, following the path of the M74 as closely as possible, but it's tricky, forensic work to get through the industrial estates of Tradeston.

There's plenty to look at, however. Huge sections of the M74 are elevated, and as the engineer enthusiasts at the Scottish Roads Archive are keen to point out, the detailing is good, and it still looks tidy and fresh. For them it is the best of Glasgow's expressways, an image of a future that never quite arrived.[78] The western section near Tradeston to Rutherglen is perhaps the most accessible, a vast, mostly elevated structure threaded through and over a busy industrial landscape. It disappears every so often and then suddenly reappears, abruptly closing down a view or leaping heroically across a railway line; rendered largely in steel and painted a uniform French blue, it's undoubtedly sculptural. Reyner Banham described the 405/10 junction in Los Angeles as a work of art, as we saw in chapter 3. This is too, in its own way, but it's a darker, heavier structure than Marilyn Jorgenson Reece's lacy intersection, instead rather more like a ship at the end of a port city's street. A dark, French blue, it has a ship's colouring. Perhaps the M74's designers thought of it like that, referencing a memory of a once common urban sight.

I feel my way through the suburbs of Polmadie and Govanhill, pausing at the Crown Street retail park, an outcrop of suburban normality. Then there's an awkward section around the Southern Necropolis, where an industrial estate blocks off the view of the expressway for a few hundred metres, before another zigzag, the Alstom train works, the thirties moderne Shawfield greyhound stadium, and some carceral-looking pubs. Then finally I reach Rutherglen and an outcrop of Victorian townscape. After the expressway world it seems upright, dense and legible. I find the M74 again here as it crosses the rail junction, a moment of real complexity as two rail lines, a station and an expressway viaduct join up. I take a train here, back to Queen Street and look at my phone to see how far I have come. Ten miles, with all the zigzags. With its scale and drama, in another time – perhaps a century into the future when the city has abandoned its cars – this might be, one of Scotland's great urban walks, a future High Line.

Walking Glasgow's expressways is a reminder on the one hand of things *not* happening: no expressway teardowns here, or tunnels, or parks built over the top, or any of the fashionable interventions of the kind described by the Congress for the New Urbanism in its *Freeways Without Futures*.[79] This is not Hamburg, or Utrecht, let alone Seoul or Madrid. On the other hand, to walk Glasgow's expressways is to be reminded of what precisely *is* there. This is a well-used landscape, much more so than might initially appear. As it passes through the industrial zone around Tradeston, you realize how densely used it is, how many businesses there are, how much this is not nowhere, but (as the anthropologist Marc Augé put it) anthropological place.[80] Around Tradeston, it frames and supports a lot of industry, catering and packaging mostly, low tech but in its way, important. Economically speaking, it could be a more productive landscape, no doubt, populated by software engineers and fund managers, in shinier buildings. But cities need cardboard boxes and food too, and these things have to go somewhere.

The M74 has big things too, such as the Alstom works servicing the West Coast Main Line's Pendolino trains. There are large areas of formal landscaping, recognized at the time of their production for their quality and worth revisiting. The junction of the M8 and M74 constitutes a species of park, and a good one, rather in the style of central Brasília, although far from accessible.[81] There are occupations and appropriations of various kinds. There's good – sometimes very good – street art on every available flat surface, with a particularly good and well-used section at the start of the M74. There was an ambitious occupation of land under the southern part of the M8 for the Kingston Skatepark, a more or less self-policed, crowdfunded, self-built park, with its own refuse collection.[82]

All along Glasgow's expressways the vegetation is planting, sometimes frustrating as it prevents access to the road, or a sight of it. But it constitutes a neo-wilderness, rougher and scarcely inhabited by humans, but alive. A sign at Townhead points out the wildlife you can routinely see in this most urban of locations: I have heard goldcrests here. Red kites, once again ubiquitous along the expressways of southern England, cannot be far behind. This landscape is not necessarily a very productive one, or especially cared for, but it's a space where things can happen. Why can cities not also be this some of the time? Does everything have to be resolved, tidied up, made polite? What if there is a value in the expressway world being precisely as it is, somewhat neglected, off the grid, a kind of wilderness?

The Expressway World is Dead – Long Live the Expressway World

In William Morris's visionary 1890 novel *News From Nowhere*, the narrator, a young man called William Guest, falls asleep in a London meeting of the Socialist League to wake up in an uncanny new world, a London of the future in which the Thames runs crystal clear and the nineteenth-century industrial city has apparently dissolved, to be replaced by a bucolic settlement in which humans exist in perfect balance with nature, all blossom and unalienated labour.[83] A deracinated, post-capital world, it is a picture of a sublime order; the odd fragment of the industrial world remains, but no longer carries any emotion; the modern world has gone, but with no regret or mourning of any kind. When it comes to imagining the post-automobile world, Morris's 1890 vision is familiar: many of the most celebrated versions of this world are calculated erasures of the modern, worlds in which industry has been replaced by nature, traffic roar with birdsong.

We have seen several of those cases here in this book, Seoul's Cheonggyecheon and Madrid Rio, as well as Boston's Rosa Fitzgerald Kennedy Greenway. There are many other examples not covered here, such as the city of Utrecht in the Netherlands, which has replaced its central expressway with a restored canal, or Hamburg in Germany, where an expressway has become a park. What could be more agreeable? In the official representations of these places, the sun shines, children play, cyclists cycle: they are pictures of a relaxed but disciplined urban order, free of dirt, or the poor. And in real life, the most successful of these reconfigured expressways teem with visitors, and bird and plant life, fine advertisements for themselves. They are also rare cases, and as we have seen in the previous chapters, have sometimes been the result of a totalizing politics, or the application of enormous amounts of money, or both; one megaproject replaces another.

The book has also shown different modes of accommodation with the expressway world. Often at the back of my mind was a quirky 2016 book by the cultural theorist Donna Haraway, *Staying with the Trouble*, in which she argues for a process-oriented approach to climate change, one that accommodates human and non-human actors, and most importantly complexity and difference. 'I am not interested in reconciliation or restoration', she writes, 'but I am deeply committed to the more modest possibilities of partial recuperation and getting on together. Call that staying with the trouble.'[84] 'Staying with the trouble' in terms of the expressway world might mean allowing quite different possibilities to co-exist and evolve (including Haraway's beloved non-human actors). It might include the hedonistic weekend occupation of the expressway surface in São Paulo, or the pragmatic occupation of the undercroft and the development of place in London, or the decades-long meditation on the expressway as culture in Los Angeles.

In Glasgow, where we began and ended, 'staying with the trouble' might help get beyond political and financial stasis. There can be no Big Dig if its cost is a third of the Scottish Government's annual budget. But other, smaller, process-oriented things might be possible, recognizing the fact that the built environment is produced as much by the care of the people who inhabit it as much as by its original designers (we might even, as we saw in the introduction, sometimes speak of 'love' for certain forms of infrastructure).[85]

It might seem unlikely in the extreme to think of Glasgow's motorways in this way, but in their current form, there are plenty of examples of care in action. A skatepark on the south side of the river may not have survived but it was an example of a community building itself. (The idea in fact returned in an expanded and official form in plans announced at the end of 2024 for a new skatepark at Tradeston under the M74.[86]) The landscape around the expressway is often a surprising wilderness, a space in which animal and plant life often flourish in the absence of human attention. Forms of activism, from the Pollok Free State onwards, even when they are ostensibly opposed to the expressway world, form in relation to it. Replace the M8 has not done anything concrete about the expressway, but it has, however incrementally, also changed the conversation around it. We have a set of ways of thinking about the future as a result.

From another, rather different perspective, the work of the Scottish Roads Archive shows how the discourse around the expressway might become more open-minded.[87] Built up by two Transport Scotland engineers, it has made neglected and often disparaged histories visible. While writing from a position of advocacy of Glasgow's expressway world, they have also been instrumental in reminding listeners and readers how and why it was built in the first place, and its complexities; they have also been critical in places, as well as open-minded to how the system has evolved. They have made the system visible as place. As have the engineers involved in the reconstruction of the Woodside viaduct, a painstaking and fine-grained process that will take almost as long (five years) as the construction of the expressway in the first place. Some have regretted the reconstruction work, for it was one of the pretexts to consider the removal of the M8. But there is no reason in principle not to think of it as a form of care, certainly at the delivery level with its innumerable small-scale decisions and improvisations, made to keep the road going.

In the medium term, the configuration of traffic will likely change too. The care that keeps the expressway going may enable different forms of traffic in half a century's time. Its traffic will certainly be more electrified, and more autonomous. It may lessen, as it did once, dramatically, during the Covid pandemic. The M8 may follow the example of São Paulo's Minhocão and stop the traffic altogether from time to time. There is no reason to suppose that what constitutes traffic now at the time of writing will still represent the traffic of 2074. There is also no reason to suppose that there cannot be improvements to the undercrofts of elevated expressways, that they cannot have better lighting and uses found for vacant bays. The Westway in London has, over a period of half a century, almost entirely filled up, as we saw in chapter 4. The undercroft of the Mancunian Way, a similar structure in central Manchester, supported a successful food village in shipping containers for years. Both have become authentic parts of their respective cities.

The expressway world might gradually come to resemble the nineteenth-century railway world, whose monuments have been so frequently restored, in the process exceeding anything its builders might have imagined. Railway infrastructure, an object of abject horror in the nineteenth century, attracts different feelings now. As Sharon Zukin wrote in her 1982 book about New York's nineteenth-century industrial buildings, they now carry connotations of the authentic and the humane, regardless of the way that they were originally produced and understood.[88] Seoullo 7017, discussed in chapter 7, is perhaps a model, however flawed.

Imagine then, a different expressway world. It's not the expressway world with which we started, the visceral horror of the Cross-Bronx. Neither is it the faux nature of the Cheonggyecheon, impressive though it is, nor Madrid's equivalent – these megaprojects are possible but rare, dependent on unusual political will. Instead, the expressway world might be thought of less as a problem than a process. It might have a general direction of travel in line with municipal and national environmental policies, away from the internal combustion engine, and the assumption of universal access to the private car. And it might be open and capacious enough to deal with the inevitable contradictions as it evolves. For Andrew Hoolachan, an academic and activist friendly to Replace the M8, this is the best imaginable future of the M8. It might be a boulevard, better able to accommodate the needs of pedestrians and non-motorized traffic, as well as a public transport corridor, perhaps not unlike the 'post-car system' envisaged by the sociologist John Urry in 2007.[89] It would certainly have fewer cars, as per that system, but it might not abolish them altogether, and whatever its final form, it would be an integrated part of the central city rather than – as in the 1965 Highways Plan – a means of emptying it out.[90] It might take thirty years to achieve, with the assistance of government at all levels. It wouldn't, significantly, be an erasure of the past but a form of accommodation with it. There ought to be some kind of acknowledgement of the boldness of the original 1965 vision, which was, for better or worse, transformative. There is a Tenement Museum in the city, Hoolachan has argued, so why not a Museum of Modernism, housed perhaps in a restored and preserved fragment of the M8?[91]

None of this alternative expressway world exactly exists, although there are elements of it in all or some of the projects discussed in the previous pages. Even in Seoul, the most totalizing of our expressway stories, the eastern fringes of the Cheonggyecheon hold radically different things simultaneously in play. It is both wild and intensely urban; distinct worlds surprisingly co-exist. The best of this book's examples is perhaps the Westway, which has, incrementally over decades, become a place, so much so that at ground level the density of human activity has made the road in some ways invisible. It has not only become a place, but a successful one that has attracted new uses even after half a century of existence.[92] The Westway is both/and, not either/or. Given the richness of its history in popular culture, it has become the object of considerable, if unexpected, affection. It has become an integral part of the city it initially seemed to erase, even adding to its possibilities. If the expressway world can evolve in this way, if it can become the city rather than threaten it, then it has some kind of future. The expressway world is dead – long live the expressway world.

Notes

Preface

1 M. Berman, *All That Is Solid Melts Into Air* (London: Verso, 1983).
2 M. Kimble, *City Limits: Infrastructure, Inequality and the Future of America's Highways* (New York: Crown, 2024), p. 277.

Chapter 1: The Expressway World Revisited

1 M. Berman, *All That Is Solid Melts Into Air* (London: Verso, 1983), p. 291.
2 *The New York Times*, 'Moses Belabors Critics on Roads' (9 May 1964), p. 29.
3 The original quotation is from chapter 1 of *The Communist Manifesto*, originally published in 1848. See K. Marx and F. Engels, *The Communist Manifesto* with an Introduction and Notes by A.J.P. Taylor (Harmondsworth: Penguin, 1985), p. 83. 'All that is solid melts into air, all that is holy is profaned, and man is at last compelled to face with sober senses, his real conditions of life and his relations with his kind.'
4 'Italy Bridge Collapse: Genoa Death Toll Rises to 43', *BBC News* (19 August 2018), https://www.bbc.co.uk/news/world-europe-45241842.
5 'Egypt is Busily Building Expressways', *The Economist* (8 October 2020), https://www.economist.com/middle-east-and-africa/2020/10/08/egypt-is-busily-building-expressways.
6 Originally published as L. Mumford, 'The Highway and the City', *Architectural Record*, 123 (April 1958). Quoted here from L. Mumford, *The Highway and the City* (New York: Harcourt, Brace and World, 1963), p. 247.
7 M. Dnes, *The Rise and Fall of London's Ringways 1943–1973* (Abingdon: Routledge, 2020), p. 1.
8 P. Hall, *Great Planning Disasters* (Harmondsworth: Weidenfeld and Nicolson, 1980), pp. 56–86.
9 Dnes, *Rise and Fall*, p. 1.
10 D. Knowles, *Carmageddon: How Cars Make Life Worse and What to Do About It* (New York: Abrams, 2023).
11 M. Kimble, *City Limits: Infrastructure, Inequality and the Future of America's Highways* (New York: Crown, 2024). See also E. Avila, *The Folklore of the Freeway: Race and Revolt in the Modernist City* (Minneapolis, MN: University of Minnesota Press, 2014).
12 P. Hall, *Cities of Tomorrow* (Oxford: Blackwell, 1996), p. 281.
13 Ibid., p. 280.
14 On the history of the Interstate system, see T. Lewis, *Divided Highways: Building the Interstate Highways, Transforming American Life* (Ithaca, NY: Cornell University Press, 2013).

15 See C. Buchanan, *Traffic in Towns* (London: HMSO, 1963), pp. 253–4. See also J. Drake, H.L. Yeadon and D.I. Evans, *Motorways* (London: Faber and Faber, 1969).
16 See R. Banham, *Theory and Design in the First Machine Age* (London: Architectural Press, 1960), pp. 99–138.
17 Translated into English as Le Corbusier, *The City of To-morrow and its Planning* (New York: Payson and Clarke, 1929), pp. 163–95.
18 See account in Le Corbusier, *The City of To-morrow* (Cambridge, MA: MIT Press, 1972).
19 See A. Amado, *Voiture Minimum: Le Corbusier and the Automobile* (Cambridge, MA: MIT Press, 2011).
20 See C.E. Crawford, *Spatial Revolution: Architecture and Planning in the Early Soviet Union* (Ithaca, NY: Cornell University Press, 2022), pp. 135–6, 145–6.
21 F.L. Wright, *The Disappearing City* (New York: William Farquhar Payson, 1932).
22 N. Bel Geddes, *Magic Motorways* (New York: Random House, 1940), cover.
23 Geddes, *Magic Motorways*, p. 239.
24 For a recent critical account of *Futurama*, see Kimble, *City Limits*, pp. 21–4.
25 On the history of the Interstate system, see Lewis, *Divided Highways*.
26 R.A. Caro, *The Power Broker* (London: The Bodley Head, 1974).
27 In W. Holford, 'Brasília, A New Capital City for Brazil', *Architectural Review*, 122 (1957), p. 402. See R.J. Williams, *Brazil: Modern Architectures in History* (London: Reaktion Books, 2009), pp. 95–132.
28 A. and P. Smithson, *Ordinariness and Light* (London: Faber, 1970), p. 148.
29 'Cumbernauld Central Area', *Architectural Design* (May 1963), p. 212.
30 Buchanan, *Traffic in Towns*, p. 11.
31 Reported in Dnes, *Rise and Fall*, p. 24.
32 Buchanan, *Traffic in Towns*, p. 11.
33 Ibid., p. 178. The full account of the Fitzrovia plan can be found on pp. 155–200.
34 Ibid., pp. 29, 56.
35 B. Larkin, 'The Poetics and Politics of Infrastructure', *Annual Review of Anthropology*, 42 (2013), p. 333. On infrastructure and power, see also *Extrastatecraft: The Power of Infrastructure Space* (London: Verso Books, 2014).
36 J. Jacobs, *The Death and Life of Great American Cities* (New York: Random House, 1961).
37 See further discussion in chapter 8, especially Paul Routledge's assessment of the success of anti-roads activism.
38 J.B. Jackson, 'The Social Landscape', in E.H. Zube (ed.) *Landscapes: Selected Writings of J.B. Jackson* (Amherst, MA: University of Massachusetts Press, 1970), pp. 146–52.
39 An indicative collection: C. Mauch and T. Zeller (eds) *The World Beyond the Windshield: Roads and Landscapes in the United States and Europe* (Athens, OH: Ohio University Press, 2008).
40 P. Merriman, *Driving Spaces: A Cultural-Historical Geography of England's M1 Motorway* (Oxford: Blackwell, 2007).
41 Avila, *The Folklore of the Freeway*, p. 177.
42 J. Moran, *On Roads: A Hidden History* (London: Profile Books, 2009).
43 H. Frichot, A. Carbonell, H. Frykholm and S. Karami, *Infrastructural Love: Caring for Our Architectural Support Systems* (Basel: Birkhäuser, 2022).
44 K. Shonfield, *Walls Have Feelings: Architecture, Film and the City* (London: Routledge, 2000), p. 154.

45 Ibid., p. 165.
46 See also P. Wollen and J. Kerr (eds) *Autopia: Cars and Culture* (London: Reaktion, 2002).
47 Shonfield, *Walls Have Feelings*, p. 115.
48 Ibid.
49 M. Augé, *Non-Places: An Introduction to Supermodernity* (London: Verso, 1995), pp. 1–2.
50 B. Van Der Haak and R Koolhaas (dirs.), *Lagos/Koolhaas* (Pieter van Huystee Films/ VPRO, 2002).
51 K. Bromwich, 'Painting the Memories Evoked by Motorways', *The Guardian* (22 May 2021), https://www.theguardian.com/artanddesign/gallery/2021/may/22/painting-the-memories-evoked-by-motorways-in-pictures.
52 J. Orpin, Conversation with the author, Manchester (July 2023).
53 B. Latour, *Down to Earth* (Cambridge: Polity, 2017), p. 19. The original French title of the book makes more of this, *Où Atterir?*, literally 'where to land?'.
54 For an overview of the implications of SB743, see https://www.sb743.org/.
55 J. Urry, *Mobilities* (Cambridge: Polity, 2007), pp. 116–17.
56 Ibid., p. 207.
57 R. Adam, 'The Greenest Building is the One That Already Exists', *Architects' Journal* (24 September 2019).
58 SAH2024 Albuquerque (17–21 April 2024), https://www.sah.org/conferences.
59 B. Calder, *Architecture from Prehistory to Climate Emergency* (London: Penguin, 2021), p. 163.
60 Ibid., p. 173. See also D. Barber, *Modern Architecture and Climate: Design Before Air Conditioning* (Princeton, NJ: Princeton University Press, 2020), p. 274.
61 Banham, *Theory and Design in the First Machine Age*.
62 H. Foster, 'Modernism in a Non-Melancholic Key', *October*, 186 (2023), pp. 197–204.
63 Ibid., p. 204.
64 Ibid.
65 'A Giant Falls', *The Economist* (4 June 2009), https://www.economist.com/briefing/2009/06/04/a-giant-falls; T. Braithwaitre and J. Reed, 'Chrysler Files for Chapter 11 Bankruptcy', *Financial Times* (3 April 2009), https://www.ft.com/content/76ccd92c-3588-11de-a997-00144feabdc0.
66 'China's BYD Overtakes Tesla's Electric Car Sales in Last Quarter of 2023', *BBC News* (2 January 2024), https://www.bbc.co.uk/news/business-67860232.
67 For example, 'The Car Industry Faces a Short-Term Crisis and Long-Term Decline', *The Economist* (25 April 2020).
68 F. Pearce, 'The End of the Road for Motormania', *New Scientist* (10 August 2011), https://institutions.newscientist.com/article/mg21128255-600-the-end-of-the-road-for-motormania/.
69 M. Crawford, *Why We Drive: On Freedom, Risk and Taking Back Control* (London: Bodley Head, 2020).
70 Among the most comprehensive historical accounts of the Big Dig is a podcast: WGBH, 'The Big Dig' (27 September–15 November 2023), https://www.wgbh.org/podcasts/the-big-dig.
71 J. Jacobs, *The Death and Life of Great American Cities* (London: Jonathan Cape, 1962), pp. 18–19.
72 Massachusetts Department of Transportation, 'Big Dig: Project Background', https://www.mass.gov/info-details/the-big-dig-project-background.

NOTES TO PP. 17–27

73 Ibid.
74 A. Goodnough, 'Settlement for Company Charged in Big Dig Death', *The New York Times* (17 December 2008), https://www.nytimes.com/2008/12/18/us/18dig.html?smid=url-share.
75 A. Flint, 'Ten Years Later Did the Big Dig Deliver?', *Boston Globe* (29 December 2015), https://www.bostonglobe.com/magazine/2015/12/29/years-later-did-big-dig-deliver/tSb8PIMS4QJUETsMpA7SpI/story.html?p1=BGSearch_Advanced_Results.
76 https://www.rosekennedygreenway.org/.
77 https://www.rosekennedygreenway.org/history/.
78 Zukin wouldn't much care for this brutal example of the expressway world – but by comparison with the Greenway, it certainly has 'authenticity'. See S. Zukin, *Naked City: The Death and Life of Authentic Urban Places* (New York: Oxford University Press, 2010).
79 Congress for the New Urbanism, *Freeways Without Futures* (Washington, DC: Congress for the New Urbanism, 2023). Available for download at www.cnu.org.
80 Congress for the New Urbanism, 'Completed Highways to Boulevards Projects', https://www.cnu.org/our-projects/highways-boulevards/completed-h2b-projects.
81 Latour, *Down to Earth*, p. 19.
82 Knowles, *Carmageddon*, pp. 215–26.
83 For an overview, see N. Whittle, *The 15 Minute City: Global Change Through Local Living* (Edinburgh: Luath Press, 2021).
84 Knowles, *Carmageddon*.

Chapter 2: New York: The Expressway in Ruins

1 'Truck and Car Fall as West Side Highway Collapses', *The New York Times* (16 December 1973), p. 76.
2 New York State Department of Transportation, *West Side Highway Project Report* (New York: New York State Department of Transportation, 1974), pp. 2–5.
3 Ibid.
4 'Indefinite Closing Is Set for West Side Highway: Northbound Road Closed', *The New York Times* (17 December 1973), p. 41.
5 A. Finstein, *Lofty Visions: The Architectural Intentions and Contrary Realities of Elevated Urban Highways in America, 1900–1959* (PhD thesis, University of Virginia, 2009), p. 28.
6 S. Giedion, *Space, Time and Architecture* (Cambridge, MA: Harvard University Press, 1941), pp. 554–5.
7 P. Hall, *Cities of Tomorrow* (Oxford: Blackwell, 1996), p. 276.
8 See historical overview in R.A. Mohl, 'Stop the Road: Freeway Revolts in American Cities', *Journal of Urban History*, 30, 5 (2004), pp. 674–706.
9 Moses is the subject of a legendary biography, and also a play. R. Caro, *Robert Moses: The Power Broker* (London: Bodley Head, 2015); D. Hare, *Straight Line Crazy* (London: Faber and Faber, 2022).
10 'Express Road Unit Opened by Miller', *The New York Times* (14 November 1930), p. 3.
11 Finstein, *Lofty Visions*, p. 217.
12 'Express Road Unit Opened by Miller', *The New York Times*.
13 Ibid.

14 Ibid.
15 'Elevated Speedway is Approved in Full', *The New York Times* (19 October 1928), pp. 1, 14.
16 Ibid.
17 Finstein, *Lofty Visions*, p. 238.
18 Ibid.
19 Ibid.
20 Ibid., p. 311.
21 A. Feininger, *West Side Highway, New York*, gelatin silver print (1940), https://whitney.org/collection/works/13750. There are rather more dilapidated images of it in D. Lyon, *The Destruction of Lower Manhattan* (New York: Aperture, 2020), originally published in 1969. The Miller Highway is a frequent image in the later, expanded edition of 2020.
22 'Asks New City Parks to Cost $20,000,000', *The New York Times* (26 February 1930), p. 1.
23 'La Guardia Opens Riverside Project', *The New York Times* (13 October 1937), p. 2.
24 Quoted in Caro, *Robert Moses*, p. 553.
25 Ibid., p. 556.
26 Ibid., pp. 555–6.
27 46th Street at West Side Highway, postcard postmarked 1942. Seymour B. Durst Old York Library Collection, Box no. 18, Item no. 269.
28 Caro, *Robert Moses*, p. 556.
29 '17 Deaths on Sharp Turn in City', *The New York Times* (23 November 1941), p. XX5.
30 Finstein, *Lofty Visions*, p. 28.
31 New York State Department of Transportation, *West Side Highway Project Report*, pp. 1-1, 2-1–2-5.
32 R. Moses, *West Side Fiasco: A Practical Proposal for the restoration of the West Side Highway and parkway to public use* (self-published, 25 November 1974), n.p.
33 Infrastructure 'becomes visible on breakdown' as Susan Star puts it. S.L. Star, 'The Ethnography of Infrastructure', *American Behavioral Scientist*, 43, 3 (1999), p. 382.
34 'Ford to City: Drop Dead', *New York Daily News* (30 October 1975), p. 1.
35 Lyon, *The Destruction of Lower Manhattan*.
36 R.A.M. Stern, D. Fishman and T. Mellins, *New York 1960: Architecture and Urbanism Between the Second World War and the Bicentennial* (New York: Monacelli Press, 1995), p. 112.
37 It could also be, intermittently, a space for homeless encampments, the last disappearing in 1989. 'Death of an Old Highway, a Home for the Homeless: Death of Road Dooms Huts of Homeless', *The New York Times* (25 May 1989), p. 2.
38 'Boy on West Side Highway Dies in Fall Through Hole', *The New York Times* (17 August 1974), p. 27.
39 F. Clines, 'About New York: The View from the West Side Highway', *The New York Times* (29 October 1977), p. 50.
40 Ibid.
41 S. Corcoran, 'From Expressway to Contemplative Oasis: The Elevated West Side Highway', Museum of the City of New York (12 November 2015), https://www.mcny.org/story/expressway-contemplative-oasis-elevated-west-side-highway.
42 R.J. Williams, *Why Cities Look the Way They Do* (Cambridge: Polity, 2019), pp. 85–7.
43 A. Shkuda, *The Lofts of SoHo* (Chicago, IL: University of Chicago Press, 2016), pp. 82, 85.
44 M. Berman, *All That Is Solid Melts Into Air* (London: Verso, 1983), pp. 290–311.

NOTES TO PP. 33–36

45 Regional Planning Association's *Regional Plan of New York and its Environs* (New York: Regional Planning Association, 1929). The RPA published a second volume on urban design in 1931. https://rpa.org/work/reports/regional-plan-of-new-york-and-its-environs.
46 See timeline in Triborough Bridge and Tunnel Authority, *Lower Manhattan Elevated Expressway* (New York: Triborough Bridge and Tunnel Authority, 1965), p. 3.
47 P. Blake, 'About Mayor Lindsay, Jane Jacobs and Peter Bogardus', *New York Magazine* (6 May 1968), p. 44.
48 'Living Big in a Loft', *Life* (27 March 1970), pp. 61–5. The classic account of the phenomenon is S. Zukin, *Loft Living: Culture and Capital in Urban Change* (Baltimore, MD: Johns Hopkins University Press, 1982), pp. 176–90. J. Schlesinger (dir. 1969), *Midnight Cowboy*, has a scene in a loft, featuring some of Andy Warhol's entourage.
49 Zukin, *Loft Living*. Zukin, correspondence with the author (August 2024).
50 On the definition of 'gray zone', see Shkuda, *The Lofts of SoHo*, p. 75.
51 Ibid., p. 71.
52 Triborough Bridge and Tunnel Authority, *Lower Manhattan Elevated Expressway*, pp. 1–2.
53 Ibid., pp. 10–11.
54 Avila, *The Folklore of the Freeway*, pp. 61–2.
55 Gerard L.A. Mountain, 'The City', *Catholic Worker*, XXIX, 7 (1963), pp. 1, 4.
56 L. Kent, 'Persecution of the City Performed by its Inmates', *Village Voice* (18 April 1968), p. 3.
57 'Marchers Protest Crosstown Road', *The New York Times* (10 August 1962), p. 8.
58 Eleanor Roosevelt, 'My Day, June 29, 1962', *The Eleanor Roosevelt Papers Digital Edition* (2017), https://www2.gwu.edu/~erpapers/myday/displaydocedits.cfm?_y=1962&_f=md005127.
59 'Mrs Roosevelt Opposes Building of LOMEX', *New York World-Telegram and Sun* (18 June 1962).
60 'New Delay Looms for Expressway', *The New York Times* (17 August 1962), p. 12.
61 Kent, 'Persecution of the City', p. 3. See also J. Jacobs, unpublished typescript of events (30 April 1968), Jane Jacobs papers, Boston College, MS1995.029, Box 26.
62 S. Gervis, 'Political Power Kills Broome St. Expressway', *Village Voice* (13 December 1962), p. 8.
63 G. Glueck, 'Artists Assail Downtown Expressway', *The New York Times* (20 June 1969), p. 37.
64 Zukin, correspondence with the author.
65 For detail, see Glueck, 'Artists Assail Downtown Expressway', and Shkuda, *The Lofts of SoHo*, pp. 89–90.
66 Shkuda, *The Lofts of SoHo*, p. 90. Zukin, correspondence with the author.
67 F. Ferretti, 'SoHo Grows Up and Grows Rich and Chic', *The New York Times* (12 October 1975), p. 184.
68 'Mayor Drops Plans for Express Roads Across 2 Boroughs', *The New York Times* (17 July 1969), p. 1.
69 'Lower Manhattan Road Killed Under State Plan', *The New York Times* (25 March 1971), p. 78.
70 Quoted in Berman, *All That Is Solid*, pp. 293–4.
71 J. Jacobs, *The Death and Life of Great American Cities* (New York: Random House, 1961), especially pp. 60–5.

72 Berman, *All That Is Solid*, pp. 312–28.
73 Avila, *The Folklore of the Freeway*, p. 99.
74 Shkuda, *The Lofts of SoHo*.
75 Ibid., pp. 89–90.
76 American Federation of the Arts, *The Evolving City* (New York: Whitney Library of Design, 1974), p. 7. 'The discreet charm of utopia: in the future, multi-layered cities – new forms for the evolving city; Architect: Paul Rudolph', *Domus*, 558 (1976), pp. 19–23.
77 Ibid.
78 R. Banham, *Megastructure: Urban Futures of the Recent Past* (London: Thames and Hudson, 1976), p. 13. Banham wrote of the LOMEX project in a note 'a mainstream megastructure if ever there was one, with its conventional A frame or Terresenhäuser section of two sloping stacks of apartments back-to-back over each carriageway of a giant transportation artery'.
79 Ibid., pp. 13–14.
80 E. Rawlings and J. Walrod, *Paul Rudolph Lower Manhattan Expressway* (New York: Cooper Union, 2010), appendix, n.p.
81 Ibid.
82 'Thrillingly futuristic', wrote Robert Stern. Stern et al., *New York 1960*, p. 259.
83 Berman, *All That Is Solid*, p. 329.
84 Stephanie Jervis, quoted in Stern et al., *New York 1960*, pp. 259–60.
85 The driver as automaton, willingly submitting to the machine remained a fantasy in Banham. See R. Banham, *Los Angeles: The Architecture of Four Ecologies* (Harmondsworth: Penguin, 1971), pp. 216–17.
86 Goldberger quoted in Stern et al., *New York 1960*, p. 116.
87 New York State Department of Transportation, *West Side Highway Project Design Report* (New York: New York State Department of Transportation, 1974), pp. 0–1, 8–13.
88 New York State Department of Transportation, *West Side Highway Project Report*. See also the similar, but expanded *West Side Highway Project Design Report* (1974).
89 'Park Extension Sought by Trump', *The New York Times* (9 May 1976), p. 43.
90 A. Lubasch, 'U.S. Judge Blocks Westway Landfill as Threat to Fish', *The New York Times* (1 April 1982), p. 1.
91 Moses, *West Side Fiasco*, n.p.
92 Ibid. See also W. Buzbee, *Fighting Westway* (Ithaca, NY: Cornell University Press, 2014), pp. 19–20.
93 Buzbee, *Fighting Westway*, pp. 192–214.
94 Vollmer Associates, *West Side Highway Replacement Study*, Draft Final Report Vol. 1, submitted to New York State Department of Transport, New York City Department of Transport, New York City Department of City Planning (New York, September 1986), p. III-1.
95 Vollmer Associates, *West Side Highway Replacement Study*.
96 Ibid., p. I-4.
97 Ibid. See, for example, section VI-6 on artists.
98 New York State Department of Transportation, Federal Highway Administration, US Department of Transportation, *Route 9A Reconstruction Project* (New York: Vollmer Associates, May 1994).
99 Ibid., appendix L, n.p.
100 Zukin, correspondence with the author.

101 Hudson River Park Conservancy, *Hudson River Park* (New York: Hudson River Park Conservancy, May 1995).
102 Ibid., p. 11.
103 Ibid., p. 12.
104 Ibid., p. 11.
105 Hudson River Park, https://hudsonriverpark.org/the-park/waterfront-transformation/.
106 Archives of the Mayor's Press Office, 'Mayor Giuliani Renames the West Side Highway in Honor of Yankee Legend Joe DiMaggio', Release #138–99 (25 April 1999), https://www.nyc.gov/html/om/html/99a/pr138-99.html.
107 New York State Department of Transportation, https://www.dot.ny.gov/route9a/history.
108 NYC Planning, Zoning Resolution, Article IX Special Purpose Districts, 'Chapter 8: Special West Chelsea District' (23 June 2005), https://zr.planning.nyc.gov/article-ix/chapter-8#98-00.
109 New York State Department of Transportation, '9A West Street Promenade', https://www.dot.ny.gov/route9a.
110 Zukin, *Loft Living*, pp. 176–90.

Chapter 3: Los Angeles: The Expressway as Art

1 Another picture of Jorgenson at the 405/10 site, taken in 1962, appeared in the exhibition *Eyes on the Road: Art of the Automotive Landscape* at the Petersen Automotive Museum, Los Angeles (March–October 2024).
2 D. Townsend, 'Freeway Builders Are Weekend Housewives: Highway Engineers Look Forward to Ordinary Suburban Chores Around Home', *Los Angeles Times* (6 April 1964), p. A1.
3 Ibid.
4 For more on the Department of Transport's women engineers, see L. Gohdes, 'Lady Engineers', *California Highways and Public Works* (January–February 1963), pp. 46–9.
5 Anne Bertolotti, interview with the author (9 August 2024). Bertolotti was that daughter. Reece's other daughter, Kristen Stahl, followed her to CalTrans as an engineer.
6 Marilyn Jorgenson Reece quoted in R. Simon, 'Four-Level Interchange Is a Four-Letter Word to Some and a Marvel to Others', *Los Angeles Times* (18 August 1995), p. VYB2.
7 Interview with Marilyn Jorgenson Reece, *CalTrans District 7 Highway News Bulletin* (October–November 1971), p. 19.
8 Bertolotti, interview with the author.
9 P. Hall, *Cities of Tomorrow*, 2nd edn (Oxford: Blackwell, 1996), p. 282.
10 Ibid., pp. 281–2.
11 W.C.S., 'New Era of the Freeway', *Los Angeles Times* (2 January 1959), p. 75.
12 S. Giedion, *Space, Time and Architecture* (Cambridge, MA: Harvard University Press, 1941), pp. 550–5.
13 For example, J.B. Jackson, 'The Public Landscape', in E.H. Zube, *Landscapes: Selected Writings of J.B. Jackson* (Amherst, MA: University of Massachusetts Press, 1970), pp. 153–60. The essay was originally given as a lecture in 1966.
14 K. Lynch, *The Image of the City* (Cambridge, MA: MIT Press, 1960), pp. 46–90.
15 Ibid., p. 23.
16 Ibid., p. 42.

17 D. Appleyard, K. Lynch and J.R. Meyer, *The View from the Road* (Cambridge, MA: MIT Press, 1965). Briefly discussed in MoMA's 2021 exhibition *Automania*. See J. Kinchin, A. Gardner and P. Galloway, *Automania* (New York: MoMA, 2021), p. 98.
18 R. Venturi, D. Scott Brown and S. Izenour, *Learning from Las Vegas* (Cambridge, MA: MIT Press, 1972).
19 Appleyard et al., *The View from the Road*, p. 3.
20 Ibid., p. 4.
21 Alfred Kinsey noted equivalences between the experience of driving at speed and sexual arousal. A.C. Kinsey, *Sexual Behaviour in the Human Male* (Philadelphia, PA: W.B. Saunders, 1948), p. 191.
22 Appleyard et al., *The View from the Road*, p. 63.
23 L. Halprin, *Freeways* (New York: Reinhold, 1966).
24 Ibid., p. 5.
25 Ibid., p. 8. Compare with Banham's remarks in 1968. Peter Hall also said something similar in 1963, although his is an imaginary scenario. P. Hall, *London 2000* (London: Faber and Faber, 1963), p. 271.
26 Halprin, *Freeways*, p. 23.
27 A.B. Hirsch, *City Choreographer: Lawrence Halprin in Urban Renewal America* (Minneapolis, MN: University of Minnesota Press, 2014), pp. 1, 156, 158.
28 Ibid., p. 156.
29 Halprin's publisher saw the parallels, writing to Jacobs in 1963 to review Halprin's *Anatomy of the City*. J. Koefoed, letter to Jane Jacobs (30 July 1963). Jane Jacobs Papers, Boston College, MS1995.029, Box 6.
30 Halprin, *Freeways*, p. 53.
31 Ibid., p. 109.
32 Tom Wolfe, *The Kandy-Kolored Tangerine-Flake Streamline Baby* (New York: Farrar, Straus and Giroux, 1965), p. 69.
33 E. Avila, *The Folklore of the Freeway: Race and Revolt in the Modernist City* (Minneapolis, MN: University of Minnesota Press, 2014), pp. 122–3.
34 Wiliam Hackman, *Out of Sight: The Los Angeles Art Scene of the Sixties* (New York: Other Press, 2015).
35 R.D. Marshall, in Museo Nacional de Arte Reina Sofia, *Edward Ruscha: Made in Los Angeles* (Madrid, 2002), p. 30.
36 Ibid., p. 14.
37 Quoted in ibid., p. 14. On subject matter, see also J. Quick, *Back to the Drawing Board: Ed Ruscha, Art and Design in the 1960s* (New Haven, CT: Yale University Press, 2022), pp. 150–1.
38 Getty, Special Collections, Edward Ruscha photographs of Los Angeles streets, 1974–2010. https://primo.getty.edu/permalink/f/19q6gmb/GETTY_ALMA21131525220001551.
39 M.B. O'Gara and T.J. Bezouska, 'Field Study of a Curved Continuous Prestressed Bridge', Division of Highways, State of California, *Bridge Notes*, 5, 7 (October 1963), p. 1. This was one of several academic journals published by the prolific Division of Highways.
40 Avila, *The Folklore of the Freeway*, pp. 126–7.
41 State of California, Department of Public Works, Division of Highways, image 10555-5, dated 8 August 1964. CalTrans Archive, Sacramento.
42 City of Los Angeles, As Built Plans, Contract 07-009-444, document 70000899 (30 April 1965), CalTrans District 7 records.

43 State of California, Department of Public Works, Division of Highways, image 10455-4, dated 10 February 1964. CalTrans Archive, Sacramento.
44 State of California, Department of Public Works, Division of Highways, image 81662-6, dated 14 January 1966. CalTrans Archive, Sacramento.
45 For negative press about expressway aesthetics at the same time, see, for example, R. Hebert, 'Maligned Freeways Hailed for Eye Appeal: But Architect Sounds Alarm on Designs Overlooking Visual Aspects', *Los Angeles Times* (17 June 1966), p. B1.
46 *California Highways and Public Works* (March–April 1965), p. 47.
47 Ibid.
48 'Governor's Design Award: Three out of Four', *California Highways and Public Works* (January–February 1967), p. 37.
49 *District 7 Highway News Bulletin* (January 1967), p. 1.
50 There were other honours, including from the pro-expressway Central City Association, who declared her one of its 'Archangels' (influential women) in 1966. 'Marilyn Reece Honored', *District 7 Highway News Bulletin* (November 1966), p. 2.
51 On Banham in general, see R.J. Williams, *Reyner Banham Revisited* (London: Reaktion Books, 2021).
52 R. Banham, *Theory and Design in the First Machine Age* (London: Architectural Press, 1960).
53 R. Banham, *Los Angeles: The Architecture of Four Ecologies* (London: Penguin, 1971), p. 23.
54 Ibid., pp. 88–9.
55 The image appears nowhere else – it is not entirely clear it is Shulman's.
56 R. Banham, 'Roadscape with Rusting Rails', *The Listener* (29 August 1968), pp. 267–8. The English architect Warren Chalk reported a similar experience: 'Up the Down Ramp', *Architectural Design*, 38, 8 (1968), pp. 404–7.
57 Mary and Ben Banham, interview with the author, London (8 May 2017).
58 J. Cooper (dir.) *Reyner Banham Loves Los Angeles* (BBC TV, 1972), https://vimeo.com/22488225. For commentary and hi-res excerpts from Banham's film, see also R.J. Williams, *Reyner Banham and the Architecture of LA: City of Fantasies* (HENI Art Talks, 2018), https://www.youtube.com/watch?v=-AeQovP7F3o.
59 Banham, *Los Angeles*, p. 213.
60 B. Conner, 'Bruce Conner Makes a Sandwich', *Artforum*, 6, 1 (1967), pp. 51–5.
61 D. Brodsly, *LA Freeway: An Appreciative Essay* (Berkeley, CA: University of California Press, 1981), p. 49.
62 Ibid., p. 42.
63 A. Betsky, 'Interstate 405-10 Interchange: Where Roadway Turns into Art', *Los Angeles Times* (24 October 1991), https://www-proquest-com.ezproxy.is.ed.ac.uk/historical-newspapers/interstate-405-10-interchange-where-roadway-turns/docview/1642357511/se-2.
64 Simon, 'Four-Level Interchange'.
65 D. McLellan, 'Marilyn J. Reece, 77; State's First Licensed Female Civil Engineer', *Los Angeles Times* (21 May 2004), p. B10.
66 California State Senate, Bill No. SCR72 (filed 15 August 2006).
67 J. Gish, 'CalTrans Dedicates the Marilyn Jorgenson Reece Memorial Interchange', *Inside Seven* (April 2008); see also J. Gish, 'Marilyn Jorgenson Reece Interchange', *CalTrans News* (June 2008). There is also a memorial plaque to Marilyn Jorgenson

Reece, presented by the American Society of Civil Engineers, on the first floor of the CalTrans District 7 Headquarters.
68 Quick, *Back to the Drawing Board*, p. 124.
69 Avila, *The Folklore of the Freeway*, p. 1.
70 'Freeway Will Ruin Homes, Board Told: Residential Areas on 80% of Route, Legislator Claims', *Los Angeles Times* (30 September 1955), p. 2. Summary of opposition in N. Masters, 'Creating the Santa Monica Freeway', *PBS SoCal* (9 September 2012), https://www.pbssocal.org/shows/departures/creating-the-santa-monica-freeway.
71 Masters, 'Creating the Santa Monica Freeway'.
72 For accounts of the riots, see J. Cohen and W.S. Murphy, *Burn, Baby, Burn! The Los Angeles Race Riots of 1965* (London: Victor Gollancz, 1966); M. Davis and J. Wiener, *Set the Night on Fire: L.A. in the Sixties* (London: Verso, 2020), pp. 204–25.
73 Banham, *Los Angeles*, p. 25.
74 Ibid., p. 173.
75 Cooper, *Reyner Banham*.
76 'UCLA Professors, Warnings on Freeways Spark Debate', *Los Angeles Times* (16 September, 1965), p. WS5.
77 Ibid.
78 Brodsly, *LA Freeway*, p. 139.
79 Brodsly apparently never wrote anything else, moving into a career in real estate.
80 See also J. Schumacher (dir.) *Falling Down* (1993), which starts with an apocalyptic freeway jam. See discussion in D.L. Ulin, *Sidewalking: Coming to Terms with Los Angeles* (Berkeley, CA: University of California Press, 2015), pp. 50–5.
81 The Photographers' Gallery, *Catherine Opie* (London: The Photographers' Gallery, 2000), p. 47.
82 Ibid., p. 7. See also discussion in Avila, *The Folklore of the Freeway*, pp. 130–2.
83 M. Davis, *City of Quartz* (New York: Verso, 1990).
84 This is the edition published as M. Davis, *City of Quartz* (London: Verso, 1998).
85 M. Davis, *Ecology of Fear: Los Angeles and the Imagination of Disaster* (New York: Metropolitan Books, 1998).
86 In spite of the apocalyptic imagery, the I-10 was actually rebuilt and returned to service in three months. See 'The 1994 Earthquake Broke the 10 Freeway. How L.A. Rebuilt it in Record Time', *Los Angeles Times* (13 November 2023), https://www.latimes.com/california/story/2023-11-13/the-1994-earthquake-smashed-the-10-freeway-how-l-a-rebuilt-it-in-record-time.
87 Davis, *City of Quartz*, pp. 232–3.
88 J.L. Wasserman et al., 'The Road, Home: Challenges of and Responses to Homelessness in State Transportation Environments', *Transportation Research Interdisciplinary Perspectives*, 21 (2023), 100890, pp. 1–13.
89 B. Schwartz, 'Life in the Slowest Lane: Some of the County's Estimated 4,000 Homeless Live Along the Freeways, Mainly, they Say, because they're Out of Sight and Not Likely to Get Rousted', *Los Angeles Times* (23 December 1988), p. 2.
90 Ibid.
91 J. Garrison, 'Finding L.A.'s Hidden Homeless', *Los Angeles Times* (23 August 2008), https://www.latimes.com/local/la-me-outreach23-2008aug23-story.html.
92 C. Hawthorne, 'No Longer Above It All: A Largely Aloof Public Must Confront Harsh Reality', *Los Angeles Times* (26 December 2015), p. A1.

93 Ibid.
94 For example, B. Rudofsky, *Architecture Without Architects: A Short Introduction to Non-Pedigreed Architecture* (New York: Doubleday, 1964).
95 G. Holland, 'Standoff Beneath the 110 Freeway', *Los Angeles Times* (24 November 2016), https://www.latimes.com/local/lanow/la-me-ln-homeless-freeway-20161115-story.html.
96 D. Miller and A. Khouri, 'Fire under 10 Freeway in Downtown L.A. Upends Traffic with No Reopening in Sight', *Los Angeles Times* (13 November 2023), https://www.latimes.com/california/story/2023-11-12/10-freeway-closed-fire.
97 B. Oreskes, 'Under Pressure, L.A. Agrees to Provide 6,000 New Beds to Clear Homeless Camps under Freeways', *Los Angeles Times* (18 June 2020), https://www.latimes.com/homeless-housing/story/2020-06-18/city-and-county-agree-to-provide-6000-new-beds-of-shelter-for-homeless-people-in-next-18-months.
98 See Ulin, *Sidewalking*, p. 45.
99 Avila, *The Folklore of the Freeway*, p. 170. Avila refers to a rather more activist situation in East Los Angeles, but the lessons are applicable here.

Chapter 4: London: The Activist Expressway

1 A note on the name: on opening in 1970 it was officially just 'Westway'. In usage it has since acquired the definite article, helpfully differentiating it from the New York scheme discussed in chapter 2.
2 J. Glancey, 'Colossus of Roads', *The Guardian* (17 July 2000), https://www.theguardian.com/culture/2000/jul/17/artsfeatures.transport.
3 The Westway has often been described as iconic. See, for example, C. Hall, 'Icon of the Month: Westway', *Icon* 087 (September 2010), pp. 22–3. See also E. Platt, *Leadville: A Journey from White City to the Hanger Lane Gyratory* (London: Picador, 2001), p. 278.
4 From Ritchie's website, and cited elsewhere: https://www.adam-ritchie-photography.co.uk/westway-scheme/westway-opposition/. Confirmed in interview with the author (6 September 2023).
5 P. Hall, *Great Planning Disasters* (London: Weidenfeld and Nicolson, 1980), p. 57. This was the same body that recommended the creation of the North and South Circular roads.
6 Ibid., p. 58.
7 Ibid., p. 59. M. Dnes, *The Rise and Fall of London's Ringways 1943–1973* (Abingdon: Routledge, 2020), pp. 14–15.
8 Hall, *Great Planning Disasters*, p. 59.
9 *The Times*, 'Motorways Plan for London' (2 April 1965), p. 10. The plan was previewed before the official announcement in *The Times*, '£450m London Roads Scheme' (25 March 1965), p. 8. The Greater London Council replaced the former London County Council.
10 *The Times*, 'New Motorways Plan for London' (2 April 1965), p. 10.
11 P. Hall, *London 2000*, 2nd edn (London: Faber and Faber, 1969), p. 271.
12 Dnes, *Rise and Fall*, p. 109.
13 Cement and Concrete Association, *Western Avenue Extension* (London: Cement and Concrete Association, 1968), p. 1.
14 For detail on key designers and contractors, see J.W. Baxter, D.J. Lee and E.F. Humphries, 'Design of Western Avenue Extension (Westway)', *Proceedings – Institution of Civil Engineers*, 51, 2 (1972), p. 177. On Holford in general, see G. Cherry and

P. Leith, *Holford: A Study in Architecture, Planning and Civic Design* (Abingdon: Routledge, 2019).
15 W. Holford, 'Brasília: A New Capital City for Brazil', *Architectural Review* (December 1957), pp. 395–402. The Costa quote appears on p. 402.
16 Cement and Concrete Association, *Western Avenue Extension*, p. 3. The maximum design speed on ramps was to be 30 mph.
17 Ibid., p. 1.
18 J.W. Baxter, D.J. Lee, E.F. Humphries and F.S. Nundy, 'Discussion of Papers 7435 and 7469, Western Avenue Extension (Westway)', *Proceedings of the Institution of Civil Engineers*, 54, 1 (1973), p. 115.
19 Baxter et al., 'Design of Western Avenue Extension', pp. 177–218; F.S. Nundy, 'Problems in the Construction of Western Avenue Extension (Westway)', *Proceedings – Institution of Civil Engineers*, 51, 2 (1972), pp. 219–50; Baxter et al., 'Discussion of Papers 7435 and 7469'.
20 Architectural Foundation, *On the Road: The Art of Engineering in the Car Age* (London: Architecture Foundation/Hayward Gallery, 1999), p. 28. See also Cement and Concrete Association, *Western Avenue Extension*, p. 3, which specifies a maximum loading of 180 tons, well in excess of the 55-ton weight of the British Army's main battle tank of the period, the Chieftain.
21 Baxter et al., 'Design of Western Avenue Extension', pp. 183–94.
22 Ibid.
23 R. Gray, letter to Hubert Bennett, Architect to the GLC (18 December 1968), Holford papers, D147 C82 1, University of Liverpool.
24 Baxter et al., 'Discussion of Papers 7435 and 7469', p. 113. Holford's own notes are slightly more detailed than the report in the Proceedings, with more on the temperature differentials and other environmental concerns. See W. Holford, Institution of Civil Engineers, 'Design of Western Avenue Extension – Notes for a Contribution to a Discussion of Papers 7469 and 7435' (28 March 1972), Holford papers, D147 C82 4, University of Liverpool.
25 Baxter et al., 'Discussion of Papers 7435 and 7469', p. 113.
26 Ibid.
27 *The Times*, 'Highway Men Design an Avenue and Produce a Desert' (11 April 1966), p. 5.
28 R. Reid, 'Under the Motorway', *Architectural Review*, 143, 852 (1968), pp. 151–4.
29 *Architects' Journal*, 'News: RIBA London Region – Architects' Sharp Criticism of GLC's 1981 Plan', 150.51 (17 and 24 December 1969), pp. 1591–2.
30 *Architects' Journal*, 'News', p. 1592. L. Mumford, *The Culture of Cities* (New York: Harcourt, Brace and Co., 1938).
31 During the Westway's construction, the *Architectural Review* published a remarkable series titled 'Manplan', setting out in detail what it saw as the profession's despair with the modern world. For a general commentary on Manplan, see S. Parnell, 'Manplan', *Architectural Review*, 235, 1405 (2014), pp. 100–1.
32 *The Times*, 'Tenants Protest at Opening of Motorway' (29 July 1970), p. 3. One of the banners is slightly misquoted as reading 'Let Us Out of this Hell', *The Times*, 'Tenants Protest'.
33 Ibid.
34 'Acklam Road Houses Near Westway to be Demolished', *The Times* (10 March 1971), p. 6.
35 'Cutting Through the Cities', *The Times* (29 July 1970), p. 7.

36 For a historical synthesis of the negative consequences of the Westway, see J. Davis, *Waterloo Sunrise: London from the Sixties to Thatcher* (Princeton, NJ: Princeton University Press, 2022).
37 Dnes, *Rise and Fall*, p. 102.
38 P. Hall, 'Where London's Roads Will Go?', *New Society* (25 March 1965), pp. 18–19.
39 R. Banham, P. Barker, P. Hall and C. Price, 'Non Plan: An Experiment in Freedom', *New Society* (20 March 1969), pp. 435–43. See discussion in R.J. Williams, *Reyner Banham Revisited* (London: Reaktion, 2021), pp. 148–59.
40 Adam Ritchie, interview with the author (6 September 2023). See also North Kensington Playscape Group, *A Scheme of Amenities, Play Facilities and Open Space for North Kensington* (1969), https://www.adam-ritchie-photography.co.uk/westway-scheme/westway-opposition/.
41 On O'Malley, see M. Mayo, 'John O'Malley Obituary', *The Guardian* (5 May 2020), https://www.theguardian.com/world/2020/may/05/john-omalley-obituary.
42 Adam Ritchie, interview with the author.
43 North Kensington Playscape Group, *A Scheme of Amenities*.
44 See T.J. Clark, *The Painting of Modern Life: Paris in the Art of Manet and his Followers* (London: Thames and Hudson, 1985), especially pp. 23–78.
45 L. Halprin, *Freeways* (New York: Reinhold, 1966).
46 R. Leigh, 'When the Road Runs Through the Middle of the House', *Daily Telegraph* (27 June 1969), pp. 6–10.
47 D. Wilcox, 'Extra Cash Plea to Brighten M-Ways', *Evening Standard* (30 October 1969), p. 10.
48 Adam Ritchie, interview with the author.
49 J.G. Ballard, *Crash* (London: Jonathan Cape, 1973). For Ballard's take on the book and subsequent film, see I. Sinclair, *Crash: David Cronenberg's Post-Mortem on J.G. Ballard's 'Trajectory of Fate'* (London: BFI Publishing, 1999).
50 J.G. Ballard, *High Rise* (London: Jonathan Cape, 1975). Ballard's model for his fictional architect, Anthony Royal, was Ernö Goldfinger who designed Trellick.
51 J.G. Ballard, 'The Car, The Future', *AA Drive* (autumn 1971), pp. 103–9.
52 Ibid., p. 103.
53 Sinclair, *Crash*, p. 96. The British Library has a first draft of *Crash*, undated by the author but identified as 1970–1. See https://www.bl.uk/collection-items/typescript-draft-of-crash-by-j-g-ballard-revised-by-hand.
54 For a commentary on the two drafts of the novel in the British Library, see C. Beckett, 'J.G. Ballard's "Elaborately Signalled Landscape": The Drafting of Concrete Island', *Electronic British Library Journal* (2015), https://bl.iro.bl.uk/concern/articles/a55369b6-4ffa-421d-9313-6c53bf088977.
55 F. Marinetti, 'Le Futurisme', *Le Figaro* (20 February 1909), p. 1.
56 J.G. Ballard, *Concrete Island* (London: Jonathan Cape, 1974), p. 13.
57 J. Raban, *Soft City* (London: Hamish Hamilton, 1974), pp. 180–211. Raban drew attention to the counter-cultural interest in the irrational and the esoteric: it was 'Magical City'.
58 Michael Moorcock, correspondence with the author (18 October 2023).
59 T. Vague, 'In Search of Place', in *Record Collector Presents Hawkwind*, special issue of *Record Collector* (2024), pp. 28–9.
60 J. Banks, *Hawkwind Days of the Underground: Radical Escapism in the Age of Paranoia*

(London: Strange Attractor Press, 2020), pp. 72–3. See also account of the Westway concerts in 'Freak Scene: The Story of Hawkwind, Deviants, Pink Fairies, Edgar Broughton Band & Early 70s Progressive Rock', *Record Collector*, 556 (April 2024).
61 Moorcock, correspondence with the author (18 October 2023).
62 Hawkwind, *Hall of the Mountain Grill* (United Artists, 1974).
63 Moorcock, correspondence with the author (11 October 2023). The battle with the police is the lyrical subject of 'Right On, Fight On', by the Pink Fairies from their 1972 album *What A Bunch of Sweeties*.
64 See R. Deakin, *Keep it Together: Cosmic Boogie with the Deviants and the Pink Fairies* (London: Headpress, 2012), pp. 201–9.
65 Moorcock, correspondence with the author (11 October 2023).
66 Moorcock interview; Banks, *Hawkwind*, p. 137.
67 The encampment has existed from the beginning of the Westway. A. Duncan, *Taking on the Motorway: North Kensington Amenity Trust 21 Years* (London: Kensington and Chelsea Community History Group, 1992), p. 33. See also I. Crowson, 'We Live on a Traveller's Site Under One of London's Busiest Roads', *Daily Mail* (20 July 2024), https://www.dailymail.co.uk/news/article-13624359/We-live-traveller-site-one-London-busiest-roads-abused-locals-NEVER-leave.html?ito=email_share_article-top.
68 For a retrospective view of the film and its difficulties, see G. Pursall, 'The Final Programme', *Blueprint Review* (23 February 2023), https://blueprintreview.co.uk/2023/02/the-final-programme/.
69 M. Moorcock, *King of the City* (London: Scribner, 2000), p. 67.
70 I. Sinclair, *Agents of Oblivion* (Dublin: Swan River Press, 2023).
71 I. Sinclair, correspondence with the author (18 October 2023).
72 Ibid.
73 T. Vague, *Getting it Straight in Notting Hill Gate: A West London Psychogeography Report* (London: Bread and Circuses, 2012). See chapter 7, 'Fifty Years of Carnival'.
74 For a definition of megastructure, see R. Banham, *Megastructure: Urban Futures of the Recent Past* (New York: Harper and Row, 1976). Banham described a number of expressway-oriented schemes, including Paul Rudolph's LOMEX study of 1970, also illustrated on the book's cover.
75 Vena Dhupa, Chief Executive Westway Trust, interview with the author (16 June 2023).
76 Duncan, *Taking on the Motorway*, p. 64.
77 Ritchie, interview with the author.
78 Duncan, *Taking on the Motorway*, p. 27.
79 https://www.westway.org/about-us/. Also Vena Dhupa, interview.
80 https://www.westway.org/about-us/. Also Vena Dupa, interview.
81 Vena Dhupa, interview.
82 Ibid.
83 https://www.westway.org/contact-us/filming-on-the-estate/.
84 Vena Dhupa, interview.
85 'Space Under the Motorway', *Concrete Quarterly* (Spring 1984), pp. 30–1.
86 Duncan, *Taking on the Motorway*, p. 57.
87 On the replacement, see https://www.basestructures.com/portfolio/portobello-market/.
88 Duncan, *Taking on the Motorway*, p. 57.
89 On the immediate causes of the fire and the initial response, see P. Apps, *Show Me the Bodies: How We Let Grenfell Happen* (London: OneWorld, 2022), pp. 9–27.

90 Vena Dhupa, interview.
91 P. Gilroy, 'Never Again Grenfell', *Steve McQueen: Grenfell* (London: Serpentine Gallery, 2023), p. 12.
92 Shown at the Serpentine Gallery in 2023. Serpentine Gallery, *Grenfell by Steve McQueen* (7 April–10 May 2023), https://www.serpentinegalleries.org/about/press/grenfellbystevemcqueen/.
93 More on the filming process can be found here: http://grenfell.film/archive/index.html. See also T. Seymour, 'A Brutal Demand for Change: Steve McQueen's Grenfell Tower Film at the Serpentine', *Art Newspaper* (4 April 2023), https://www.theartnewspaper.com/2023/04/04/steve-mcqueen-grenfell-film-serpentine-gallery-review.
94 It is officially the Maxilla Memorial and Healing Space: https://www.westway.org/about-us/maxilla-memorial-healing-space/.
95 A more permanent memorial to Grenfell takes the form of a community centre in Bay 20, another symbolic and actual linkage between the two sites. See I. Priest, 'New Heart for Grenfell: How a Limbo Space Was Returned to the Community; Architects: Featherstone Young', *RIBA Journal*, 125, 12 (2018), pp. 6–8.
96 Gilroy, 'Never Again Grenfell', pp. 8–9.
97 Ibid.
98 Platt, *Leadville*, p. 278. See also Glancey, 'Colossus of Roads'.
99 Platt, *Leadville*, p. 283.
100 J. Bell, *Carchitecture* (Basel: Birkhäuser, 2001), p. 74.
101 R. Venturi and D. Scott Brown, *Complexity and Contradiction in Modern Architecture* (New York: MoMA, 1966).
102 Duncan, *Taking on the Motorway*, p. 64.
103 R. Waite, 'Turner Works Reveals Contest-winning Imperial Student Hub below Westway', *Architects' Journal* (21 June 2024), https://www.architectsjournal.co.uk/news/turner-works-reveals-contest-winning-imperial-student-hub-below-westway.
104 Vena Dhupa, interview.

Chapter 5: São Paulo: The Expressway Occupied

1 'Calor de hoje poderá ser o mais forte deste verão', *Folha de São Paulo* (1 January 1971), p. 6.
2 'Elevado Costa e Silva: a maior obra da capital depois do Metrô', *Folha de São Paulo* (1 January 1971), p. 8.
3 'Paulo Maluf anuncia construção do Minhocão' (1969), https://www.youtube.com/watch?v=j44cTNnDHps.
4 'Entregue à cidade a via Presidente Costa e Silva', *Folha de São Paulo* (25 January 1971), p. 7.
5 'Cidade recebeu a via elevada', *Folha de São Paulo* (25 January 1971), p. 1.
6 N. Chomsky, *Occupy!* (London: Penguin Books, 2012).
7 J. Perlman, *The Myth of Marginality: Urban Poverty and Politics in Rio de Janeiro* (Berkeley, CA: University of California Press, 1976).
8 R. Rolnik, *São Paulo: O Planejamento da Desigualdade* (São Paulo: Editora Fósforo, 2022), pp. 88–103.
9 T. Phillips, 'Brazil's Roofless Reclaim the Cities', *The Guardian* (23 January 2006),

https://www.theguardian.com/world/2006/jan/23/brazil.uknews1. See also Rolnik, *São Paulo*, p. 98.
10 35 Bienal de São Paulo, 'Cozinha Ocupação 9 de Julho', https://35.bienal.org.br/en/participante/cozinha-ocupacao-9-de-julho/.
11 On an earlier Bienal, see V. Bevis, 'Brazil's Occupying Artists Propel Bienal São Paulo's Theme', *Los Angeles Times* (8 November 2014), https://www.latimes.com/entertainment/arts/la-et-cm-ca-brazil-art-20141109-story.html.
12 N. Nascimento, 'Conheça cinco ocupações culturais de São Paulo, da 9 de Julho à Ouvidor 63', *Folha de São Paulo* (11 May 2023), https://guia.folha.uol.com.br/passeios/2023/05/conheca-cinco-ocupacoes-culturais-de-sao-paulo-da-9-de-julho-a-ouvidor-63.shtml.
13 N. Millington, 'Public Space and *Terrain Vague* on São Paulo's Minhocão: The High Line in Translation', in C. Lindner and B. Rosa (eds) *Postindustrial Urbanism and the Rise of the Elevated Park* (New Brunswick, NJ: Rutgers University Press, 2017), pp. 201–18.
14 Ibid., pp. 216–17.
15 On Augusta, see also Rolnik, *São Paulo*, p. 97.
16 Millington, 'Public Space and *Terrain Vague*', p. 213 on Caldeira. See also J. Holston, *The Modernist City: An Anthropological Critique of Brasília* (Chicago, IL: University of Chicago Press, 1989), pp. 312–13.
17 Millington, 'Public Space and *Terrain Vague*', pp. 216–17.
18 H. Menezes, 'Choreographies of the Impossible, Crossroads of Time', *35ª Bienal de São Paulo* (São Paulo: Bienal de São Paulo, 2023), pp. 14–19.
19 R. Rolnik, *São Paulo: O Planejamento da Desigualdade* (São Paulo: Fosforo, 2022).
20 M.A. Lagonegro, *Metrópole sem metrô: transporte público, rodoviarismo e populismo em São Paulo (1955–1965)* (PhD thesis, University of São Paulo, 2003). See also L.R.A. Florence, *Arquitetura e Autopia: Infraestrutura Rodoviária em São Paulo 1952–1972* (PhD thesis, University of São Paulo, 2020), pp. 228–322.
21 L. Costa, *O Relatório do Plano Piloto de Brasília*, 4th edn (Brasília: IPHAN, 2018), p. 127.
22 E. Vasconcellos, *Urban Transport, Environment and Equity: The Case for Developing Countries* (London: Earthscan, 2001), p. 156.
23 Lagonegro, *Metrópole sem metrô*, p. 446. See also M. Bastos, *Pós-Brasília: Rumos da Arquitetura Brasileira* (São Paulo: Editora Perspectiva, 2003), p. 24.
24 Florence, *Arquitetura e Autopia*, pp. 339–42.
25 On the Futurist City, see R. Banham, *Theory and Design in the First Machine Age* (London: Architectural Press, 1960), pp. 127–38.
26 Florence, *Arquitetura e Autopia*, p. 349.
27 Prefeitura Municipal de São Paulo, *Anteprojeto de um Sistema de Transporte Rápido* (São Paulo: Prefeitura Municipal de São Paulo, 1956).
28 Ibid., pp. 98–9. See also Florence, *Arquitetura e Autopia*, p. 153.
29 Prefeitura Municipal de São Paulo, Lei no. 7.113 (11 January 1968) and Lei no. 7.386 (19 November 1969).
30 C. Lévi-Strauss, *Tristes Tropiques* (London: Jonathan Cape, 1973), p. 122.
31 Florence, *Arquitetura e Autopia*, p. 360.
32 Ibid., p. 507.
33 COGEP is the Coordenadoria de Gestão de Pessoas, or Co-ordination of Human Resources Management.

34 F. Motta and M. Nitsche, *Superfícies Habitáveis* (1974), https://www.youtube.com/watch?v=3wonAAgqTBA.
35 F.L. Motta, 'Superfíceis Habitáveis', *O Estado de São Paulo*, Suplemento Literário (12 May 1974), p. 5.
36 *O Estado de São Paulo*, 'Pilastras Pintadas, vacas de concreto. É a arte das ruas' (12 May 1974).
37 Motta, 'Superfíceis Habitáveis'.
38 Ibid.
39 'DSV fecha o elevado durante a madrugada', *Folha de São Paulo* (30 December 1976), p. 14.
40 'Moradores de São João querem elevado interditado à noite', *Folha de São Paulo* (29 December 1976), p. 9.
41 'DSV fecha o elevado', *Folha de São Paulo*.
42 Prefeitura de São Paulo, Lei no. 16.833 (7 February 2018), https://legislacao.prefeitura.sp.gov.br/leis/lei-16833-de-7-de-fevereiro-de-2018.
43 K.M. Yamashita, *Minhocão: Via de Práticas Culturais e Ativismo Urbano* (PhD thesis, University of São Paulo, São Carlos, 2019), p. 33. Author's translation.
44 R. Artigas, J. Mello and A.C. Castro (eds) *Caminhos do Elevado: Memória e Projetos* (São Paulo: IMESP, 2008).
45 On the Minhocão on film, see ibid., p. 51; N. Pinazza and L. Bayman (eds) *World Film Locations São Paulo* (Bristol: Intellect, 2013), pp. 100–2; R.J. Williams, 'São Paulo's Minhocão on Film', *SOPHIA*, 8, 1 (2023), pp. 79–96.
46 Cited by Yamashita as a key cultural event. See Yamashita, *Minhocão*, p. C8.
47 L.R. Florence, 'Estréia documentário "Elevado 3.5"', *Vitruvius* 032, 3 (June 2010), https://vitruvius.com.br/revistas/read/drops/10.032/3441.
48 The comparison was widely made. See 'Melancólia, Decadência e Solidão', *Piauí* (28 June 2010), https://piaui.folha.uol.com.br/elevado-35-melancolia-decadencia-e-solidao/.
49 Florence, 'Estréia documentário'.
50 Comolatti, interview.
51 Ibid.
52 Millington, 'Public Space and *Terrain Vague*', p. 209.
53 Ibid., p. 211.
54 On the High Line question, see also Millington, ibid., p. 216.
55 Associação Parque Minhocão, 'Modos de Negociar', *Monolito*, 17 (2013), pp. 118–19.
56 Felipe S.S. Rodrigues, 'O que é a Associação Parque Minhocão?', wall text, Associação Parque Minhocão headquarters, São Paulo (2013). The wall text was still there in 2022.
57 J. Deodoro, 'O Minhocão pode se transformar em uma gentileza para São Paulo', *Veja São Paulo* (24 September 2013), https://vejasp.abril.com.br/cidades/robert-hammond-high-line-sao-paulo.
58 See description in 'Carrópolis', *Monolito*, 17 (2013), pp. 40–4.
59 R.J. Williams, 'The Politics of Public Space at São Paulo's Parque Minhocão', *City* 28, 3–4 (2024), pp. 512–24.
60 C. Miguel, interview with the author (29 September 2023).
61 Ibid.
62 Ibid.
63 R. Senra, 'Água, Cloro e Asfalto', *Folha de São Paulo* (1 December 2013), p. 31.
64 L. Galani, 'Jaime Lerner comandará transformação do Minhocão em parque suspenso',

Gazeta do Povo (26 February 2019), https://www.gazetadopovo.com.br/haus/urbanismo/minhocao-sao-paulo-jaime-lerner-parque-linear-pedestres/.
65 F. Rodrigues, 'Razões do Parque Minhocão', *Vitruvius* (October 2017), https://vitruvius.com.br/revistas/read/arquitextos/18.209/6751.
66 Ibid.
67 Ibid.
68 On the High Line question, see also Millington, 'Public Space and *Terrain Vague*', p. 216.
69 This is the view of Simone Scifoni of USP. See Mariana Da Silva Nito and Simone Scifoni, interview with the author, São Paulo (1 April 2022); see also, for example, M. da Silva Nito and S. Scifoni, 'O Patrimônio Contra a Gentrificação: A Experiência do Inventário Participativo de Referências Culturais do Minhocão', *Revista do Centro da Pesquisa e Formação*, 5 (2017), pp. 82–94.
70 L. Costa, 'Razões da Nova Arquitectura', *Revista da Directoria de Engenharia*, 3, 1 (1936), pp. 3–9.
71 Rodrigues, 'Razões'.
72 See also the discussion of polling in Millington, 'Public Space and *Terrain Vague*', p. 217.
73 Diário Oficial, Cidade de São Paulo, 140 (1 August 2014), p. 18.
74 Prefeitura de São Paulo, Lei No. 16.833 (7 February 2018), https://legislacao.prefeitura.sp.gov.br/leis/lei-16833-de-7-de-fevereiro-de-2018.
75 Comolatti, interview.
76 Ibid. Artist, and sometime chair of the Associação Parque Minhocão, Felipe Morozini, underlined that view: 'I just want the traffic to stop.' Morozini, interview with the author, São Paulo (17 March 2022).
77 A. Hochuli, 'The Brazilianization of the World', *American Affairs* (20 May 2021), https://americanaffairsjournal.org/2021/05/the-brazilianization-of-the-world/.
78 For example, La Bienale di Venezia, 10 Mostra Internazionale di Architettura, *Cities Architecture and Society* (Venice: Marsilio, 2010), pp. 100–1.
79 Rolnik, *São Paulo*, pp. 70–8.
80 Ibid., pp. 79–87.
81 F. Neto, 'População de rua cadastrada no Brasil cresceu quase 10 vezes na última década, aponta Ipea', *Folha de São Paulo* (11 December 2023), https://www1.folha.uol.com.br/cotidiano/2023/12/populacao-de-rua-no-brasil-cresceu-quase-10-vezes-na-ultima-decada-aponta-ipea.shtml.
82 K. Watson, 'As famílias de SP que moram em microcasas para escapar da vida nas ruas', *BBC News Brasil* (30 August 2023), https://www.bbc.com/portuguese/articles/c51j8x1yx48o.amp.
83 Rede Nosso São Paulo, Mapa de Desigualdade 2022 (2022), https://www.nossasaopaulo.org.br/wp-content/uploads/2022/11/Mapa-da-Desigualdade-2022_Tabelas.pdf.
84 Hochuli, 'Brazilianization'.
85 V. Mendes, '"Avenida São João, sem número": os moradores que construíram casas inteiras nas ruas de São Paulo', *BBC Brasil* (22 April 2017), https://www.bbc.com/portuguese/brasil-39661329.
86 C. Pereira, 'Embaixo do Elevado, a luta dos mais pobres é para sobreviver a cada dia', *O São Paulo* (26 January 2022), https://osaopaulo.org.br/sao-paulo/embaixo-do-elevado-a-luta-dos-mais-pobres-e-para-sobreviver-a-cada-dia/. The work features in the anthology film *All the Invisible Children* (2005), in the episode directed by Kátia Lund.
87 P. Dias, 'Moradores do centro protestam no Minhocão contra a cracolândia, *Folha*

de São Paulo (20 May 2022), https://www1.folha.uol.com.br/amp/cotidiano/2022/05/moradores-do-centro-protestam-no-minhocao-contra-a-cracolandia.shtml#.
88 'Prédios ao redor do Minhocão recebem projeções de pessoas em situação de rua', *Folha de São Paulo* (20 April 2022), https://guia.folha.uol.com.br/shows/2023/04/predios-ao-redor-do-minhocao-recebem-projecoes-de-pessoas-em-situacao-de-rua.shtml.
89 'Projeções em famosos murais no Minhocão dão visibilidade a pessoas em situação de rua debaixo do elevado', *Mariana Kotscho* (20 April 2022), https://marianakotscho.uol.com.br/inclusao/projecoes-em-famosos-murais-no-minhocao-dao-visibilidade-a-pessoas-em-situacao-de-rua-debaixo-do-elevado.html.
90 'Mar360: Museu de arte de rua de SP', https://www.mar360.art.br/pt/.
91 On this new typology, see also Rolnik, *São Paulo*, pp. 99–100.
92 The development's Facebook page can be found here: https://www.facebook.com/CosmopolitanHigienopolis/?locale=pt_BR.
93 Comolatti, interview.
94 Prefeitura de São Paulo, Lei No. 16.833.
95 Including the 1996 attempt by Paulo Maluf to reinstate the original traffic hours. Rodrigues, 'Razões do Parque Minhocão'.
96 Rolnik, *São Paulo*, pp. 79–87.
97 https://cineminhocao.com.br/.

Chapter 6: Madrid: The Expressway as Public Space

1 For an account of the situation in 2024, see 'Madrid is Booming. Growing While Keeping its Cool Will Be the Tricky Part', *The Economist* (6 February 2024), https://www.economist.com/europe/2024/02/06/madrid-is-booming-growing-while-keeping-its-cool-will-be-the-tricky-part.
2 Especially indicative are R. Rogers with P. Gumuchdjian, *Cities for a Small Planet* (London: Faber, 1996); P.G. Rowe, *Civic Realism* (Cambridge, MA: MIT Press, 1999); general discussion of 1990s trends in public space including the UK government's Urban Task Force in R.J. Williams, *The Anxious City: English Urbanism at the End of the Twentieth Century* (London: Routledge, 2004), pp. 129–53. See also J. Lerner, *Acupunctura Urbana* (Rio de Janeiro: Editora Record, 2005).
3 O. Bohigas, '10 Points for an Urban Methodology', *Architectural Review*, CCVI, 1231 (1999) pp. 88–91. See also P. Buchanan, 'Regenerating Barcelona with Parks and Plazas', *Architectural Review* (1984), pp. 32–6.
4 See, for example, Rowe on Siena, *Civic Realism*, pp. 24–41.
5 See, for example, M. Kimmelman, 'In Madrid's Heart, Park Blooms Where a Freeway Once Blighted', *The New York Times* (27 December 2011), p. 2.
6 Julio Salvador (dir.) *Ya Tenemos Coche* (1958).
7 E. de Blaye, *Franco and the Politics of Spain* (London: Pelican 1976), p. 229.
8 M. Pallares-Barbera, 'Changing Production Systems: The Automobile Industry in Spain', *Economic Geography*, 74, 4 (1998), p. 349.
9 R. Carr and J.P. Fusi, *Spain: Dictatorship to Democracy* (London: Unwin, 1979), p. 59.
10 A.C. Sánchez, *Fear and Progress: Ordinary Lives in Franco's Spain* (Oxford: Wiley Blackwell, 2010), p. 12.
11 Ibid., p. 13.

12 M. Castells, *The City and the Grassroots* (London: Edward Arnold, 1983), p. 219.
13 Ibid., p. 220.
14 M. Davis, *City of Quartz* (London: Verso, 1998).
15 Ministerio de la Gobernación, Junta de Reconstrucción de Madrid, *Plan General de Ordenación de Madrid* (28 March 1943), pp. 13–16.
16 See also F. Burgos, G. Garrido and F. Porras-Isla (eds) *Landscapes in the City. Madrid Río: Geography, Infrastructure and Public Space* (Madrid: Turner, 2014), p. 32.
17 Decreto 2655/1963, *Boletín Oficial del Estado*, 10 (11 January 1964), p. 493.
18 Colegio Oficial de Arquitectos de Madrid (COAM), *Exposición sobre el Plan Especial Avda. de la Paz* (Madrid: COAM, 1976).
19 Madrid, *Boletín Oficial del Estado*, 126 (25 May 1968), p. 7558.
20 For example, advertisement for La Colina development, *ABC* (21 March 1969), p. 13.
21 C. Galindo, 'Ampliación de los Parques Madrileños', *ABC* (4 February 1968), pp. 26–7.
22 Burgos et al., *Landscapes in the City*, p. 32.
23 *ABC* (13 November 1974), p. 1.
24 A. Díaz, 'Treinta Años de M-30', *El Pais* (11 November 2004), https://elpais.com/diario/2004/11/11/madrid/1100175864850215.html.
25 'El Presidente del Gobiernio Inauguro Los Treinta y Seis Kilometros Este, Sur y Oeste del Tercer Cinturón de la Ciudad', *ABC* (13 November 1974), p. 57. The fourth belt was built in 1996 as the M-40.
26 'Madrid al Dia', *ABC* (19 January 1975), p. 39.
27 Burgos et al., *Landscapes in the City*, p. 32.
28 COAM, *Exposición sobre el Plan Especial*.
29 Ibid., p. 25. Translation by the author.
30 Ibid., p. 3. Translation by the author.
31 Ibid., p. 90. Translation by the author.
32 'La Expropriación', COAM, *Exposición sobre el Plan Especial*, pp. 55, 72–3. Of the 72,000 already living in the area at the start of the project, a third were forcibly removed.
33 G. Ruiz Cabrero, 'Las Holandesas Perdidas: Elogio de la M-30', *Arquitectura*, 235 (1982), pp. 51–3. See also Burgos et al., *Landscapes in the City*, p. 41.
34 Cabrero, 'Las Holandesas Perdidas', pp. 51, 52.
35 José María Ezquiaga, 'La Ciudad: Pliegues y Piezas', *AV Monografías*, 74 (1998), p. 5.
36 Ibid., p. 9.
37 See P. Buchanan, 'Regenerating Barcelona with Parks and Plazas', *Architectural Review* (June 1984), pp. 32–6; P.G. Rowe, *Civic Realism* (Cambridge, MA: MIT Press, 1999), pp. 46–57.
38 Ezquiaga, 'La Ciudad', p. 9. It was also, arguably, nothing very new, rather the continuation of processes initiated in the Franco period. See Burgos et al., *Landscapes in the City*, p. 32.
39 See Gehry's own Santa Monica residence of 1991, a suburban bungalow turned into a fortified enclave.
40 'Arquitectura espanola 1993', *Croquis*, 12, 5 (1993), p. 104.
41 'Housing on the M-30 Highway, Madrid', *AV Monografías*, 79–80 (1999), pp. 16–17.
42 Rowe, *Civic Realism*.
43 A. Cañas, 'Qué fue de Alberto Ruiz-Gallardón, el alcalde de Madrid que abandonó la primera línea política', *AS online* (23 May 2023), https://as.com/actualidad/politica/que-fue-de-alberto-ruiz-gallardon-el-alcalde-de-madrid-que-abandono-la-primera-linea-politica-n/.

44 Interview with Ginés Garrido.
45 Ibid. See also B. Villanti, 'Subway Lessons from Madrid', *City Journal* (Spring 2010), https://www.city-journal.org/article/subway-lessons-from-madrid.
46 Compare Ruiz-Gallardón's approach with that of 'bulldozer' Lee Myung-bak in Seoul at the same time. See chapter 7.
47 Interview with Ginés Garrido.
48 On Brasília, see J. Holston, *The Modernist City: An Anthropological Critique of Brasília* (Chicago, IL: University of Chicago Press, 1989); R.J. Williams, *Brazil: Modern Architectures in History* (London: Reaktion Books, 2009), pp. 95–132.
49 Burgos et al., *Landscapes in the City*, p. 50.
50 M. Contreras, 'Gallardón: La Reforma de la M-30 es el Metrosur de la Próxima Legislatura' (14 May 2003). Dietrich Braess's original 1968 article, after which the phenomenon has come to be named, was published in an English translation in 2005: D. Braess, A. Nagurney and T. Wakolbinger, 'On a Paradox of Traffic Planning', *Transportation Science*, 39, 4 (2005), pp. 446–50.
51 S. Medialdea, 'Ruiz-Gallardón Propone Rehacer la M-30', *ABC* (5 March 2003), p. 38.
52 Ibid.
53 Contreras, 'Gallardón: La Reforma de la M-30', p. 37.
54 Burgos et al., *Landscapes in the City*, p. 50.
55 'PSOE e IU creen que la reforma de la M-30 prometida por el PP la colapsará', *El Pais* (6 March 2003), https://elpais.com/diario/2003/03/06/madrid/1046953461_850215.html.
56 Ibid.
57 Burgos et al., *Landscapes in the City*, pp. 100–3.
58 Contreras, 'Gallardón: La Reforma de la M-30'.
59 Braess et al., 'On a Paradox of Traffic Planning'.
60 J. Sérvulo González, 'El Manzanares se despide de los coches', *El Pais* (26 March 2007), https://elpais.com/diario/2007/03/26/madrid/1174908260_850215.html#.
61 Interview with Ginés Garrido.
62 Massachusetts Department of Transportation, 'Big Dig: Project Background', https://www.mass.gov/info-details/the-big-dig-project-background.
63 Interview with Ginés Garrido.
64 P.G. Rowe, 'Mas que una autopista', *Arquitectura Viva*, 106–108 (2006) pp. 42–51.
65 Burgos et al., *Landscapes in the City*, pp. 60–1.
66 Interview with Ginés Garrido.
67 Ibid. See also Burgos et al., *Landscapes in the City*, pp. 158–63.
68 Dobrick quoted in J.C. Kucharek, 'Thin Green Line', *RIBA Journal* (April 2010), p. 52.
69 Interview with Ginés Garrido.
70 Ibid.
71 Burgos et al., *Landscapes in the City*, p. 32.
72 For a straightforward account of the design principles by the West 8 lead, see C. Dobrick, 'Landscape Architecture as a Political Means', *Topos*, 73 (2010) pp. 28–35. See also Kucharek, 'Thin Green Line'.
73 Interview with Ginés Garrido. See also Burgos et al., *Landscapes in the City*, p. 63.
74 Burgos et al., *Landscapes in the City*, pp. 302–3.
75 Interview with Ginés Garrido. On the financing, see also Dobrick, 'Landscape Architecture', p. 32.
76 'Besos en Madrid Rio', *El Pais* (15 April 2011), https://elpais.com/diario/2011/04/15/madrid/1302866656_850215.html.

77 Kimmelman, 'In Madrid's Heart'.
78 E. Mangada, 'Madrid Rescata su Rio', *Arquitectura Viva*, 136 (2011), pp. 26, 32–3.
79 Ibid., pp. 27–8.
80 Veronica Rudge Green Prize in Urban Design, https://urbandesignprize.gsd.harvard.edu/madrid-rio/.
81 'La nueva M-30 revaloriza un 24% el precio de los pisos en la zona desde 2003', *ABC* (6 June 2007), p. 65.
82 'El Misterio de las Columnas Griegas de la M-30', *ABC* (18 November 2015), https://www.abc.es/espana/madrid/abci-misterio-columnas-griegas-m-30-201511180056_noticia.html.
83 'Centro de Creación Matadero, Madrid', *AV Monografías*, 159–60 (2013), pp. 28–53.
84 Interview with Ginés Garrido.
85 Burgos et al., *Landscapes in the City*, p. 122.

Chapter 7: Seoul: The Return of Nature

1 The so-called Braess Paradox. See, for example, J.H. Chung, K.Y. Hwang and Y.K. Bae, 'The Loss of Road Capacity and Self-compliance: Lessons from the Cheonggyecheon Stream Restoration', *Transport Policy*, 21 (2012), pp. 165–78. See also A. Biggs, 'Seoul Gets Image of Soft City with Cheonggyecheon', *Korea Times* (28 June 2010), https://www.koreatimes.co.kr/www/nation/2023/11/123_68399.html.
2 Seoul Biennale of Architecture, *4th Seoul Biennale of Architecture and Urbanism: Land Architecture and Urbanism* (Seoul: Seoul Biennale of Architecture, 2023), p. 33.
3 See also M. Cho, 'The Politics of Urban Nature Restoration: The Case of Cheonggyecheon Restoration in Seoul, Korea', *International Development Planning Review*, 32, 2 (2010), p. 149.
4 Seoul Biennale of Architecture, *4th Seoul Biennale*, p. 19.
5 Ibid., pp. 39, 157. The site was a 'pine forest during the Joseon dynasty, a residential area during Japanese period, a US military base, then left empty for 70 years'.
6 Ibid., p. 31.
7 J. Lerner, *Acupunctura Urbana* (Rio de Janeiro: Editora Record, 2005), pp. 15–17. 'Urban Acupuncture' in English.
8 Seoul Metropolitan Government Cheonggyecheon Museum, *Back to a Future Seoul: Cheonggyecheon Restoration Project* (Seoul: Seoul Metropolitan Government Cheonggyecheon Museum, 2011).
9 P.G. Rowe and M. Sypkens, *Emergent Architectural Territories in East Asian Cities* (Basel: Birkhäuser, 2012), p. 149.
10 C. Jeon and Y. Kang, 'Restoring and Re-Restoring the Cheonggyecheon: Nature, Technology, and History in Seoul, South Korea', *Environmental History* 24, 4 (2019), p. 742.
11 P.G. Rowe (ed.), *A City and Its Stream: The Cheonggyecheon Restoration Project* (Seoul: Seoul Development Institute 2011), p. 32.
12 The phrase was apparently first used by prime minister Chang Myon in 1961.
13 B. Kim and E.F. Vogel (eds) *The Park Chung-hee Era: The Transformation of South Korea* (Cambridge, MA: Harvard University Press, 2011).
14 Jeon and Kang, 'Restoring and Re-Restoring the Cheonggyecheon', p. 744.

15 Rowe, *A City and Its Stream*, p. 24.
16 'Park Opens Samil Highway', *Korea Times* (23 March 1969), p. 1.
17 Ibid.
18 N.Y. Lee, 'The Automobile Industry', in Kim and Vogel, *Park Chung-hee Era*, pp. 295–321.
19 'Park Opens Samil Highway', *Korea Times*.
20 https://www.youtube.com/watch?v=CTJK7TPlxM8. On Kim in general, see David Belcher, 'A Founding Father of Korean Multimedia Comes to Maastricht', *The New York Times* (15 June 2022), https://www.nytimes.com/2022/06/15/arts/kim-kulim-tefaf-maastricht.html.
21 C. Shin, 'Summer of 1969, Seoul: Film The Meaning of 1/24 Second and Kim Ku-lim's Urban Imaginaries' (28 March 2019), http://kimkulim.com/home/bbs/board.php?bo_table=a2&wr_id=9.
22 Guggenheim Museum New York, Description of The Meaning of 1/24 Second, 1969 (31 August 2023), https://www.guggenheim.org/audio/track/description-of-the-meaning-of-1-24-second-1969.
23 A. Vila, 'Under-Recognized South Korean Artists Come into Focus at the Hammer Museum', *Art News* (28 February 2024), https://www.artnews.com/art-news/artists/under-recognized-south-korean-artists-focus-og-guggenheim-museum-show-1234678898/. The exhibition started at the Guggenheim Museum in New York, before touring to the Hammer in Los Angeles.
24 Shin, 'Summer of 1969'. For technical reasons the multimedia part never came off – but the intentions were certainly spectacular.
25 Ibid.
26 Ibid. For a definition of megastructure, see Reyner Banham, *Megastructure: Urban Futures of the Recent Past* (London: Thames and Hudson, 1976).
27 P.G. Rowe, Y. Fu and J. Song, *Korean Modern: The Matter of Identity* (Basel: Birkhäuser, 2012), pp. 148–55.
28 For a commentary on its refurbishment, see Owen Hatherley, 'What is Happening at Sewoon Plaza is Quietly, Quite Extraordinary', *Dezeen* (4 January 2018), https://www.dezeen.com/2018/01/04/owen-hatherley-sewoon-sangga-seoul-extraordinary-revamp-brutalist-megastructure/.
29 The film was shown at the National Museum of Modern and Contemporary Art, Seoul, in 2023. For more on *The Lost Voyage*, see https://www.mmca.go.kr/collections/collectionsDetailPage.do?menuId=0000000000&wrkinfoSeqno=8838&artistnm=%EC%84%9C%ED%98%84%EC%84%9D. Sewoon Sangga also appears repeatedly in *Pietá* (Kim Ki-duk, 2012).
30 Rowe, *A City and Its Stream*, p. 32.
31 'Han River Bridge Collapses: 32 Killed', *Korea Times* (22 October 1994), p. 1.
32 For example, Andrei Lankov, 'Collapse of Sampoong Department Store', *Korea Times* (15 October 2004), p. 10.
33 T. Robinson and M. Ji, *Sustainable, Smart and Solidary Seoul: Transforming an Asian Megacity* (Cham: Springer International, 2022), pp. 43–4.
34 Ibid., pp. 43–5.
35 H. Shin, 'Uncovering Chonggyecheon: The Ruins of Modernization and Everyday Life', *Korean Studies*, 29, 1 (2005), p. 97.
36 K. Park, *Land*, trans. A. Tennant (Abingdon: Routledge, 1996). There are varied anglicizations of the name – for consistency I use Park Kyung-ni.

37 G. Kim, 'Writer Park Kyung-ni, Who Raised the Topic of Life/"Restoration" in Cheonggyecheon', *Hanyoreh* (1 January 2002), available in Korean at https://www.kinds.or.kr/v2/news/newsDetailView.do?newsId=01101001.2002010100002401.
38 Kim, 'Writer Park Kyung-ni'; W. Morris, *News From Nowhere and Other Writings* (London: Penguin, 1993) (first published in 1890).
39 Jeon and Kang, 'Restoring and Re-Restoring the Cheonggyecheon', p. 745.
40 Kim, 'Writer Park Kyung-ni'.
41 Jeon and Kang, 'Restoring and Re-Restoring the Cheonggyecheon', p. 744.
42 Cho, 'The Politics of Urban Nature Restoration', p. 151.
43 'Who is Lee Myung-bak?', *Hankyoreh* (21 August 2007), https://web.archive.org/web/20130615103617/http://english.hani.co.kr/arti/english_edition/e_national/230316.html. For a recent, much more critical assessment, see also H. Seong, 'The Two Faces of Lee Myung-bak', *Hankyoreh* (7 November 2023), https://english.hani.co.kr/arti/english_edition/english_editorials/335467.
44 Jeon and Kang, 'Restoring and Re-Restoring the Cheonggyecheon', p. 745.
45 For example, R. Florida, *The Rise of the Creative Class* (New York: Basic Books, 2002). On Seoul as a creative city, see K. Spence, 'Creative Seoul: A Lesson for Asian Creative Cities', in X. Gu, M.K. Lim and J. O'Connor (eds) *Re-Imagining Creative Cities in Twenty-First Century Asia* (Cham: Palgrave Macmillan, 2021), pp. 203–19.
46 Rowe, *A City and Its Stream*, p. 214.
47 See Seoul Metropolitan Government/Cheonggyecheon Museum, *Back to a Future Seoul* (Seoul: Seoul Metropolitan Government/Cheonggyecheon Museum, 2011), pp. 76–81.
48 Seong, 'The Two Faces'.
49 Jeon and Kang, 'Restoring and Re-Restoring the Cheonggyecheon', pp. 746–8.
50 R. Kim, 'Cheonggyechon: New Stream of Seoul', *Korea Times* (30 September 2005), pp. 14–15.
51 Jeon and Kang, 'Restoring and Re-Restoring the Cheonggyecheon', p. 737.
52 Cho, 'The Politics of Urban Nature Restoration', p. 163.
53 On the background to the Dongdaemun redevelopment, see J.W. Lee, 'Competing Visions for Urban Space in Seoul: Understanding the Demolition of Korea's Dongdaemun Baseball Stadium', in N. Koch (ed.) *Critical Geographies of Sport* (London: Routledge, 2017), pp. 158–72.
54 O. Norimitsu, 'The Evolution of a Man Called Bulldozer', *The New York Times* (20 December 2007), p. A8.
55 F. Burgos, G. Garrido and F. Porras-Isla (eds) *Landscapes in the City. Madrid Río: Geography, Infrastructure and Public Space* (Madrid: Turner, 2014), p. 21.
56 M. Weiss in J. Busquets (ed.) *Deconstruction/Construction: The Cheonggyecheon Restoration Project in Seoul* (Cambridge, MA: Harvard University Graduate School of Design, 2011), p. 52.
57 Rowe, *A City and Its Stream*, p. 16.
58 C. Reed in Busquets (ed.) *Deconstruction/Construction*, p. 35.
59 Ibid., p. 41. On insects, see also L. Choe et al., 'Temporal Changes in Benthic Macroinvertebrates and Their Interactions with Fish Predators after Restoration in the Cheonggyecheon, a Downtown Stream in Seoul, Korea', *Entomological Research*, 44, 6 (2014), 338–48.
60 J. Roe and L. McCay, *Restorative Cities: Urban Design for Mental Health and Wellbeing* (London: Bloomsbury, 2021), pp. 58–9.

61 Reported in Burgos et al., *Landscapes in the City*, p. 20.
62 Busquets (ed.) *Deconstruction/Construction*, pp. 62–3.
63 Cho, 'The Politics of Urban Nature Restoration', p. 163. Useful, brief summary also here: R. Kim, 'Mayor Following Predecessors', *Korea Times* (8 October 2015), p. 8.
64 Rowe, *A City and its Stream*, p. 100. On Garden Five, see 'The Humiliation of "Garden Five" ... Change of Use of Remaining Land after the Failure of Sale', *Korea Economic Daily* (25 March 2010), https://www.hankyung.com/news/app/newsview.php?aid=2010032539191 (in Korean).
65 'Many of these businesses do not seem to have kept pace with the times and are becoming obsolete.' Rowe, *A City and its Stream*, p. 52.
66 Cho, 'The Politics of Urban Nature Restoration', p. 159.
67 Seong, 'The Two Faces'.
68 Cho, 'The Politics of Urban Nature Restoration'; Jeon and Kang, 'Restoring and Re-Restoring the Cheonggyecheon'. There are numerous informal critiques of Cheonggyecheon online too.
69 S. Park, 'Controversy Continues over Chosen Cheonggye Sculpture', *Korea JoongAng Daily* (16 February 2006), https://koreajoongangdaily.joins.com/2006/02/16/features/Controversy-continues-over-chosen-Cheonggye-sculpture/2686192.html.
70 Cho, 'The Politics of Urban Nature Restoration', pp. 145–65.
71 Ibid., pp. 155, 163.
72 K. Park, 'Special Contribution by Novelist Park Gyeong-ri/Cheonggyecheon, Was It Development?' *Dong-a Ilbo* (5 March 2004), https://n.news.naver.com/mnews/article/028/0000050440?sid=102.
73 https://n.news.naver.com/mnews/article/028/0000050440?sid=102.
74 Jeon and Kang, 'Restoring and Re-Restoring the Cheonggyecheon', pp. 737, 755.
75 H.K. Lee, *'Difficult Heritage' in Nation Building South Korea and Post-Conflict Japanese Colonial Occupation* (Cham: Springer International, 2019), pp. 159–210.
76 Ibid.
77 See also *Pietá* (dir. Kim Ki-duk, 2012) for a similar fictional representation of the Cheonggyecheon district.
78 https://www.mvrdv.com/projects/208/seoullo-7017-skygarden.
79 Seoul Metropolitan Government, Press Release: 'New Pedestrian Road "Seoullo 7017" in a Walkable City – Preserving History and Memory of Seoul through Urban Regeneration' (10 October 2017), https://www.prnewswire.com/news-releases/new-pedestrian-road-seoullo-7017-in-a-walkable-city---preserving-history-and-memory-of-seoul-through-urban-regeneration-300532913.html.
80 'Elevated Highway, Tunnel Dedicated', *Korea Times* (16 August 1970), p. 8.
81 K.M. Lee, 'Seoul to Launch Overpass Remodelling Next Month' (6 November 2015), p. 3.
82 'Park Won-soon, Seoul Mayor and Human Rights Lawyer, Dies at 64', *Korea JoongAng Daily* (12 July 2020), https://koreajoongangdaily.joins.com/2020/07/12/national/socialAffairs/Park-Wonsoon-obituary-human-rights-activist/20200712174607471.html.
83 Kim, 'Mayor Following Predecessors'.
84 M. Jung, 'Seoul Will Have its Own "High Line Park"', *Korea Times* (24 September 2014), p. 6.
85 H. Hartman, 'Seoullo Performance', *Architectural Review*, 1447 (2017), https://www

.architectural-review.com/buildings/seoullo-performance-seoullo-7017-skygarden-seoul-south-korea-by-mvrdv.
86 'EU to Hold Eurovillage Event on Seoul's Overpass Park', *Korea Times* (31 May 2017), https://www.koreatimes.co.kr/www/nation/2017/05/113_230366.html.
87 Seoul Metropolitan Government, 'New Pedestrian Road "Seoullo 7017"'.
88 'Seoul Redeemed', *Icon*, 178 (2018), pp. 104–12.
89 R. Moore, 'A Garden Bridge that Works: How Seoul Succeeded where London Failed', *The Guardian* (20 May 2017), https://www.theguardian.com/cities/2017/may/19/seoul-skygarden-south-korea-london-garden-bridge.
90 https://time.com/collection/worlds-greatest-places-2018/5366679/seoullo-7017-skygarden-seoul-south-korea/.
91 A. Fifield, 'Seoul, a City "with no Soul", Builds its own High Line on an Old Overpass', *Washington Post* (14 May 2017), https://www.washingtonpost.com/world/asia_pacific/seoul-a-city-with-no-soulbuilds-its-own-high-line-on-an-old-overpass/2017/05/14/6b398ae6-3684-11e7-ab03-aa29f656f13e_story.html.
92 Robinson and Ji, *Sustainable, Smart and Solidary Seoul*, p. 60.
93 Hartman, 'Seoullo Performance'.
94 'Foreigner Leaps to Death from New Overpass Park in Seoul', *Korea Times* (30 May 2017), https://www.koreatimes.co.kr/www/nation/2023/10/113_230260.html.
95 '2 years later, Seoullo 7017 holds little appeal for visitors', *Korea Times* (29 May 2019), https://www.koreatimes.co.kr/www/nation/2019/05/113_269668.html.
96 Ibid.
97 S. Bak, 'Seoul's Pedestrian Overpass Gets Mixed Reactions One Year On', *Korea Herald* (27 May 2018), https://www.koreaherald.com/search/list_reporter.php?byline=Bak+Se-hwan. This was a common news story after the opening.
98 'Park Won-soon Discovered Dead at 64', *Hankyoreh* (10 July 2020), https://english.hani.co.kr/arti/english_edition/e_national/953184.html.
99 See discussion of the 'artistic mode of production' in S. Zukin, *Loft Living* (Baltimore, MD: Johns Hopkins University Press, 1982).
100 Robinson and Ji, *Sustainable, Smart and Solidary Seoul*, p. 39.
101 The 2023 figures are provided by statistica.com: https://www.statista.com/statistics/584968/leading-car-manufacturing-countries-worldwide/.
102 'Seoul Struggles with Nation's Steepest Population Decline', *Korea Times* (17 July 2023), https://www.koreatimes.co.kr/www/biz/2023/11/602_355105.html. Data from Korean Statistical Information Service. Seoul's core urban population in 2022 was 9.42 million, down 1.2 million from a postwar peak of 10.6 million in 1990.
103 '"Korea is so screwed!": The Statistic Making Foreign Scholars' Heads Spin', *Hankyoreh* (25 August 2023), https://english.hani.co.kr/arti/english_edition/e_national/1105828.html. The Korean Statistical Information Service projects a decline in population from 51.8 million in 2022 to 40 million in 2070. See https://kosis.kr/eng/.

Chapter 8: Glasgow: Living with the Expressway

1 S. Bryce-Wunder, 'Glasgow, Anti-Urbanism and the Scottish Literary Renaissance', *European Journal of English Studies*, 18, 1 (2014), pp. 86–98.
2 R. Olcayto, 'Welcome to the Shipwreck', *The Drouth* (9 January 2024), https://

www.thedrouth.org/welcome-to-the-shipwreck-by-rory-olcayto/. Originally published as R. Olcayto, 'Glasgow Cheerleaders Should Admit It: The City is on its Knees', *Architects' Journal* (19 December 2023).
3   A. Arnold (dir.) *Red Road* (2006).
4   Glasgow City Council figure, based on 2021 population estimate: https://www.glasgow.gov.uk/article/6088/Population-and-Projections#:~:text=Tables%201%2D12%20illustrate%20key,recent%20population%20estimates%20(2021).
5   On COP26 and its outcomes, see https://webarchive.nationalarchives.gov.uk/ukgwa/20230401054904/https://ukcop26.org/.
6   J. Rodger, *Glasgow Cool of Art: 13 Books of Fire at the Mackintosh Library* (Glasgow: The Drouth, 2022).
7   BBC Radio, 'Archive on 4: Motorway City' (3 February 2024), https://www.bbc.co.uk/programmes/m001vzm7.
8   Transport Scotland, 'M74 Completion', https://www.transport.gov.scot/projects/m74-completion/.
9   Glasgow's current, reform-friendly approach to the M8 can be found in Glasgow City Council, Meeting Minute (30 March 2023). See also the 2016 report on Glasgow's city centre by MVRDV, who were the architects of Seoullo 7017: MVRDV, Y(our) City Centre (2016), https://www.mvrdv.com/projects/258/your-city-centre.
10 Transport Scotland, 'Woodside Viaducts Project', https://www.transport.gov.scot/projects/m8-woodside-viaducts-project/project-details/.
11 'Workmen Run to Safety', *Glasgow Herald* (5 March 1969), p. 1.
12 P. Kelly, interview with the author (7 June 2024).
13 R. Bruce, *First Planning Report to the Highways and Planning Committee of the Corporation of the City of Glasgow* (Glasgow: Glasgow Corporation, 1945).
14 Ibid., p. 13.
15 Ibid.
16 Ibid., p. 14.
17 P. Abercrombie and R. Matthew, *The Clyde Valley Regional Plan 1946: a Report Prepared for the Clyde Valley Regional Planning Committee* (Edinburgh: HMSO, 1949). An internal version was available in 1947; this is the version available to the general public.
18 Ibid., p. 159.
19 Ibid., p. 7.
20 Ibid., p. 11. It also has something of Moses's plans for Long Island, a region remade in the image of leisure. See R. Caro, *Robert Moses: The Power Broker* (London: Bodley Head, 2015), pp. 143–71.
21 Corporation of the City of Glasgow, and Scott & Wilson, Kirkpatrick & Partners, *Report on a Highway Plan for Glasgow* (Glasgow: Corporation of Glasgow (Scotland). Corporation of Glasgow, 1965). For official appointment of SWK, see Corporation of Glasgow, Planning Committee, Minutes (27 January 1960), pp. 1841–2.
22 J. McCafferty in M. Glendinning (ed.), *Rebuilding Scotland: The Postwar Vision, 1945–1975* (East Linton: Tuckwell Press, 1997), p. 75. On Scotland's 'colossal' ambitions, see also Glendinning in the same volume, p. xi.
23 Corporation of the City of Glasgow, *Report on a Highway Plan for Glasgow*, pp. 67, 69. See also commentary in O. Saumarez Smith, *Boom Cities: Architect Planners and the Politics of Radical Urban Renewal in 1960s Britain* (Oxford: Oxford University Press, 2019), p. 170.

24 The Corporation of the City of Glasgow, Scott & Wilson, Kirkpatrick & Partners, *Interim Report on the Glasgow Inner Ring Road* (Glasgow: Glasgow Corporation, 1962), p. 13.
25 See also the similar, earlier use of an aerial view of working-class housing in London in Le Corbusier, *The City of To-morrow and its Planning* (New York: Payson and Clarke, 1929), p. xx.
26 Identified as ramps J and K at the opening of the Townhead viaduct. See Corporation of Glasgow, *Glasgow Inner Ring Road Townhead Stage 1*, booklet marking opening (Glasgow: Corporation of Glasgow, 5 April 1968), unpaginated.
27 Corporation of the City of Glasgow, Scott & Wilson, Kirkpatrick & Partners, *Interim Report*, p. 32.
28 Corporation of the City of Glasgow, *Report on a Highway Plan for Glasgow*, p. 83. See later assessment in McCafferty in Glendinning, *Rebuilding Scotland*, p. 81.
29 Corporation of the City of Glasgow, *Report on a Highway Plan for Glasgow*, p. 83.
30 Lord Esher, *Conservation in Glasgow* (Glasgow: Corporation of Glasgow, 1971), p. 17.
31 See the same tactics in P. Abercrombie and D. Boyd, *A Civic Survey and Plan for the City and Royal Burgh of Edinburgh* (Edinburgh: Oliver and Boyd, 1949).
32 Corporation of the City of Glasgow, *Report on a Highway Plan for Glasgow*, p. 217.
33 See Corporation of Glasgow, *Recent Shopping Developments in Europe Area* (Glasgow: Glasgow Corporation, 1971). The Corporation party was particularly impressed by the Stockholm branch of IKEA. Also Gerald Eve and Co., *Glasgow: Report on Aspects of Future Shopping Provision* (London: Gerald Eve and Co., 1971), pp. 10, 57.
34 Corporation of the City of Glasgow, *Souvenir Booklet of the Opening of the North and West Flanks of the Inner Ring Road* (Glasgow: Corporation of the City of Glasgow, 1972), p. 10.
35 'New Ring Road Section Hailed as Vital Central Link', *Glasgow Herald* (5 February 1972). p. 5.
36 'Rings of Roads', *Glasgow Herald* (5 February 1972), p. 6.
37 C. McKean and J.M. McKean, 'Motorway City', *Architects' Journal* (27 October 1971).
38 Ibid.
39 Ibid.
40 Ibid.
41 For a historical account of the breakdown, see S. Mass, 'Cost-Benefit Break Down: Unplannable Spaces in 1970s Glasgow', *Urban History*, 46 (2019), 309–30.
42 Scottish Roads Archive, 'From Concept to Cancellation: The Story of Glasgow's Inner Ring Road', https://www.scottishroadsarchive.org/inner-ring-road.
43 McCafferty in Glendinning, *Rebuilding Scotland*, p. 83. McCafferty remained an optimist. From the same source: 'it is, in my opinion, a green, pleasant, yet at the same time dramatic motorway. Lots of trees, landscaping, spiral ramps – the planting has come on well.'
44 Paul Routledge, interview with the author (20 May 2024). The cars for the ceremony mysteriously 'appeared'.
45 See film of the process in Undercurrents Alternative News Video, *To Pollok With Love* (1995), https://www.youtube.com/watch?v=Vueb1vF4C18.
46 'Motorway Protest Beds In More Firmly', *Herald* (1 October 1994), p. 9.
47 P. Routledge, 'The Imagineering of Resistance: Pollok Free State and the Practice of Postmodern Politics', *Transactions of the Institute of British Geographers*, 22 (1997), p. 360.

NOTES TO PP. 177–181

48 'M77 Motorway Glasgow to Kilmarnock', *Scottish Roads Archive*, https://www.scottishroadsarchive.org/m77#:~:text=A%20Public%20Local%20Inquiry%20was,in%20Britain%20at%20that%20time.
49 Colin McLeod, in BBC Alba, *The Birdman of Pollok* (2019), https://www.bbc.co.uk/programmes/m000ct1t.
50 McIntosh, in BBC Alba, *The Birdman of Pollok*. The original Thatcher quotation can be found here, among other places: https://www.margaretthatcher.org/document/108038.
51 Routledge, 'The Imagineering of Resistance', pp. 369, 372.
52 Ibid., p. 363.
53 BBC Alba, *The Birdman of Pollok*.
54 Routledge, 'The Imagineering of Resistance', p. 360.
55 Ibid., p. 369.
56 This and previous quotations from Routledge, interview.
57 Routledge, interview. On Reclaim the Streets, see D. Wall, *Earth First and the Anti-Roads Movement* (London: Routledge, 1999).
58 'M74 Completion', Scottish Roads Archive, https://www.scottishroadsarchive.org/m74-completion. See also *M74 Completion: Makes Complete Sense* (Glasgow: Scottish Office, Glasgow City Council, Renfrewshire Council, South Lanarkshire Council, 2003).
59 D. Gogishvili, 'Urban Infrastructure in the Framework of Megaevent Exceptionalism: Glasgow and the 2014 Commonwealth Games', *Urban Geography*, 43, 4 (2022), 589–612.
60 'Glasgow 2014: Red Road Flats Demolition Dropped from Opening', *BBC News* (13 April 2014), https://www.bbc.co.uk/news/uk-scotland-glasgow-west-27009806.
61 'Great Deal to Admire but also to Cause Concern', *Herald* (29 June 2011), https://www.heraldscotland.com/opinion/13032207.great-deal-admire-also-cause-concern-m74-link/.
62 'Mo Town Low Down', *Prospect (Scotland)*, 186 (Autumn 2009), p. 28.
63 Kelly, interview with the author.
64 For indicative images of the 'boulevard' concept, see J. Mitchell, 'Campaigners Want M8 Scrapped and Replaced with Urban Boulevard', *STV News* (15 February 2022), https://news.stv.tv/west-central/campaigners-want-m8-scrapped-and-replaced-with-urban-boulevard.
65 New Glasgow Society, *Replace the M8* (December 2022).
66 A. Hoolachan, 'Replace the M8? A Public Conversation', report on a public event at the University of Glasgow (June 2022), https://www.gla.ac.uk/colleges/socialsciences/research/interdisciplinaryresearchthemes/headline_877918_en.html.
67 C. Silver, 'The Politics of Traffic Are a Dead-End: Why It's Time to Replace the M8', *Bella Caledonia* (12 September 2021), https://bellacaledonia.org.uk/2021/09/12/the-politics-of-traffic-are-a-dead-end-why-its-time-to-replace-the-m8/.
68 Kelly, interview with the author.
69 Angus Millar, interview with the author, Glasgow (23 January 2023).
70 Councillor Angus Millar, submission of 18 July 2023 PE1906/G: *Investigate options for removing and reducing the impact of the central Glasgow section of the M8*, https://www.parliament.scot/get-involved/petitions/view-petitions/pe1906-investigate-options-for-removing-and-reducing-the-impact-ofthecentralglasgowsectionofthem8. The author also submitted brief written evidence for this petition.
71 Millar, interview.

NOTES TO PP. 181–189

72 Olcayto, 'Welcome to the Shipwreck'; 'Glasgow City Council to Pay £770m to Settle Equal Pay Dispute', *BBC News* (11 November 2022), https://www.bbc.co.uk/news/uk-scotland-glasgow-west-63584376.
73 Glasgow City Council, Minutes of Glasgow City Council (30 March 2023).
74 D. Hinde, 'Looking for Scottish Modern', *The Drouth* (no date, 2021), https://www.thedrouth.org/looking-for-scottish-modern-by-dominic-hinde/.
75 I. Sinclair, *London Orbital* (London: Granta Books, 2002).
76 I. Spring, *Phantom Village: The Myth of the New Glasgow* (Edinburgh: Polygon, 2001), pp. 140–1. For the same idea, see also N. Gray, *Neoliberal Urbanism and Spatial Composition in Recessionary Glasgow* (PhD thesis, University of Glasgow, 2015), p. 134.
77 Corporation of the City of Glasgow, *Souvenir Booklet*.
78 'The M74: From Roman Road to Multi-Lane Motorway', *The Scottish Roadscast* (22 April 2022), https://podcasts.apple.com/gb/podcast/the-scottish-roadscast/id1447302966?i=1000558357695.
79 Congress for the New Urbanism, *Freeways Without Futures* (Washington, DC: Congress for the New Urbanism, 2023).
80 M. Augé, *Non-Places: An Introduction to Supermodernity* (London: Verso, 1995).
81 A.M. Doak and A.M. Young, *Glasgow at a Glance* (London: Robert Hale, 1977), p. 231.
82 'Our Skatepark Cleaned Up Crime – Now It's Being Closed', *BBC News* (22 June 2024), https://www.bbc.co.uk/news/articles/c3ggqke5wxgo.
83 W. Morris, *News From Nowhere and Other Writings* (London: Penguin, 1993) (first published in 1890).
84 D. Haraway, *Staying with the Trouble* (Durham, NC: Duke University Press, 2016), p. 10.
85 H. Frichot, A. Carbonell, H. Frykholm and S. Karami, *Infrastructural Love: Caring for our Architectural Support Systems* (Basel: Birkhäuser, 2022).
86 'Design Unveiled for Urban Sports Park Under M74 Motorway', *BBC News* (2 October 2024), https://www.bbc.co.uk/news/articles/ckgn6jmxgoyo.
87 https://www.scottishroadsarchive.org/.
88 S. Zukin, *Loft Living: Culture and Capital in Urban Change* (Baltimore, MD: Johns Hopkins University Press), pp. 58–9. 'Ironically the mass production of an earlier industrial era looks to us like individuality.'
89 J. Urry, *Mobilities* (Cambridge: Polity, 2007), p. 284.
90 A. Hoolachan, interview with the author (28 June 2024).
91 Hoolachan, interview.
92 R. Waite, 'Turner Works Reveals Contest-winning Imperial Student Hub below Westway', *Architects' Journal* (21 June 2024).

Select Bibliography

Includes sources with general application. For more detail, see the references to the individual chapters.

Amado, A., *Voiture Minimum: Le Corbusier and the Automobile* (Cambridge, MA: MIT Press, 2011).
Appleyard, D., K. Lynch and J.R. Meyer, *The View from the Road* (Cambridge, MA: MIT Press, 1965).
Architectural Foundation, *On the Road: The Art of Engineering in the Car Age* (London: Architecture Foundation/Hayward Gallery, 1999).
Artigas, R., J. Mello and A.C. Castro (eds), *Caminhos do Elevado: Memória e Projetos* (São Paulo: IMESP, 2008).
Asher, W., *Rings Around London: Orbital Motorways and the Battle for Homes Beyond Roads* (London: Capital History Publishing, 2008).
Augé, M., *Non-Places: An Introduction to Supermodernity* (London: Verso, 1995).
Avila, E., *The Folklore of the Freeway: Race and Revolt in the Modernist City* (Minneapolis, MN: University of Minnesota Press, 2014).
Ballard, J.G., *Concrete Island* (London: Jonathan Cape, 1974).
Banham, R., *Los Angeles: The Architecture of Four Ecologies* (Harmondsworth: Penguin, 1971).
Banham, R., *Theory and Design in the First Machine Age* (London: Architectural Press, 1960).
Bel Geddes, N., *Magic Motorways* (New York: Random House, 1940).
Bell, J., *Carchitecture* (Basel: Birkhäuser, 2001).
Berman, M., *All That Is Solid Melts Into Air* (London: Verso, 1983).
Brodsly, D., *LA Freeway: An Appreciative Essay* (Berkeley, CA: University of California Press, 1981).
Buchanan, C., *Traffic in Towns: The Specially Shortened Edition of the Buchanan Report* (London: HMSO, 1963).
Burgos, F., G. Garrido and F. Porras-Isla (eds), *Landscapes in the City. Madrid Río: Geography, Infrastructure and Public Space* (Madrid: Turner, 2014).
Caro, R., *Robert Moses: The Power Broker* (London: Bodley Head, 2015).
Crawford, M., *Why We Drive: On Freedom, Risk and Taking Back Control* (London: Bodley Head, 2020).
Davis, M., *City of Quartz: Excavating the Future in Los Angeles* (London: Verso, 1990).
Davis, M., *Ecology of Fear: Los Angeles and the Imagination of Disaster* (New York: Metropolitan Books, 1998).
DiMento, J.F.C. and C. Ellis, *Changing Lanes: Visions and Histories of Urban Freeways* (Cambridge, MA: MIT Press, 2011).
Dnes, M., *The Rise and Fall of London's Ringways 1943–1973* (Abingdon: Routledge, 2020).
Drake, J., H.L. Yeadon and D.I. Evans, *Motorways* (London: Faber and Faber, 1969).
Easterling, E., *Extrastatecraft: The Power of Infrastructure Space* (London: Verso Books, 2014).
Frichot, H., A. Carbonell, H. Frykholm and S. Karami (eds), *Infrastuructural Love: Caring for our Architectural Support Systems* (Basel: Birkhäuser, 2022).
Giedion, S., *Space, Time and Architecture* (Cambridge, MA: Harvard University Press, 1941).
Grindrod, J., *Concretopia* (London: Old Street Publishing, 2013).
Hall, P., *Cities of Tomorrow*, 2nd edn (Oxford: Blackwell, 1996).

SELECT BIBLIOGRAPHY

Hall, P., *Great Planning Disasters* (London: Weidenfeld and Nicolson, 1980).
Halprin, L., *Freeways* (New York: Reinhold, 1966).
Hirsch, A.B., *City Choreographer: Lawrence Halprin in Urban Renewal America* (Minneapolis, MN: University of Minnesota Press, 2014).
Jacobs, J., *The Death and Life of Great American Cities* (New York: Random House, 1961).
Jellicoe, G.A., *Motopia* (London: Studio Books, 1961).
Kimble, M., *City Limits: Infrastructure, Inequality and the Future of America's Highways* (New York: Crown, 2024).
Kinchin, J., A. Gardner and P. Galloway, *Automania* (New York: MoMA, 2021).
Knowles, D., *Carmageddon: How Cars Make Life Much Worse and What to Do About It* (New York: Abrams, 2023).
Le Corbusier, *The City of To-morrow and its Planning* (London: J. Rodker, 1929).
Lerner, J., *Acupuntura Urbana* (Rio de Janeiro: Editora Record, 2005).
Lewis, T., *Divided Highways: Building the Interstate Highways, Transforming American Life* (Ithaca, NY: Cornell University Press, 2013).
Lynch, K., *The Image of the City* (Cambridge, MA: MIT Press, 1960).
Mauch, C. and T. Zeller (eds), *The World Beyond the Windshield: Roads and Landscapes in the United States and Europe* (Athens, OH: Ohio University Press, 2008).
Merriman, P., *Driving Spaces: A Cultural-Historical Geography of England's M1 Motorway* (Oxford: Blackwell, 2007).
Moran, J., *On Roads: A Hidden History* (London: Profile Books, 2009).
Mumford, L., *The Highway and the City* (New York: Harcourt, Brace and World, 1963).
Platt, E., *Leadville: A Journey from White City to the Hanger Lane Gyratory* (Basingstoke: Picador, 2001).
Raban, J., *Soft City* (London: Hamish Hamilton, 1974).
Rogers, R. with P. Gumuchdjian, *Cities for a Small Planet* (London: Faber, 1996).
Rowe, P.G. (ed.), *A City and Its Stream: The Cheonggyecheon Restoration Project* (Seoul: Seoul Development Institute, 2011).
Rowe, P.G., *Civic Realism* (Cambridge, MA: MIT Press, 1999).
Saumarez Smith, O., *Boom Cities: Architect Planners and the Politics of Radical Urban Renewal in 1960s Britain* (Oxford: Oxford University Press, 2019).
Shkuda, A., *The Lofts of SoHo* (Chicago, IL: University of Chicago Press, 2016).
Shonfield, K., *Walls Have Feelings: Architecture, Film and the City* (London: Routledge, 2000).
Sinclair, I., *London Orbital* (London: Granta Books, 2002).
Smithson, A. and P., *Ordinariness and Light: Urban Theories 1952–1960 and their Application in a Building Project 1963–1970* (London: Faber and Faber, 1970).
Spring, I., *Phantom Village: The Myth of the New Glasgow* (Edinburgh: Polygon, 2001).
Starkie, D., *The Motorway Age* (London: Pergamon Press, 1982).
Tetlow, J. and A. Goss, *Homes, Towns and Traffic* (London: Faber, 1965).
Urry, J., *Mobilities* (Cambridge: Polity, 2007).
Venturi, R. and D. Scott Brown, *Complexity and Contradiction in Modern Architecture* (New York: MoMA, 1966).
Williams, R.J., *Reyner Banham Revisited* (London: Reaktion Books, 2021).
Wolfe, T., *The Kandy-Kolored Tangerine-Flake Streamline Baby* (New York: Farrar, Straus and Giroux, 1965).
Wright, F.L., *The Disappearing City* (New York: William Farquhar Payson, 1932).
Zube, E.H. (ed.), *Landscapes: Selected Writings of J. B. Jackson* (Amherst, MA: University of Massachusetts Press, 1970).
Zukin, S., *Naked City: The Death and Life of Authentic Urban Places* (New York: Oxford University Press, 2010).

Index

Abalos, Iñaki and Juan Herreros 133
Abercrombie, Patrick 75, 77, 173, 217, 218
Almodóvar, Pedro, *Qué He Hecho Yo Para Merecer Esto?* 131, 132, 142, 143
Ant Farm, *Cadillac Ranch* 177
Augé, Marc 184, 192, 220
Avila, Eric 10, 34, 36, 57, 62, 71, 190, 191, 195, 196, 198, 200, 201

Babenco, Héctor, *Kiss of the Spider Woman* 11, 110
Ballard, J.G. 32, 85, 86
  Concrete Island 83, 84, 88
  Crash 83, 203
Baltrop, Alvin 32
Banham, Reyner x, 19, 191, 192, 199, 200, 206
  Los Angeles: The Architecture of Four Ecologies 60, 61, 62, 63, 64, 70, 183
  Megastructure: Urban Futures of the Recent Past 37, 196, 204, 213
  'Non-Plan' 81, 203
Barcelona, Spain 123, 125, 127, 133, 209, 210
Bel Geddes, Norman 6, 191
Bendixson, Terence 82
Berlin, Germany 4, 7
Berman, Marshall ix, 1, 2, 20, 26, 33, 36, 40, 190, 194, 195, 196
Betsky, Aaron 61, 199
Birmingham, England xi, 75
Blake, Peter 33, 195
Bong, Joon-ho, *Parasite* 166
Boston, USA 16, 17, 52, 54, 122, 137, 138, 155, 158, 179, 186, 193, 195, 198
  The Rose Fitzgerald Kennedy Greenway 16
Brasília, Brazil xi, 1, 6, 7, 77, 101, 135, 173, 185, 191, 202, 206, 211
Brodsly, David 61, 64, 199, 200

Brutalism 60, 107
Bubbles, Barney 86, 87
Buchanan, Colin, *Traffic in Towns* 8, 191, 209, 210
Buro Happold 91

Cabrero, Gabriel Ruiz 130, 131, 210
Cairo, Egypt 2
Calder, Barnabas 14, 192
California Division of Highways 9, 49
Car industry 5, 15, 101, 123–5, 149, 192
Caro, Robert, *The Power Broker: Robert Moses and the Fall of New York* 6, 29, 30, 191, 193, 194, 217
Castells, Manuel 126, 127, 209
Chazelle, Damien, *La La Land* 11, 69
Comolatti, Athos 109, 110, 114, 119, 207, 208
Congress for the New Urbanism (CNU) 18, 20, 184, 193, 220
COP26 170, 180, 181, 217
Corbusier, Le 5, 191, 218
Costa, Lucio 7, 77, 101, 114, 202, 206, 208
Coutinho, Eduardo, *Edifício Master* 107
Crowther, Sir Geoffrey 8
Cumbernauld, Scotland 7, 191

Davis, Mike, *City of Quartz* 66, 67, 127, 200, 210
Detroit, USA 3
Dhupa, Vena 88, 89, 92, 204, 205
Dnes, Michael 3, 76, 190, 191, 201, 203

Edinburgh, Scotland xii, 171
Eindhoven, Netherlands 19
Elefante, Carl 13
Esher, Lord 174, 176, 218

Federal-Aid Highway Act 4, 26
Feininger, Andreas 28, 194

INDEX

Foster, Hal 14, 292
Franco, General Francisco 126, 127, 128, 129, 134, 136, 139
Freeway revolts 3, 26, 193
Fuest, Robert, *The Final Programme* 87
Futurama exhibition 5, 6, 8, 191
Futurism xii, 5, 7, 39, 60, 61, 84, 91, 102, 122, 206

Garrido, Ginés 135, 138, 139, 157, 201, 211, 212, 214
Gehry, Frank 133, 210
Giedion, Sigfried 26, 52, 193, 197
Giuliani, Rudy 43, 197
Glasgow, Scotland
  Bruce Report 172, 173, 175, 217
  Charing Cross xi, 168, 169, 172, 175, 176, 180
  Clyde Valley Regional Plan 173, 217
  Glasgow School of Art 175
  M77 extension 3, 10, 168, 177, 179, 219
  M8 motorway x, xi, 20, 168, 169–85, 187–9
  Mitchell Library 168, 174
  Pollok Free State 175, 178, 179, 185, 218
  Replace the M8 campaign 172, 180, 187, 188, 219
  Tradeston 168, 179, 182, 183, 184, 187
Godard, Jean-Luc, *Two or Three Things I Know About Her* 11, 12
Goldberger, Paul 40, 196

Hall, Peter 3, 4, 26, 76, 81, 190, 193, 197, 198, 200, 201, 203
Halprin, Lawrence 52, 54, 55, 83, 198, 203
Hamburg, Germany 184, 186
Haraway, Donna 186, 220
Hawkwind 85–7, 203, 204
Heatherwick, Thomas 44, 45
Hochuli, Alex 114, 116, 208
Holford, William 77, 78, 173, 191, 201, 202
Hoolachan, Andrew 188, 189, 219, 220
Houston, USA 2, 65

Jackson, John Brinckerhoff 10, 52, 191, 197
Jacobs, Jane 3, 10, 16, 17, 35, 55, 198
  Death and Life of Great American Cities 9, 16, 34, 36, 191, 192, 195
Jervis, Stephanie 40, 196

Kim, Hyun-ok 149, 154, 163
Kim, Ku-lim, *The Meaning of 1/24 Second* 150, 213
Kim, Swoo-geun 151
Kimble, Megan xi, 3, 190, 191
Knowles, Daniel 3, 20, 190, 193
Koolhaas, Rem and Bregtje van der Haak, *Lagos/Koolhaas* 12, 192
Korean War 146, 148

Larkin, Brian 9, 191
Latour, Bruno 13, 19, 192, 193
Lee, Hyun Kyung 161
Lee, Myung-bak 9, 154, 211, 214
Lerner, Jaime 113, 147, 207, 208, 209, 213
London, England
  Grenfell Tower 72, 92, 205
  Motorway Box 3, 75
  Ringways Project 76, 80, 84, 173
  Trellick Tower 83, 203
  Westway (A40(M)) 19, 78, 83, 92–100, 188, 189, 201–4
Long Island Parkway 26
Los Angeles, USA x, 4, 11, 19, 26, 48–71, 76, 126, 127, 132, 170, 183, 186, 196, 197, 198, 200, 206, 213
  Arroyo Seco Parkway 4, 52
  Homelessness 66–70
  Northridge Earthquake 2, 66, 69
  Watts riots 63, 64
Lumet, Sidney, *Serpico* 32
Lynch, Kevin, *Image of the City* 52, 53, 197
  with Donald Appleyard and John R. Meyer, *The View from the Road* 53, 198

Maas, Winy 162, 164
Maastricht, Netherlands 213
Madrid, Spain
  Avenida de la Paz 127, 128, 129, 136
  COAM 129, 210
  Las Colmenas 120, 124, 128, 142
  M-30 expressway 18, 20, 120–43, 155, 170, 171
  Madrid Rio 121, 132–43, 147, 157, 186, 210, 211, 212, 214
  Manzanares river 121, 122, 127, 128, 129, 137, 139, 140, 141, 211
  Matadero Municipal 120, 141, 212

INDEX

Puente de Arganzuela 120, 133, 141
Puente de Toledo 120, 121, 123, 139, 142
Maluf, Paulo 97, 99, 103, 107, 113, 205, 209
Manchester, England
Mancunian Way 188
Marples, Ernest 8
McLeod, Colin ('The Birdman of Pollok') 178, 219
McQueen, Steve 92, 205
Meirelles, Fernando 11, 107
Merriman, Peter 10, 191
Miguel, Ciro 111, 112, 113, 207
Millar, Angus 180, 181, 219
Miller, Julius 27, 28
Millington, Nate 100, 110, 206, 207, 208
MNLA (landscape architects) 45
Moorcock, Michael 85–7, 91, 203, 204
Moreno, Carlos 20
Morozini, Felipe 110, 117, 118, 208
Morris, William 153, 185, 214
Moses, Robert 1–2, 6, 9, 26–9, 33–4, 36, 40–1, 134, 170, 190, 193, 194, 196, 217
Motorway Development Trust 81, 83, 89
  see also North Kensington Amenity Trust
Motta, Flávio 104, 105, 207
Mumford, Lewis 2, 80, 190, 202
MVRDV 162, 164, 215

New York City, USA
  Artists Against the Expressway 35
  Downtown-Lower Manhattan Association (DLMA) 34
  High Line 22, 44, 46, 110, 111, 113, 157, 163, 164, 184, 206, 207, 208, 215, 216
  Hudson Yards 44
  Little Island 22, 44–6
  Lower Manhattan Expressway (LOMEX) 19, 22, 32–40, 42, 43, 195, 196, 204
  Miller Highway 25–31, 44
  SoHo 22, 33–7, 194, 195, 196
  Triborough Bridge and Tunnel Authority 1, 6, 26, 34, 195
  West Side Highway 44–6
  Westway (New York City) 40–3
North Kensington Amenity Trust 89, 204
Nugent, Richard 76

Occupation, squatting 10, 24, 88, 89, 99–101, 104–19, 171, 185, 186
Oíza, Francisco Sáenz de 134
Okhitovich, Mikhail and Moisei Ginzburg 5
Oldenburg, Claes and Coosje Van Bruggen 156, 159
O'Malley, John 81, 82, 203
Opie, Catherine 65, 66, 200
Orpin, Jen 13, 192

Paris, France xi, 8, 11, 18, 20, 82, 83, 89, 127, 136, 137
Park, Chung-hee 147, 149, 159, 163, 212, 213
Park, Kelvin Kyung Kun, *Cheonggyecheon Medley* 161
Park, Kyung-ni 151, 154, 159, 160, 213, 214
Park, Won-soon 163, 165, 215, 216
Perlman, Janice 19, 205
Perrault, Dominique 133, 138, 141
Piano, Renzo 44
Pink Fairies, The 85, 204
Platt, Edward 94, 201, 205
Prestes Maia, Francisco 106

Raban, Jonathan 85, 203
Reece, Marylin Jorgenson 49–51, 57, 59, 60, 62, 70, 71, 183, 197, 199, 200
Ritchie, Adam 73–5, 81, 82, 87, 89, 201, 203, 204
Rodrigues, Felipe S. S. 110, 111, 113, 114, 207, 208, 209
Rogers, Richard 89, 123, 129
Rolnik, Raquel 100, 115, 119, 205, 206, 208, 209
Routledge, Paul 177–8, 191
Rowe, Peter 134, 138, 155, 158, 201, 209, 211, 212, 213, 214, 215
Rudolph, Paul 37–40, 196, 204
Ruiz-Gallardón, Alberto 134, 139, 143, 210, 211
Ruscha, Ed 4, 56–7, 61, 198

Safdie, Moshe 17
Sant'Elia, Antonio 5, 91
São Paulo, Brazil 12
  9 de Julho occupation 100, 101, 102, 206
  Associação Parque Minhocão 96, 109

INDEX

São Paulo, Brazil (*cont.*)
   Elevado Presidente Costa e Silva/Elevado
      João Goulart (Minhocão) xi, 19, 94,
      96–119, 147, 188, 205, 206, 207, 208,
      209
   Ouvidor 63 occupation 100, 206
   Praça Roosevelt 96, 97, 102, 103, 108,
      109, 115
   Praça da Sé 100
   São Paulo Bienal 100, 101, 111, 114, 206
Schumaker, Carol 49, 50
Scorsese, Martin, *Taxi Driver* 32
Scott Wilson Kirkpatrick (SWK) and
   Partners 173–6, 217
Scottish Roads Archive 183, 187, 218, 219
SEAT 600 123–5
Seoul, South Korea
   Cheonggyecheon Museum 144, 148, 152,
      155, 212, 214
   Cheonggyecheon river 144, 160
   Dongdaemun Design Plaza 156
   Gyeongbokgung Palace 147, 161
   Han river 146, 213
   Sampoong Department Store 152, 213
   Seongsu Bridge 152
   Seoul Architecture Biennale 146
   Seoullo 7017 144, 161, 162, 165, 188, 215, 216
   Sewoon Sangga 144, 151, 152, 156, 213

Shonfield, Katherine 11–12, 191, 192
Shulman, Julius 57, 60, 199
Sinclair, Iain 88, 181, 203, 204, 220
Smith, Al 27
Smithson, Peter and Alison 7, 191
Sodré, João, Paulo Pastorelo and Maíra
   Bühler, *Elevado 3.5* 12, 106, 107, 117,
   207
Staller, Jan 32

Tarkovsky, Andrei, *Solaris* 12
Toronto, Canada 10
Transport Scotland 171, 181, 182, 187, 217
Trump, Donald 41, 42, 196
Trux, Jon 85, 86, 191
Twyford Down 10

Urry, John 13, 188, 192, 220
Utrecht, Netherlands 184, 186

Vasconcellos, Edouardo 102, 206
Venturi, Robert and Denise Scott Brown
   41, 53, 94, 198, 205

Wenders, Wim, *Paris, Texas* 11, 65
Wisnik, Guilherme 111
Wolfe, Tom 55, 198
Wright, Frank Lloyd 5